Organizing Insurgency

'In these depressing times, when the neoliberal consensus has acquired an aura of inevitability akin to the Laws of Physics, it is a breath of fresh air to read serious scholarship that challenges this consensus.'
—Norman Finkelstein

'The rising anti-imperialist struggles in both the underdeveloped and developed countries are signalling the resurgence of the world proletarian-socialist revolution. Immanuel Ness makes a just call for forging a global workers' movement by reinvigorating and further developing the trade union movement, the workers' parties and political movements to fight for the rights and interests of the working class and the rest of the suffering people.'
—Professor Jose Maria Sison, Chairperson Emeritus of the International League of Peoples' Struggle, Founding Chairman, Communist Party of the Philippines and Co-Founder of the National Democratic Front of the Philippines

'Important.'
—Richard Wolff, Professor Emeritus of Economics at the University of Massachusetts Amherst

'Timely and relevant. The theoretical framing around political organisation of the working class for social transformation is much-needed. Its energetic, provocative scholarship with insightful case studies from across the South makes it essential reading for academics and activists alike.'
—Anita Hammer, Senior Lecturer of Organisational Studies and Human Resources, University of Essex

'A valuable book that addresses the necessity of revolutionary organization in times of socialist ideological resurgence. Essential reading to anyone wishing to understand the proletarianization of the Global South. Its in-depth examination of modern forms of imperialist exploitation and revolts contribute to comprehending areas rarely covered by mainstream social science.'
—Ali Kadri, National University of Singapore

'A rich combination of theoretical insights and valuable case-studies from the Global South – a much-needed reminder that the agenda of social transformation requires a strong and sustained political intervention to turn protests into a powerful movement.'
—Prabhat Patnaik, Jawaharlal Nehru University

'Challenges the prevailing racializing perception of the Southern worker held in the North as powerless and without agency. "Organizing Insurgency" is a must read for an understanding of imperialism, which has normalized a lack of awareness of the sustaining role of the southern agricultural and industrial workers in global capitalism.'
—Himani Bannerji, York University

Wildcat: Workers' Movements and Global Capitalism

Series Editors:
Immanuel Ness (City University of New York)
Peter Cole (Western Illinois University)
Raquel Varela (Instituto de História Contemporânea [IHC]
of Universidade Nova de Lisboa, Lisbon New University)
Tim Pringle (SOAS, University of London)

Also available:

Organizing Insurgency

Workers' Movements in
the Global South

Immanuel Ness

PLUTO PRESS

First published 2021 by Pluto Press
345 Archway Road, London N6 5AA

www.plutobooks.com

Copyright © Immanuel Ness 2021

The right of Immanuel Ness to be identified as the author of this work has been
asserted in accordance with the Copyright, Designs and Patents Act 1988.

British Library Cataloguing in Publication Data
A catalogue record for this book is available from the British Library

ISBN 978 0 7453 4360 0   Hardback
ISBN 978 0 7453 4359 4   Paperback
ISBN 978 0 7453 4363 1   PDF
ISBN 978 0 7453 4361 7   EPUB
ISBN 978 0 7453 4362 4   Kindle

Typeset by Stanford DTP Services, Northampton, England

Simultaneously printed in the United Kingdom and United States of America

Contents

Figures and Tables

Abbreviations

AFL	American Federation of Labor
AFP	Armed Forces of the Philippines
AMCU	Association of Mineworkers and Construction Union
AMSA	ArcelorMittal South Africa
ANC	African National Congress
ARB	Agrarian Reform Beneficiary (programme)
BMD	Bharat Mukti Dal
CARP	Comprehensive Agrarian Reform Programme
CCMA	Commission for Conciliation, Mediation and Arbitration
CITU	Centre of Indian Trade Unions
CIW	Coalition of Immokalee Workers
COSATU	Confederation of South African Trade Unions
CPI	Communist Party of India
CPI(M)	Communist Party of India (Marxist)
CSR	corporate social responsibility
CWAO	Casual Workers Advice Office
DLC	Delhi Labour Commissioner
DOLE	Department of Labour and Employment
EPI	export promotion industrialization
EPZ	Economic Processing Zone
FAO	Food and Agriculture Organization
FAWU	Food and Allied Workers Union
FMS	Faridabad Majdoor Samachar ('Faridabad Workers Newspaper')
GCC	global commodity chain
GEAR	Growth, Employment and Redistribution (programme)
GRMES	Garam Rolla Mazdoor Ekta Samiti
IMF	International Monetary Fund
INR	Indian rupee
INTUC	Indian National Trade Union Congress
ISI	import substitution industrialization

ITUC	International Trade Union Confederation
IUF	International Union of Food, Agricultural, Hotel, Restaurant, Catering, Tobacco and Allied Workers' Associations
IWW	Industrial Workers of the World
KMU	Kilusang Mayo Uno ('May First Movement')
MNC	multinational corporation
NAFLU	National Federation of Labor Unions
NAMASUFA	Nagkahiusang Mamumuo sa Suyapa Farm
NCT	National Capital Territory
NDF	National Democratic Front
NDP	National Development Plan
NFWOs	new forms of worker organization
NGO	non-governmental organization
NPA	New People's Army
NTUI	New Trade Union Initiative
NUM	National Union of Mineworkers
NUMSA	National Union of Metalworkers of South Africa
R	South African rand
Rs	Indian rupees
SACP	South African Communist Party
SAFTU	South African Federation of Trade Unions
SAPS	South African Police Service
SEWA	Self Employed Women's Association
SMSEs	small and medium-sized enterprises
SRWP	Socialist Revolutionary Workers Party
SWF	Simunye Workers' Forum
TES	temporary employment services
TNC	transnational corporation
UAW	United Auto Workers
UCW	Union Carriage & Wagon
UF	United Front
UMA	Unyon ng mga Manggagawa sa Agrikultura
WIA	Wazirpur Industrial Area

Series Preface

Workers' movements are a common and recurring feature in contemporary capitalism. The same militancy that inspired the mass labour movements of the twentieth century continues to define worker struggles that proliferate throughout the world today.

For more than a century, labour unions have mobilized to represent the political-economic interests of workers by uncovering the abuses of capitalism, establishing wage standards, improving oppressive working conditions, and bargaining with employers and the state. Since the 1970s, organized labour has declined in size and influence as the global power and influence of capital have expanded dramatically. The world over, existing unions are in a condition of fracture and turbulence in response to neoliberalism, financialization, and the reappearance of rapacious forms of imperialism. New and modernized unions are adapting to conditions and creating class-conscious workers' movements rooted in militancy and solidarity. Ironically, while the power of organized labour contracts, working-class militancy and resistance persist and are growing in the global South.

Wildcat publishes ambitious and innovative works on the history and political economy of workers' movements, and is a forum for debate on pivotal movements and labour struggles. The series applies a broad definition of the labour movement to include workers in and out of unions, and seeks works that examine proletarianization and class formation; mass production; gender, affective, and reproductive labour; imperialism and workers; syndicalism and independent unions, and labour and Leftist social and political movements.

Acknowledgements

I wish to thank and acknowledge all those who have supported me in making this book possible. Due to the sensitive nature of this work, many of those who have helped this research become a reality must remain anonymous. If we are serious about the possibility of revolutionary transformation, it is essential that we protect our sources in India, the Philippines, and South Africa. I am grateful to you all and greatly appreciate all your assistance in making this project a reality. We share a common struggle and hope that our collective work will bring about a genuine transformation in each society.

I have also received much assistance from all of those who have provided access and logistic support to make this book a reality. In South Africa, I would like to thank Luke Sinwell, Trevor Ngwane, Pragna Ragunanan, Trevor Mbatha, and Bruce Mellado. Chapter 4 on the struggle in Mindanao was made possible by the indefatigable support of Sarah Raymundo, who expended so much energy in facilitating access to key informants in the Philippines. I am grateful to my close comrades in India for their unflinching support in providing access to activists and workers. In the US, I thank Sarika Chandra for many conversations about this work, and most importantly, for teaching me the art of personal discipline and attention to detail. I thank Honghui Park for illuminating and revealing the oppressive and stultifying conditions and struggles of young women labourers in electronics factories producing for consumers in the global North.

At Pluto Press, I thank David Shulman, Emily Orford, Robert Webb, and Huw Jones.

Finally, I would like to thank all those who have read and provided advice in sharpening the arguments of this work. I alone take responsibility for the narratives and arguments of this book, which I hope will contribute to debate on the significance of the political and social organization of labour in the global South to build a better world. If we are to improve the conditions of life for all humanity, we must start with understanding and prioritizing all those who struggle every day in oppressive workplaces of the poorest countries and mobilize democratically into strong working-class anti-imperialist organizations. I dedicate this book to the workers and activists in the global South who continuously struggle for an egalitarian world and to the memory of Carlos Jopson Raymundo Jr, whose spirit lives on in our struggle.

Introduction: Forging a New Global Workers' Movement

This book argues that the contemporary era of imperialism is marked by the extension of exploitation of the global South's workers in core sectors of the economy: agriculture, mining, and industry. Indeed, incidences of protest are expanding in absolute numbers as industrial production shifts to the global South, where 84 per cent of the world's population of 7.8 billion people reside. In this Southern region, manufacturing workers are subjected to far more onerous and dangerous labour conditions than industrial workers in the developed metropolitan and settler countries. This book demonstrates that in recent years, workers have engaged in mass protests at a higher rate than ever and seek to obtain political power. In the 2010s, mass protests occurred unabated throughout the global South, in a range of contexts. The struggles are in large and small factories that have directly disrupted global supply chains essential to the production and distribution of goods and services in advanced economies.

Second, this book contends that workers in the rural and urban informal sectors of the global South are integrated into global commodity chains, and that their labour is essential to the maintenance of profit rates worldwide. This work supports the contention that profits are extracted from workers in rural regions as well as those who migrate back and forth from rural to urban areas for economic sustenance. The chapters will show that informal workers surrounding major economic centres in the rural and urban sectors are crucial to corporate profit margins and are major sites of economic contestation between labour and capital. While arable lands are located in regions of the global North and South, the production of key agricultural commodities like coffee, cocoa, and tropical foodstuffs takes place in regions where wages are low due to imperialist underdevelopment and where, as a consequence, there is an oversupply of labour from rural regions. But, on a planetary level, urban migration has not reduced the total population of agrarian workers. In fact, the evidence shows that rural labour has expanded in the first two decades of the twenty-first century. Indeed, the agrarian population has continued to grow over the last century, and even over the last 50 years, as rural populations continue to rely on agricultural production for sustenance, and worldwide demand for agricultural commodities continues to expand. Population growth in rural regions challenges the dominant narrative generated by Mike Davis and others who focus on ineluctable urban growth globally. While urban growth is indeed expanding, the rate of rural population growth is also expanding. Concomitantly, mass urbanization over the past century has increased populations in major urban centres in the global North and South. The vast majority of populations in many major cities of the South live in abject poverty without basic necessities such as electricity, running water, sanitation, and access to basic services. Thus, while the planet is growing in urban areas, it is also expanding in rural regions: a dynamic that is too often ignored.

Third, this book affirms the significance of strong organization for the working class to advance its interests: political and economic representation of the working class is crucial to improving the quality of life in the global South and building the power of labour. The case studies in this book show that worker unrest and popular social movements in the global South are ubiquitous in contemporary neoliberal capitalism. Indeed, research demonstrates that the size and intensity of protests are expanding in the contemporary era as industrial labour has expanded dramatically from the 1990s to the present. The research will also show that even as workers in urban and rural areas engage in mass mobilization, the disconnected nature of protests does not ensure that successful strikes are consolidated to become the basis for the development of socialism, solidarity, and equality.

WAITING FOR THE GLOBAL WORKING-CLASS UPSURGE

Most current popular and academic interpretations of the state of the world's working class brood over the absence of resistance and protest against labour exploitation and low wages. This book contends that workers indeed do engage in protest against employers in a range of contexts in urban and rural regions. Researchers (e.g. Munck and Silver, among others) are awaiting the moment when an upsurge of worker protest will occur.[1] In sharp contrast, this book argues that, over the past 50 years, labour protest is ever expanding as the world's working class has grown dramatically.

This book argues that a paucity of social and political working-class organization is a defining feature of protests in rural and urban areas alike. The argument is not new, but is often missing in the literature on contemporary labour movements. As existing trade unions and political parties have declined, much scholarship has overwhelmingly focused on new formations. In part, this is a result of the aversion to past and present socialist and communist working-class organizations that have disillusioned many on the Left. In this way, scholarship has sought to identify these new forms of amorphous and nebulous working-class organization that are said to have emerged from a new form of transcendent autonomous popular activity as somehow embodying popular power through an 'assembly' of the 'multitude' (to link two Hardt and Negri titles seeking to describe this new kind of workers' control).

If workers are protesting against conditions, then why is there no tangible improvement in the conditions of workers? This book argues that socialist organizations have eroded dramatically due in part to a fear of seizing power, which requires a strong and assertive working-class movement that actively challenges the paradigm of capitalist rule. In promoting political power for workers, it is necessary to take into consideration a wide range of literature by theorists and protagonists of popular struggles in the twentieth century. Yet a vocabulary of anti-socialism is the leading form of accepted knowledge with respect to socialist states of the past, so that analyses of actually existing socialism or communism typically focus on failures rather than major achievements. The resulting ideological disillusion militates against the attainment of power by the working class.

As we enter the 2020s, the nature of labour and work has transformed irrevocably as more and more people are forced into the labour market. On a global scale, wages, conditions, and working-class organization have declined dramatically. In rich countries of the global North, the outsourcing of capital and the closure of manufacturing have pushed more workers into services and commerce. In the global South, foreign investment and outsourcing have increased the share of workers employed in manufacturing industries which primarily supply commodities and natural resources to the global North.

IMPORTANCE OF POLITICAL AND ECONOMIC
WORKING-CLASS ORGANIZATION

Neoliberal capitalism has taken hold throughout the world over the five decades since 1970. Political and economic interpretations of the state of the global working class have reflected the diminishing resilience of social democratic programmes and the flagging influence that labour unions have over business and the state. As Left parties have adopted market-based policies, financialization and privatization have produced a general transfer of wealth to the upper classes, and opportunities to achieve public solutions to growing poverty and inequality have decreased dramatically.

Even if driven by electoral support for social programmes to reverse the distribution of social resources to the wealthy, liberal and social democratic political parties are unwilling and unable to shift course due to the overwhelming power of finance capital. In the global North, neoliberal policies have created greater inequality, but have not significantly reduced the standard of living for most workers, as consumption rates of workers have increased. In the global South, where abject poverty is systemic, political parties and governments are incapable of challenging the dominance of capital and finance in the global North. United Nations (UN) and World Bank data show that from 2000 to the present, the absolute number of people living in abject poverty has grown significantly. Without hesitation, Western capital can withdraw, sanction, and isolate countries seeking to redistribute wealth to the poor through nationalizing industry or the regulation of national markets and investments.

As global inequality and poverty have reached the highest levels today, this book presents a comparative study of labour in the global South, providing a highly accessible contribution to understanding the history, theory, and political economy of labour across continents and regions. The book includes three case studies of the global South. In the global North, neoliberal policies have afforded increased consumption of low-wage imports from the global South, while underpaid migrant workers provide essential food, transport, and care services, thus sustaining relatively high, though unevenly distributed, living standards. Resentment is very often directed against 'foreigners', particularly as they come to reside in the imperialist countries. As working-class shares of 'national' income have decreased in the metropolitan and settler-colonial countries since the 1980s relative to those of capital, international value transfer has ensured that this has not resulted in significant proletarianization. Building on the analysis set forth in my previous book, *Southern Insurgency: The Coming of the Global Working Class*, which examined internal migration and class struggles, this work examines the expansion and proliferation of temporary labour in the capitalist world system and its effects on the dynamics of the global class structure. It describes and explains the significance of: (1) the international division of labour, (2) national and regional labour supply and employment and unemployment (the 'reserve army of labour'), and (3) the importance and magnitude of migrant labour in the global system.

ORGANIZATION OF THE BOOK

This book is divided into two parts.

Part I, 'Theories and Concepts of Labour in the Global South', comprises an exposition and theorization of the impoverished state of labour in the global South, an examination of the status of labour following four decades of neoliberal capitalism, and a critique of the dominant development narrative. While some countries and regions within countries have achieved economic gains, the majority of workers in the global South remain in positions of poverty. Part I also examines the enduring significance of rural workers, whose population is larger today than at any time in history. In urban areas, workers are employed under highly unstable conditions and constitute what Jan Breman calls 'footloose labour' with strong ties to the rural regions and living in underdeveloped and highly exploitative urban locations. Part I concludes with a defence of the necessity for strong political and economic organization to advance the material conditions of most of the world's population. This book rejects the dominant labour literature that views local autonomous configurations and lack of strong organization as a virtue.

Part II, 'Case Studies: Rural and Informal Labour Struggles', examines three case studies drawn from the global South which demonstrate the major arguments of this book. In each case, under neoliberal practices forged from the 1980s to the present, workers are employed in unstable contract and informal work, and multinational corporations (MNCs) and employers seek to further disrupt the status quo and make ever more onerous demands on workers while weakening their institutional and organizational attachments. The case studies are based on direct research in India, the Philippines, and South Africa from 2016 to 2019. The chapters show that workers are eager to mobilize and strike to improve their conditions if they have sustenance from a political organization.

CHAPTER OUTLINE

Introduction

This introduction briefly presents the major arguments of the book, focusing on how neoliberal capitalism has impoverished workers in the Third World, as well as theoretical and conceptual perspectives on improving and transforming the condition of labour and the working class.

Part I: Theories and Concepts of Labour in the Global South

Chapter 1: The Labour Atlas: The Southern Working Class Holding Up the World. In Greek mythology, Atlas, the defeated Titan, is doomed to carry the whole weight of the world on his shoulders. This chapter claims that the Atlas metaphor applies to the global economy today, as workers in the Third World are doomed through economic imperialism to carry the burden of the entire world. The chapter examines the global state of the working class through focusing on the most exploited workers in the countries of the global South. While inequality is growing worldwide, a new consensus is emerging among political economists that the surplus labour of the working class in the 'periphery' is sustaining the world economy.

The chapter also examines the weakening of labour movements in the South under neoliberal capitalism, which demonstrates that strong labour organization, reaching a peak in the second half of the twentieth century, is more of a historical exception than a rule. In response to the ossification and decline of trade unions, labour scholars have espoused autonomous labour organization as a democratic alternative. By contrast, this chapter views rank-and-file labour organization as constant in nearly every historic epoch and geographic space. In view of the universal presence of autonomous labour activity, the chapter analyses the need for strong and committed organizations capable of sustaining incremental gains and holding out the hope of genuine social transformation.

Chapter 2: Workers' Movements in the South: Inequality, Poverty, and Enduring Relevance of Rural Proletariat and Informal Sector Workers. The importance of agrarian and informal workers is stressed in this chapter. Industrial workers have never comprised a majority of all workers under capitalism, and the Fordist system of production is an exception within manufacturing, especially today as global commodity supply chains rely on the dispersal of labour in plants across countries. This chapter examines the informal and rural sectors as major sites of class conflict that have been mostly neglected within labour research. In absolute terms, as the global population approaches 8 billion, the rural population is not declining in Asia and Africa, where demographic growth is higher today than in any era in history. In parallel, impoverished undeveloped settlements, which form part of major urban agglomerations, are growing at the most dramatic rate in history and constitute the largest component of urban centres in the global South. Conditions bear a resemblance to those of rural regions, in many cases lacking access to water, sanitation, electricity, and other basic services. Indeed, conditions in urban settlements are typically more dangerous than in rural zones. Drawing on the scholarship of Jan Breman, Jeffrey Paige, and other scholars of the agrarian and urban semi-proletariat, this chapter examines the significance of these workers to national economies and to the global economy.

Part II: Case Studies: Rural and Informal Labour Struggles

Chapter 3: Primitive Steel Manufacturing for the Global Consumer Market: Capital, Super-exploitation, and Surplus Value in Wazirpur, India. This chapter examines the crucial importance of informal workers in India. The Indian working class does not exemplify the confident image of Indian economists as comprising a skilled labour force trained in modern production techniques; often depicted by Thomas Friedman, among other Western political observers, as having higher skills in medicine, programming, and engineering and key fields; workers whose wages will eventually outpace Western workers, who do not have equivalent professional training. On the contrary, while India has high-technology centres, India's workforce is predominantly semi-proletarian and agrarian and is not leapfrogging over labourers in the US, Western, and even emerging economies of East and Southeast Asia. The vast majority of industrial activity in India is characterized by primitive forms of productive activity under extreme conditions of poverty, both in the rural countryside and in the major urban centres. The daily conditions of workers in Delhi's Wazirpur Industrial Area are resonant of Dickensian nineteenth-century England, rather than the cutting-edge high-technology image that promoters of India's economy seek to depict. Yet, as the industrial zone relies on highly exploited labour working for low wages under dangerous conditions, the stainless steel kitchen utensils and tableware goods produced are decisively integrated into global commodity supply chains for high-quality products in restaurants and households.

The chapter chronicles the development of Wazirpur as a major cog in the kitchen utensil and tableware global commodity supply chain through supplying the products to the international market for these goods. It examines the unbroken struggles of steelworkers over a two-decade period, which continue to the present. While informal sector workers engage in persistent job actions and combativeness against employers, their capacity to convert everyday resistance into concrete gains in wages and working conditions has only come about with the support of powerful and militant political organization with a strong commitment to mobilizing workers. In two instances, this chapter on Wazirpur's labouring poor demonstrates that the unification of an amorphous semi-proletariat labour force is only possible through strong organization applying political and economic mobilizing tactics to a common struggle against employers and state authorities.

Chapter 4: The Enduring System of Global Agricultural Commodity Production and First World Commodity Extraction: The Case of Mindanao, the Philippines. The Philippines represents an archetypal economy in the global South, exemplary rather than an anomaly in Southeast Asia and the world as a dependent capitalist country reliant on the extraction of natural resources, agricultural commodities, and on migrant labour for national economic development and growth. Unlike other countries in Southeast Asia and population centres in the global South, the Philippines is not developing a large manufacturing sector, but depends highly on exports of agricultural products, natural resources, and foreign remittances from skilled, semi-skilled, and unskilled migrants who work primarily outside the region. The Philippines' agricultural and mineral products are crucial for the development of global commodity chains. Resting at the bottom of the chain, the Philippines is the primary source and producer of commodities. However, due to the Philippines' subordinate position in global commodity chains, the value of the products is transferred to destination regions in the rich countries of Europe, North America, Japan, and beyond. The vast majority of the Philippines' population reside in agrarian regions where surplus is extracted from the land and people by comprador oligarchs and multinational corporations for the benefit of residents in the global North. The extraction of the land and labour of the Philippines by a privileged oligarchy with the support of foreign MNCs has endured from the era of Spanish and US colonization, through independence, and continued even after the 1986 popular protests which dislodged the dictator Ferdinand Marcos from power.

This chapter examines the organization of exploited rural agrarian workers in the southernmost island of the Philippines: Mindanao. The chapter documents the persistence of poverty and destitution through control of the land and natural resources by MNCs and oligarchs, with the unwavering support of the Philippines' state legal and security apparatus. The chapter documents how, even after the land reforms of the 1980s and 1990s, the rural proletariat has remained highly marginalized by a fraudulent land reform policy which has pushed landless workers into precarious working conditions through the institutionalization of a system of labour contracting. Through a case study of the Sumifru banana packing workers' strike of 2018–19, the chapter demonstrates that banana workers on plantations and in packing houses have lost their status as regular workers, and have been shifted into labour contracting through a duplicitous worker cooperative system. Worker cooperatives in Mindanao exploit labour for MNCs through avoiding labour laws, safe working conditions, and pensions while also obliging workers to pay for the right to join their organizations. Rural worker cooperatives in Mindanao are even more exploitative than the corporate farms they replaced in the early 2000s, while remaining subservient to the demands of MNCs. On fertile land that could potentially be cultivated to provide food and sustenance for the Philippines' population of 110 million, workers labour to produce bananas, pineapples, mangos, and other exotic tropical fruits to conform to the latest culinary tastes of First World populations. The global commodity supply chain for bananas and other tropical fruit reinforces exploitation in rural regions where workers are farthest removed from the point of consumption and exchange. Profits are realized in the bustling markets of Japan, Korea, Oceania, and the Gulf States where consumers buy tropical fruit exports from Mindanao. The case study examines the resilience of Kilusang Mayo Uno (KMU), a militant union aligned with popular struggles throughout the Philippines. In view of the Philippines' semi-colony status as a source of natural resources, agricultural commodities, and migrant labourers to the global capitalist economy, KMU recognizes the significance of rural labour in enriching economic imperialism. The chapter also examines the worker cooperative system in the Philippines, which has been co-opted by multinational corporations like Del Monte, Dole, Fyffes, and Sumitomo. In effect, the cooperatives operate as labour subcontractors.

The chapter examines the organizational power of the KMU as a political and economic counter-hegemonic force which mobilizes the most marginal workers, achieving gains *vis-à-vis* employers, and demanding the transformation of an unjust system where wealth is monopolized by local comprador classes and multinationals in the advanced economies of the world.

Chapter 5: Global Capitalism: Corporate Restructuring, Labour Brokering, and Working-class Mobilization in South Africa. More than 25 years after the end of apartheid, black South Africans, constituting more than 90 per cent of the nation's 60 million residents, remain mired in poverty and destitution. The post-apartheid period granted political equality devoid of economic rights. In this context, South Africa has become the most unequal major country in the world, with a small minority holding on to control over agricultural lands and natural resources. The failings of the post-apartheid era became visible in the 2010s as workers in the mining industry engaged in major struggles against the corrupt National Union of Mineworkers and the ruling African National Congress (ANC) and Tripartite Alliance which imposed and reinforced inequality. The April 2012 Marikana Massacre demonstrated that the Tripartite Alliance Government was representing the economic interests of the white minority, black comprador elites, and multinational corporations at the expense of the black South African majority. The polarized economy soon led to deep fissures within the Tripartite Alliance and within the ANC, South African Communist Party, and Confederation of South African Trade Unions ruling alliance. In particular, this chapter focuses on the growing acrimony which punctuated the era as the National Union of Metalworkers of South Africa (NUMSA) broke with the ANC and then was expelled from the Congress of South African Trade Unions (COSATU). These internecine political conflicts reflected growing resentment and a sense of futility among black South African workers seeking to challenge the dominant neoliberal order. Government bureaucrats with networks in government personally benefited financially.

NUMSA, representing urban manufacturing workers, was the major force in the development of an opposition to the Tripartite Alliance, helping form the United Front of community organizations, the South African Federation of Trade Unions, and the fledgling South African Revolutionary Workers Party to galvanize the black working class throughout the economy. In 2020, this new apparatus remains inchoate and requires broader participation among the dispersed working class which is now engaged in struggles throughout South Africa. As NUMSA seeks to galvanize a strong opposition party and movement, South African workers have formed independent organizations to challenge the state's shift to neoliberalism, which supports subcontracting of work to informal workers in the settlements surrounding Johannesburg, Durban, Cape Town, and South Africa's major economic centres. While NUMSA stands in political opposition, committed to social transformation, nationalization of strategic industries, redistribution and collectivization of lands, and the end of economic imperialism by foreign multinationals, workers are often engaged in autonomous struggles against avaricious employers who have subordinated workers into the subcontracting system in the informal economy.

This chapter on South Africa examines the struggles of informal workers to gain status as regular workers through examining organization of the autonomous Casual Workers Advice Office (CWAO) and NUMSA. CWAO was formed in 2011 as an independent labour organization in Germiston, on the East Rand, an old manufacturing centre in Gauteng Province undergoing industrial restructuring and the recomposition of its labour force from formal to informal sector workers. A decade earlier, large factories and mills employing hundreds of workers began to be replaced by smaller facilities that employed non-union and temporary workers. The primary campaigns have focused on mobilizing the growing number of impoverished workers seeking equity with full-time workers at major private businesses, including subsidiaries of major MNCs. CWAO is filling a major gap which established unions have neglected in the period from 1995 to 2010, especially the vastly growing number of workers employed for labour contractors, brokers, and in small and dispersed factories. While COSATU had been critical of the rise of labour brokers from 2000 to 2010, following Marikana and the expulsion of NUMSA, COSATU's defence of non-union workers employed for labour brokers has vanished. The labour brokering practice is supported by leading

South African state and business interests seeking to lower the cost of labour in manufacturing, services, and logistics.

The chapter chronicles key organizing and legal campaigns of NUMSA and CWAO against the state and multinationals to defend the most impoverished workers mired in the labour broking system without legal status as regular workers. The chapter surveys the competing organizing campaigns: NUMSA seeking to directly organize workers into the union, and CWAO mobilizing workers as an autonomous force through the Simunye Workers' Forum, which holds regular meetings and presses demands for labour actions against specific employers. The former seeks to consolidate the struggles of workers into a strong union, the latter opposes all organization in favour of worker rank-and-file activity in one enterprise at a time.

Chapter 6: Conclusion: Labour Struggles and Political Organization. This chapter recapitulates the major findings of the book on the growing significance of informal sector workers in urban settlements and agrarian regions to global supply chains, and assesses the significance of labour mobilization and political struggles in these crucial geographic zones of the world. The chapter reiterates the significance of robust political organization in consolidating the gains of grassroots struggles and the practical potential in advancing effective struggles that conceivably may contribute to egalitarian social transformation.

PART I

THEORIES AND CONCEPTS OF LABOUR IN THE GLOBAL SOUTH

1
The Labour Atlas: The Southern Working Class Holding Up the World

In Greek mythology, Atlas, the leader of the Titans, is doomed to carry the whole weight of the heavens on his shoulders after his people's defeat in their struggle against Zeus. The symbolism of Atlas holding up the world is apt in signifying the present global order where the labouring classes of the Third World hold up the entire world: both the 90 per cent of the world's population living in poor countries and the workforce of the First World, which continues to profit from the toiling working classes in Southern countries. Like Titan, global South workers are condemned to the fate of work; they are also forced to exist under the most unbearable conditions of extreme suffering.

GLOBAL NEOLIBERALISM AND INCREASING MISERY OF THE SOUTHERN WORKING CLASS

As global neoliberalist capitalism has expanded in the 50 years from 1970 to 2020, the absolute power of capital has grown *vis-à-vis* labour. Working-class organizations and trade unions have been unable to curb the absolute growth in corporate power in a local, state, regional, and global context. In turn, working-class organizations have eroded dramatically and have become marginal in most countries of the world. The consequence of the decline in working-class organization is far more deleterious for workers in poor countries of the South than it is for those in the wealthy metropolitan and settler states. At the height of capitalist development in Western Europe and North America, workers developed labour organizations to advance their material interests. Yet today, with a severe shortage of working-class organization, global South workers lack the power to build defensive organizations to challenge a far more rapacious form of multinational capital. Thus, the disparity of wealth, wages, and income between North and South is expanding at a faster pace than any time in the last 50 years.

This book asserts that the deterioration of conditions of workers in the global South is directly related to the decline in working-class organizations, many of which expanded during the period of decolonization from the 1940s to the 1970s. Labour unions which emerged and gained power in this era have been under relentless attack by the logic of capitalist profitability under neoliberalism and the modern state. Working-class organizations are eschewed by capital and the state as a constraint on profits and development. Thus, under neoliberalism, states which freely permit working-class organizations are bypassed in the commodity supply chains for products primarily for consumers in the rich countries. As labour unions' state social programmes complicate the production of low-cost consumer goods, states striving for integration into the global capitalist system view working-class organizations as anathema to development. Moreover, since foreign direct investments are also likely to go to countries with the weakest social safety nets, even products sold for national consumption must abjure the formation of strong labour unions. Thus, even in states with robust labour and social protection, social programmes advocated by the UN's International Labour Organization, and beyond, are fiercely resisted by local capitalists and state regulatory bodies as capital mobility permits the freedom to invest and withdraw capital. States challenging the global neoliberal regime risk losing capital investments that are essential for economic expansion and growth. Yet, concomitantly, these very policies cause mass global poverty and economic inequality.

Thus, throughout the global South, trade unions which came of age from the 1940s to 1970s as strong and vigorous guardians of an incipient working class have now been eroded or rendered impotent in defending the broader working-class rights. Prior to the implementation of neoliberal reforms, strong unions sought to defend the rank and file and organize the most deprived workers. Today, unions are unable to even defend their own members, let alone organize the hundreds of millions of workers who have entered the labour force in the first two decades of the twentieth century.

The dominant pattern on a global level is the withdrawal of trade unions from the sphere of work in all but a few sectors. Yet the fading of strong and responsive trade unions has not diminished the aspirations of workers for strong labour and effective representation. Today, in the absence of strong trade unions, the dominant trend among scholars of labour movements is to demonstrate that the working class is engaged in new forms of organization. These scholars posit that workers reject the *old* form of labour organization, which was deficient in democratic participation and as a rule engaged in labour–management cooperation, which weakened the power of workers. The claim that trade unions had devolved into ossified organizations benefiting only labour leaders, thwarting the foundation of trade unions in the post-war era that was directly related to mass waves of labour protests and demands for representation. Thus, labour scholarship asserts that because established trade unions ineluctably ensconce themselves into serving the interests of capital or compromising with it, workers have formed independent, autonomous trade unions to advance their class interests.

Consequently, optimistic observers point to class struggle emerging under new agency: the autonomous force of workers' self-activity, the development of workers' assemblies external to existing trade unions, and other organizations expressing the unique identity of workers. In addition, labour scholars identify a workers' movement which is far more radical, as it is unconstrained by the bureaucratic and organizational constraints of established trade unions. They point to the explosion of workers' movements on a world scale, including for-hire transportation and delivery, garment manufacturing, high-technology production workers, dockworkers, and beyond, encompassing every sector of national economies. At times, these worker mobilizations congeal into unconstrained rank-and-file organizations, and other times, they may fade away, only to return in different forms.

This book affirms the expansion of new forms of working-class organizations today as established union representatives decline in influence and power. However, the book also asserts that workers have always been in motion and are no more likely to engage in struggle against capital than in the past. The reason why we see these multifarious actions is that the working classes lack strong organization, thus protests are not seen as contained in the framework of organizational demands.

The book also argues that with stronger organization, labour struggles would expand dramatically, as workers are prone to engage in disruptive activity under the umbrella of a class-wide organization which has the capacity to defend and advance conditions, prevent the setting of one segment of the workforce into opposition against another, and act as a class-wide force. Thus, the labour scholarship is misplaced, as it fails to integrate the significance of strong unions and parties. Thus, we must distinguish between the quotidian protests which occur openly today and real class power, reflected in organization.

WORKER MOBILIZATION, RESISTANCE, AND ORGANIZATION

As the vast majority of the world's workers are employed in the global South, this book provides three crucial case studies that have been derived from research across major economic regions of economic production. The case studies provide tangible examples so that readers can grasp the constraints faced by workers in context. Key questions include:

- How do workers resist oppression on a regular basis? Why is this resistance not translated into unified and militant social protest movements?
- What organizational triggers contribute to the cohesion of quotidian labour struggles into mass movements?
- How do these mass movements differ from expected social mobilization against injustice and oppression?
- What are the institutions of working-class solidarity that transform protest movements into robust social organizations capable of challenging capital and the state?

THE SIGNIFICANCE OF THE RURAL WORKING CLASS

A second major contention of this book is that rural labour retains an enduring presence into the twenty-first century. Rural labour is conceived as workers who rotate between work and non-work. In this way, in rural regions, labour has never been fully employed throughout the year. Work is guided by agricultural seasons, planting, tilling, and harvesting. The agrarian sector has never had labourers who have been working year-round. By contrast, capitalist production has compelled labour to be constantly working, and during periods of joblessness or irregular work, the livelihood of urban workers and their families comes under severe threat. The Left has come to view irregular employment as a major threat to the existence of workers, but this risk is derived from capitalism, which separates workers from agrarian zones. This book contends that agrarian regions are crucial to comprehending labour struggles today, as they have not declined, but have expanded.

In absolute terms, the rural sectors have expanded in the global South. These regions comprise 51 per cent of the population in poor countries of the South. Moreover, as the urban regions have encroached on agrarian zones in major urban metropolises, these key agglomerations have encompassed agricultural zones. The largest cities of the global South blend urban and rural. As a consequence, labour researchers have conceived of workers as irregular or precarious. Precariousness has permeated the entire planet as workers have become redundant even in the rich countries of the global North, but it primarily depicts and comprises the vast majority of the workers who reside in the global South, as the commodification of rural areas pushes rural residents into urban zones where they must work. And work is almost always temporary and lacking in job security.

The agrarian working class has been neglected in practically all the recent scholarly analysis dealing with the transformation of labour. Indeed, this is a major omission in diagnosing the contemporary status of the labour movement and its capacity to improve its material and social conditions through social change. This inattention to rural labour is principally driven by the prominence given to new technology by social scientists, and Marxists in particular. Consequently, the focus has been trained on the modern economy, high technology, etc.

The rapid pace of global urbanization fails to consider three major countercurrents which suggest that the trajectory out of rural regions is not inexorable:

- *Expansion of urban conglomerations into adjacent areas in the countryside* – large tracts of land once in rural regions have been designated by government authorities as coterminous with urban zones.
- *Correspondingly, the typical urban zone in the global South bears a resemblance to rural areas* – in many cases, newly designated urban tracts are deficient in the characteristics of urban areas, for example they do not have running and potable water, sanitation services, electricity, health services, paved roads, security and crime prevention, education, public and private enterprises, or access to nearby markets.
- *Return migration to rural regions* – unable to survive and live sustainable lives in urban zones, labourers often return to rural regions upon

completion of their work or when industries close and unemployment rises. The ethnographic research of Jan Breman dating back to the 1990s reveals widespread poverty and absence of basic services in urban areas in South Asia, a feature that is even more prevalent in new 'urban' areas of Africa and Southeast Asia.[1]

Scarcity of critical daily necessities of life pushes the working classes of the global South into a peripatetic existence in the interstices between urban and rural life. Consequently, the developmental jargon proffered by established political economists is inaccurate in defining the stark disparities between the conditions of abject poverty of the global South and the relative prosperity of the global North. In the global South, work which is defined as 'informal' was always 'informal' per se, in both urban and rural regions. Rural workers always laboured under harsh conditions without standards. Accordingly, the scholarly use of the terminology 'informal' and 'precarious' fails to recognize the conditions of workers in poor countries who produce commodities for local, regional, and international markets. As we shall see in Chapter 3 on India, some industries with a very low subsumption of capital produce commodities for consumption in the rich countries of the global North through the super-exploitation of highly precarious labourers who have recently moved to major urban agglomerations.

Moreover, as we shall see in Chapter 4 on the Philippines, the agricultural sector remains a strong part of the political economy of the global South. Mike Davis's pioneering work on global urbanization, *Planet of Slums*, posits a sharply rising urban population as the rural regions are depopulated.[2] The global economic development literature endorses and reaffirms this view of an urbanizing world.[3] Yet the discourse fails to acknowledge the enduring presence of a large and growing rural population. The UN projects that population growth in urban areas will outpace rural regions from 2020 to 2050. See Table 1.1 for urban–rural population change from 1950 to 2050 in more developed and less developed regions, and Table 1.2 for the distribution of rural populations on a regional basis. Both tables demonstrate that urban conglomerates will grow quickly over the next 30 years to 2050. However, rural areas, which have expanded rapidly since 1950, will not substantially decline. UN projections show that rural populations may in fact grow through higher density rates and the development of agglomerations. It is highly unlikely that the new urban areas will provide the basic services necessary for basic subsistence of rural populations. These estimates are based on natural increase, rural–urban migration, and geographic expansion of urban settlements. Thus, UN demographers agree that sheer population growth will transform rural localities into urban settlements in the countryside.[4] A decisive factor in Third World urbanization from 1950 to the present is the enduring connection between the urban proletariat and rural regions. In addition, basic services and urban infrastructure do not accompany the growth of urban zones in these regions. The designation 'urban' does not denote access to clean water, sanitation, electricity, transportation, healthcare, education, or even food stocks. Unsurprisingly, planetary population growth is associated with higher density rates, which are often likely to change rural zones into urban settlements, but density does not imply basic services that are typically present in the global North.

As the Earth's human population has grown under capitalism, both urban and rural regions have grown, though urban areas are growing at a faster pace and rural hinterlands are often absorbed into the city limits. Mike Davis details that the urban sphere has grown dramatically in the global South, contributing to poverty and inequality and deepening divisions between urban and rural regions. Thus, while Davis correctly views urban regions as growing, we must also consider the vast growth in the rural regions, where population growth has not declined, but expanded, contributing to greater poverty. Moreover, Davis does not consider the degree to which urban zones or 'slums' are often marked by a 'rural' character and geography. These urban settlements are often visible through their lack of rudimentary attributes: unpaved roads, lack of running water, electricity, transportation, healthcare, and public amenities that are typically considered urban. The urban agglomerations have grown dramatically as 'cities' grow exponentially, but this does not translate into what is typically considered *urban*.

The meaning of precariousness differs greatly between the global North and global South, and must be situated in context. We must use the term 'precarious' as a form of expectation of living. If we mean by 'precarious' a routine everyday life of lack of opportunity, few expectations for increased wealth accumulation, and lack of growth, and the term applies to a sector of global North workers, then declining expectations can be considered precarious as workers do not have a sense that capitalist economies will increase their opportunity for the accumulation of wealth. But 'precarious' also includes access to basic standards of existence: food, health care,

Table 1.1 Total, urban, and rural populations and their average annual rates of change for the world and development groups, selected years and periods, 1950–2050

Development group	Population (billions)						Average annual rate of change (%)				
	1950	1970	1990	2018	2030	2050	1950–1970	1970–1990	1990–2018	2018–2030	2030–2050
Total population											
World	2.54	3.70	5.33	7.63	8.55	9.77	1.89	1.83	1.28	0.95	0.67
More developed regions	0.81	1.01	1.15	1.26	1.29	1.30	1.07	0.64	0.34	0.17	0.03
Less developed regions	1.72	2.69	4.18	6.37	7.26	8.47	2.23	2.21	1.50	1.09	0.77
Urban population											
World	0.75	1.35	2.29	4.22	5.17	6.68	2.95	2.63	2.18	1.69	1.28
More developed regions	0.45	0.67	0.83	0.99	1.05	1.12	2.06	1.04	0.64	0.46	0.34
Less developed regions	0.30	0.68	1.46	3.23	4.12	5.56	4.02	3.82	2.83	2.03	1.50
Rural population											
World	1.79	2.35	3.04	3.41	3.38	3.09	1.37	1.30	0.41	-0.07	-0.45
More developed regions	0.37	0.33	0.32	0.27	0.24	0.17	-0.48	-0.27	-0.58	-0.95	-1.61
Less developed regions	1.42	2.01	2.72	3.14	3.14	2.92	1.75	1.52	0.51	0.00	-0.37

Source: United Nations, Department of Economic and Social Affairs, *World Urbanization Prospects: The 2018 Revision* (New York: United Nations, 2019), https://population.un.org/wup/Publications/Files/WUP2018-Report.pdf, accessed 20 February 2020, p. 9.

Table 1.2 Evolution of the urban, rural, and total populations of the world by geographic region, selected years, 1950–2050

	Population (millions)					% geographic region				
	1950	1990	2018	2030	2050	1950	1990	2018	2030	2050
A. Urban population										
World	751	2290	4220	5167	6680	100.0	100.0	100.0	100.0	100.0
Africa	33	200	548	824	1489	4.3	8.7	13.0	15.9	22.3
Asia	246	1040	2266	2802	3479	32.8	45.4	53.7	54.2	52.1
Europe	284	505	553	573	599	37.8	22.0	13.1	11.1	9.0
Latin America and the Caribbean	70	315	526	600	685	9.3	13.8	12.5	11.6	10.3
Northern America	110	211	299	335	387	14.7	9.2	7.1	6.5	5.8
Oceania	8	19	28	33	41	1.1	0.8	0.7	0.6	0.6
B. Rural population										
World	1785	3041	3413	3384	3092	100.0	100.0	100.0	100.0	100.0
Africa	196	434	740	880	1039	11.0	14.3	21.7	26.0	33.6
Asia	1158	2182	2279	2144	1778	64.9	71.8	66.8	63.4	57.5
Europe	265	217	190	167	117	14.9	7.1	5.6	4.9	3.8
Latin America and the Caribbean	99	131	126	118	95	5.6	4.3	3.7	3.5	3.1
Northern America	62	69	65	61	48	3.5	2.3	1.9	1.8	1.6
Oceania	5	8	13	15	16	0.3	0.3	0.4	0.4	0.5
C. Total population										
World	2536	5331	7633	8551	9772	100.0	100.0	100.0	100.0	100.0
Africa	229	635	1288	1704	2528	9.0	11.9	16.9	19.9	25.9
Asia	1404	3221	4545	4947	5257	55.4	60.4	59.5	57.8	53.8
Europe	549	722	743	739	716	21.7	13.5	9.7	8.6	7.3
Latin America and the Caribbean	169	446	652	718	780	6.7	8.4	8.5	8.4	8.0
Northern America	173	280	364	395	435	6.8	5.3	4.8	4.6	4.4
Oceania	13	27	41	48	57	0.5	0.5	0.5	0.6	0.6

Source: United Nations, Department of Economic and Social Affairs, *World Urbanization Prospects: The 2018 Revision* (New York: United Nations, 2019), https://population.un.org/wup/Publications/Files/WUP2018-Report.pdf, accessed 20 January 2020.

housing, running water, electricity, transportation, etc. While employment opportunities and wage rates have declined for some workers, capitalist restructuring under neoliberalism has created the tendency for wealth to be accumulated through the ownership of assets that can be clearly enumerated in financial terms.

In contrast, in the global South, precariousness and precarity have a wholly distinctive nature, with severe and unyielding consequences for workers and peasants. The principal contrast in the South is that precarity is the standard for the vast majority of labour. Precarious labour typically does not extend to more than 10–20 per cent of the working populations of advanced capitalist economies in the global North. Yet the vast majority of scholarship on precarious scholarship is focused on these advanced capitalist economies.[5] Thus, precariousness is the norm as opposed to the exception to the rule. Furthermore, established working patterns of the past have always been the standard: long and arduous hours of work, low wages that are often too low for survival, and harsh and dangerous conditions of work. In addition, the share of the population working is far larger and includes a larger share of women in manufacturing production. The legal restrictions stipulating the conditions of work are non-existent or frequently unenforced. Thus, child labour is rampant, exposure to hazardous materials commonplace, and dangers extend to those not in the workforce. For example, women may take their children to work in unsafe buildings or fields sprayed with dangerous pesticides.

Further, given that urban agglomerations have grown so rapidly in the 50 years from the 1970s to the present, there is a far greater propensity for residents to live where they work. Thus, whole communities may be sites of danger. As we shall see in Chapter 3, Wazirpur, a steel-producing community in northeast New Delhi of some 200,000 people, is a site of distress in workplaces and in homes. The air pollution caused by 24-hour operation of hundreds of small steel mills is at dangerous levels. Children live with their families in small, wooden, fire-prone flats behind the factories, purchasing food in the market requires crossing the railway tracks, and youngsters may wander away from their adults and be struck and killed by trains. This is standard, not exceptional. Precarious workers in the global South do not have access to basic social and economic services, nor did they ever have them.

Further, in the global North, there is an implication that 'precarious' implies working in an economy which does not have opportunities as in the past, and workers are employed for far fewer hours per week and lack the job stability that once existed. In the global South, job instability has been the norm, but work time has not diminished. Workers must eke out a living or starve.

Conditions for the vast majority of workers labouring in the global South have remained impoverished in the post-independence era as economic imperialism has dominated the world economy from the end of the Second World War to the 2010s. This structural inequality has been intensified in the 1980s and 1990s by the international imposition of neoliberal policies, as national development and import substitution industrialization (ISI) schemes were removed and replaced by export promotion industrialization (EPI). Colonialism and economic imperialism had always been based on the transfer of wealth to the metropolitan and settler economies through the extraction of natural resources and agricultural commodities in Asia, Africa, and Latin America. These practices of extraction and *value transfer* from the global South to the global North have been extended and deepened from the 1980s and 1990s through the relocation and expansion of EPI in the global South for consumption in the global North. The growth of the workforce in the global South disproves the claim by economists in the global North that workers are being replaced by robots. Rather, the absolute size of the working class has expanded in the South through industrial development and urbanization. Thus, the greater part of value transfer from the South to the advanced developed countries is a corollary of the direct exploitation of labour. Even if commodities produced in the South are consumed in the South, profits are realized by multinational corporations and concentrated in financial centres of the North.

Therefore, labour struggles in the imperialist North, where e-commerce and the service sector have expanded dramatically, are of far less consequence. Most observers of labour in the metropolitan and settler economies of the global North focus on the decline in labour and growing inequality, but not poverty. Attribution for the decline in the labour movement in Western Europe and North America by Moody and other labour commentators is directed at rapacious capital and the failures of trade unions themselves to respond to the challenges posed to the working class by the consolidation of multinational capital.[6] While Moody is correct that the working class is not disappearing in the US and the West, and that the 'new terrain' has expanded to new jobs in the service sector, he discounts the relative benefits that accrue to workers in the imperial centre obtaining from the transfer of value and wealth from workers and resources on the periphery. Income inequality within the US has grown since the 1970s, but the major disparity in working-class wealth is between the rich and poor countries. The claim that working-class membership in trade unions is declining reveals this relative prosperity, and not simply a corollary of the rise of corporate influence.

Up until the 1980s and 1990s, rising unemployment was a positive force on capital, as an enlarged reserve army of labour moderates wage demands. In the international economy, capital markets benefit from affluent workers who represent the market for the goods produced by a low-wage working class in the South.[7] Conversely, when wages rise in the South, finance capital will withdraw investments for lower-wage regions. Undeniably, the beneficiaries of capitalist globalization are both corporations and affluent workers in the West. Little or no attention is given to the fact that while inequality is growing dramatically within the rich countries of the world, poverty is not expanding, while the level of absolute poverty is expanding in the global South. In the South, unions which formed and expanded in the independence era were severely weakened by capitalist states that were intent on imposing neoliberal policies to retain and attract industry and foreign direct investment.

Even as trade unions are in a decades-long downward spiral, sociologist Ronaldo Munck and others have claimed that globalization generates new openings for international working-class solidarity in the present interregnum of inertia. Accordingly, he maintains that worker organizations and trade unions must remain resilient under the most adverse political and economic conditions.[8] We must credit Munck for his recognition of the significance of international labour solidarity in re-establishing a strong working-class movement on national and global scales. Careful delineation of the growing divisions in the working classes within countries is necessary to precisely understand the nature of the working class, especially the growth of contingent and non-standard labour. A desiccated labour movement has grown under neoliberalism, and it is necessary to recognize the significance of differentiating standard, informal, contract, and precarious work in today's world. Serious scholarship is built upon a resolute refutation of the latest fads that captivate labour intellectuals, which only confuse and distort a vivid conceptualization of the stark divisions that are appearing globally. Most recently, conceptual distortion of workers, the working class, and working-class organization has emerged as scholars conjure up terms such as 'the precariat' and 'autonomous unions'.[9] There are no new discoveries about the nature of labour and working-class organization. Concomitantly, we must reject the dominant view in the West that the working class is disappearing as a social force through the introduction of new technology and its application in the material world. Digitization and robotization are the latest iterations, but they will not change the calculus of class antagonism and the necessity for working-class and peasant organization.

Globalization and the application of technological change are accelerating at an unprecedented rate, and employers are relentlessly seeking to lower wage costs. Marx and Engels were cognizant that these developments would bring new challenges to working-class solidarity. These challenges are formidable in stymieing class unity on a local and regional basis: for example, the recent resistance to placing Amazon's vaunted second headquarters, which pitted construction workers against retail and government employees. Likewise, the Keystone pipeline controversy showed that trade unions are often indifferent to the ecological impact of new development. Twenty years ago, the Battle in Seattle displayed a faint possibility of cooperation.

A growing strand of contemporary labour research focuses on positive outcomes of transnational labour union mobilization and strike action that lead to higher wages and improved working conditions.[10] While studies of trade union victories in strategic sectors may provide hope and optimism for revival of a labour movement, they are the exception to the general rule of systemic long-term decline in working-class organizational power.

But in the absence of working-class parties, trade unions are unable to restrain the national chauvinism and racism that have dangerously erupted in Europe and North America and among the bourgeois and comprador classes in poor countries of the South. Indeed, as international solidarity has waned over the past five decades, the most privileged sections of workers in metropolitan and settler countries have promoted nationalism and intensified global poverty and inequality.

We *do* have a historical legacy of international working-class solidarity. While Global Union Federations and the International Trade Union Confederation (ITUC) are periodically challenging multinational capitalists to improve conditions, these labour organizations will not transform the calculus of ruling-class domination on national and international levels. The 200 million members of ITUC represent about 5 per cent of all global workers, and their militancy varies along national and sectoral lines, reflecting the significance of states and global capital.

It is a formidable task to develop international working-class solidarity. Labour scholars have impressively marshalled compelling examples of valiant trade unions and labour organizations mobilizing and organizing against extreme exploitation to achieve workers' rights. In doing so, they have presented specific examples of international solidarity in logistics and among the most vulnerable workers earning poverty wages. Best practices are advanced by labour scholars, and come and go, but a genuine organizational commitment to advancing the interests of the working classes in these most vulnerable positions is rooted in class struggle and the struggle for solidarity that is established and consolidated over a long time. In the 1990s through to the 2010s, labour organizers have sketched a myriad of tactics and campaigns for trade unions based on persuading state actors and capitalists to grant workers greater power. However, these largely ephemeral efforts to improve organizational practices, frame new organizing strategies, and establish innovative approaches to labour union action have been unsuccessful for trade union and working-class organizations.[11] However, under neoliberalism we have not seen 'workers of the world unite' through existing labour organizations.

The potential for building international working-class solidarity in the transport and logistics sectors, from air transport and rail to shipping, provides a new redoubt for organization, but given the vast divisions between rich and poor countries, the outcomes of work stoppages and strikes vary greatly. But the cases of international solidarity, while impressive in themselves, are nebulous, and do not define the dominant impediment to global solidarity in the present era. Munck has pointed to worker strikes at Ryanair and non-governmental organization (NGO) advocacy campaigns for worker rights, which appear to be corporate foundational alternatives to independent trade unions, and to temporary migrant labour organizing in Malaysia.

But these examples are anaemic, few and far between, and do not collectively build a major movement for transnational working-class solidarity.

Some labour scholars take solace in isolated and discrete organizing campaigns culminating in the recruitment of workers into trade unions and the negotiation of bargaining agreements which marginally increase wages and working conditions.[12] These labour campaigns are often achieved through a form of 'trade union arbitrage': to wit, labour unions negotiate with multinational corporations and exchange the rights of workers in one location for organizing relatively small numbers of workers in another location, for example the G4S Security campaign organizing South African security guards.

The most notable recent examples of global solidarity in the last five years, such as Ryanair, have benefited relatively privileged workers in the rich countries of the North, and have not encompassed the vast majority of global workers in the South. Campaigns have been waged in the last 40 years of neoliberal capitalism which, while impressive, do not build a strong case for an emergent movement for a nascent transnational labour solidarity. To build working-class solidarity, we cannot rely on technocrats and trade union administrators. Though competence and commitment are crucial in building workers' organization, most of these new formations do not provide the basis for a new transnational solidarity.

THE WORKING CLASS AND POLITICAL TRANSFORMATION

Advocates for global working-class solidarity should be given credit for calling on 'workers of the world to unite' and looking for opportunity and possibility amid the gloom. We need to foster hope rather than criticize even faint attempts at solidarity if we do not have a grounded solution. But history does provide powerful examples of international working-class solidarity. And these examples are drawn from the major transformative movements in the global South, namely the Bolshevik Revolution and the Chinese Revolution.

We must start by identifying the divide between rich and poor as the most powerful working-class force for global solidarity over the last century. Global North workers must understand and act on the oppression that undergirds the capitalist system: the divide between workers in affluent regions and the 90 per cent of the global working class living outside Western Europe, North

America, and the rest of the settler world. This is why imperialism and the Third World are still crucial concepts and realities.

The problems encountered by First World workers pale in comparison to the reality faced by workers in the Third World. What examples can we draw on? How can we build unity between the global North and global South? International working-class solidarity has always required socialist political organization. We can expect workers to engage in autonomous self-activity, innovative struggles, and strikes, but these forms of militancy can only succeed with cohesive leadership that arises from a revolutionary political perspective. Out of the Bolshevik and Chinese Revolutions, new movements and organizations emerged dedicated to the struggle against global capitalism and imperialism. At the moment, no such organization or movement exists. Thus, while agreement exists among Marxist trade unions in the global South on the necessity for social transformation and anti-imperialism, few organizations have emerged with the capacity or will to challenge state power to build a broader movement against monopoly capitalism propelled by the imperialist states. If a communist or socialist party intent on building socialism takes power in the global South, it will boost the spirits of workers on a global basis. The year 2019 was the hundredth anniversary of the Comintern, which sought to build an internationalist movement. Challenging global capitalism was initiated by first taking power in key regions of the colonized world.

Today's socialists and workers can learn critical lessons that the most important struggle is against capitalist and imperialist oppression. The question then emerges: What kind of workers' movement? Munck takes solace in the existing architecture of labour organizations in the contemporary capitalist system. But they do not possess the capacity or the willingness to change the calculus of state and world power as the Bolsheviks and Chinese Communists did. Both were intent on openly resisting capitalism and imperialism. Marx and Engels recognized the vast inequality between British and Irish workers. Lenin and Mao clearly identified the vast gap between the metropolitan countries of Europe and North America and workers and the peasantry in Asia, Africa, and Latin America. They recognized that the most glaring struggle was between the imperialist countries and workers in oppressed nations. Yet ending European colonial domination was only the first step in a broader struggle for economic equality for the impoverished masses today in the South that live on a fraction of the wages of workers in the developed North.

Munck and other optimists in the contemporary labour movement are correct to note that the size of the world's working class is growing dramatically, more than doubling in the last 25 years. However, the absolute number of industrial workers is not declining, but growing as it moves from North to South, where nearly 600 million labour, mostly as informal, irregular, and temporary workers – often migrating from rural to urban, and back again. Today, the aspirations of workers and peasants in the Third World to satisfy basic needs remain unrequited as the disparity between North and South widens. While we are living in an urbanizing world, the population is continuing to grow in rural areas of Africa, Asia, and Latin America as they continue to struggle for land.

Global working-class solidarity must require recognition of this vast disparity in wealth and income between North and South. Although it is true that good jobs are disappearing from the North too, the global chasm is growing far more rapidly. To build international solidarity, we cannot fight for First World internationalism, but for world socialism. First World workers and their leaders must join with popular worker and peasant struggles in the South. The only concrete, non-utopian hope is for the construction of a major socialist state (or entity) in the South that can galvanize working-class support in the Third World.

The Bolshevik and Chinese revolutions captured the imagination of workers worldwide and triggered the major upsurge in labour mobilization and organization in Western Europe and North America and the major reform movements that followed. Thus, today, as Torkil Lauesen suggests, if a resurgent working class in China were to reject capitalist forms and re-embrace socialism and collective ownership of factories, land, and commerce, this could embolden labourers worldwide to follow.[13]

To be sure, there will be socialist revolutions in the twenty-first century. But labour solidarity cannot be built on the shoals of higher consumption and living standards in the North at the expense of poverty, inequality, and environmental degradation in the South. This requires a socialist movement propelled by militant anti-imperialist political organization in the South. Today's privileged global North unions, which Zak Cope shows represent a labour aristocracy, will not willingly support a redistribution of the world's resources to the majority of the planet.[14] They will be pushed reluctantly to recognize that the future of humanity depends on a struggle against economic imperialism and monopoly capitalism.

THE FIRST WORLD AND THIRD WORLD RURAL WORKING CLASS

A central argument of this book is that rural regions in the Third World remain a major point for the growth of material and class interests between the global North and global South, arising out of the expansion of the rural regions as a source of commodity production and social reproduction. For more than a century, rural populations have been migrating to urban centres; rural populations have also grown in rural regions, notably in the global South; and agriculture remains a fundamental source of sustenance for peasants. Correspondingly, rural regions in the global South have experienced an intense and extensive transformation as subsistence forms of production have given way to commodity production. Above all, the replacement of feudal and semi-feudal modes of production in rural regions of the global South by the capitalist mode of production has launched a far-reaching transformation of social class relations in agricultural zones.

Karl Marx depicts the capital relation as the 'Secret of Primitive Accumulation' and the guiding force of the landless rural proletariat as a divorce of the peasant from the land:

> The process, therefore, which creates the capital relation can be nothing other than the process which divorces the worker from the ownership of the conditions of his own labour; it is a process which operates two transformations, whereby the social means of subsistence and production are turned into capital, and the immediate producers are turned into wage-labourers. So-called primitive accumulation, therefore, is nothing else than the historical process of divorcing the producer from the means of production. [...] The economic structure of capitalist society has grown out of the economic structure of feudal society.[15]

Marx's explanation of the process of expropriation of the agricultural producer from the land is indeed the foundation for understanding the process of capitalist production and the development of industry. In *Capital*, Volume I, Marx plainly recognizes capitalist development as taking place in urban as well as rural regions. Accordingly, investigation of the conditions of the rural proletariat and semi-proletariat is necessary in the late nineteenth century. Yet, while examination of the rural worker remains crucial to comprehending the contemporary working class, urbanization over the past century has categorically directed the spotlight onto urban regions and has generated significant data and analysis on urbanization. The UN's 2018 *World Urbanization Prospects* report baldly asserts: 'The future of the world's population is urban.'[16] The rural proletariat is mostly ignored by scholarly and professional observers. The city and urban areas have replaced the town and countryside as the centre of research, evinced by the UN, multilateral institutions, and popular scholarship. Yet the literature fails to recognize that the planet's rural population has expanded dramatically over the last century, 50, and even 25 years.

Moreover, what is considered an urban settlement is often a squatter camp and slum that bears both urban and rural features. Landlessness and indigence are common features that span both rural and urban zones. Sometimes urban zones overrun rural zones, and in far more instances zones designated as urban are unalloyed rural areas within a metropolitan zone. Thus, the study of urbanization has neglected the significant dynamics of capitalism in the countryside. For Marx, the extinction of primitive accumulation is mainly a class relation, and not an account of the form of industrialization. The obliteration of primitive accumulation has engendered dynamic class relations on a local, regional, national, and international basis whereby workers are consigned to extreme levels of exploitation, as will be revealed in this book's case studies of India, the Philippines, and South Africa.

The capitalist mode of production in rural regions of the South manifests itself in different ways across the world. Thus, in the global North, capital and corporations have gained nearly absolute control of rural lands through industrial farming. In the South, arable land is distributed unequally between classes. In most regions, landlessness is pervasive among large proportions of the rural population. Where land has been redistributed, peasants typically receive the meagre broken and discontinuous plots of the least fertile land which is least likely to significantly improve living standards. Consequently, a rural proletariat has emerged to work as contract labourers on plantations owned by large landowners or controlled by major multinational corporations.

In this way, the landless peasants and rural workers with inadequate plots often resort to renting land from larger landowners, and others migrate to and from cities for work. To patch together a means of survival, rural workers are often forced to work on small plots without seeds, fertilizer, pesticides, and other necessities while also working in rural agricultural plantations, packing plants, transport, and logistics. As we shall see in Chapter 4, in the Philippines, rural land reform of the 1980s to 2000s did not lead to a noticeable improvement in the quality of life and standard of living of rural peasants in Mindanao. Rural workers owned small detached plots of land producing inferior-quality produce for the local economy while also working on plantations operated by oligarchs and multinational corporations which controlled the entire agricultural production chain, where profits are realized in the rich countries of the global North. Under current labour regimes in the Philippines and other agricultural commodity producing countries, peasants are transformed into rural workers domiciled in the countryside. Undeniably, rural workers are proliferating through-out the rural regions, and are not inevitably moving to urban areas as Marx predicted in *Capital*.

So what is the capital-relation in these rural zones, both in the countryside and cities? First and foremost, rural workers are subordinated to capitalist enterprises. Sociologist Jeffrey Paige shows that non-cultivators control and profit from rural production. Rural workers can technically own the land they till or rural agricultural enterprises through rural cooperatives, yet be deprived of the benefits of ownership by the class relation with non-cultivators who, as Jeffrey Paige claims, 'typically control the critical means of production whether they be land, capital, or commercial marketing channels' in more affluent consumer countries.[17] The endurance of the non-cultivator classes as the upper class and cultivators as the lower class is the major class relation in rural zones.[18] Over the last 50 years, this class relationship has held constant, according to Paige, who asserts:

The economic strength of commercial and industrial classes in export agriculture makes special land tenure privileges considerably less essential. In fact in small holding systems the control of the land itself is not an issue, since the upper-class income depends on marketing, and not producing the crop. In plantation systems the powerful corporate interests which constitute the agrarian upper classes are clearly capable of buying out even powerful members of the landed aristocracy, to say nothing of small landholders.[19]

In the context of South Asia, social anthropologist Jan Breman identifies workers caught in this unremitting form of rural–urban–rural migration as 'footloose labour' persistently moving from one worksite to another. The scale of the human population transfer from rural to urban areas is reminiscent of the social upheaval of late eighteenth-century England, as portrayed in Karl Polanyi's *The Great Transformation*: the vast majority of newcomers to urban centres are crowded into massive urban slums, facing imminent death and sure injury at work, and squalor and deprivation in nearby neighbourhoods.[20] Yet, as noted, 'urban' slums are often redolent of rural conditions, and South Asian and other global South workers often move back to the countryside when there is a shortage of urban jobs. These methods of labour contracting produce enduring and expansive reserve armies of labour which are continuously called upon to work at a fraction of the wages paid to most permanent workers performing the very same jobs. On completion of the work assigned, these labourers travel back to their rural regions of origin, some to stay and others to return just as others migrate to urban areas to begin work projects.

THE PERSISTENCE AND GROWTH OF THE RURAL PROLETARIAT

The peripheries of urban agglomerations and commodified rural regions are a focal point of poverty and destitution. Global multinational endorsement of urban migration as the remedy for national poverty is highly dependent on the circumstances under which rural workers leave the land. As is well documented and established in the political economy literature, urbanization may have benefits under conditions of equitable land reform.[21] If rural labourers are involuntarily forced from the land due to poverty and destitution, the probability is far greater for migration to urban slums lacking in amenities and basic amenities, where conditions are often far worse and jobs are often informal and scarce.

In the global South, rural regions are universally viewed as focal points of poverty, social desolation, and dislocation for the vast majority of inhabitants. Consequently, political economists view the shift in population from the rural hinterland to urban areas as the most important factor in eradicating poverty and increasing economic development. In the first two decades of the twentieth century, urbanization is held out as the remedy to the stultifying conditions of life in rural areas.

Economic development for the advanced capitalist countries was highly dependent on land reform, land tenure, preventing land degradation, and the consolidation of dispersed plots, public provision of irrigation, transport, fertilizers, seeds, and prices.

The question of control and ownership of both land and means of production, access to transportation, seed, fertilizer, etc. are crucial in reducing structural inequities and maintaining liveable income in rural regions. In the late twentieth century, control over the global supply chain eclipsed the extension of land tenure to the poor, as income and living standards depended increasingly on marketing and distribution by transnational corporations, dominated by multinational financial corporations seeking to enforce low wages for peasants and rural workers while dominating the system of trade and the sale of commodities in the consumer markets of the West. Land reform, while crucial to improving living standards of subsistence farmers, did not assure rural labourers' living wages on the countryside. As Third World countries became increasingly reliant on the sale of agricultural commodities, control of logistics and markets took precedence over control over land. Writing in 1978, sociologist Jeffery M. Paige documented the unlimited control of non-cultivators over peasants:

Whatever the income sources of cultivators and non-cultivators, however, it is the non-cultivators who typically control the critical means of production whether they be land, capital, or commercial marketing channels, and the two groups are separated by differences in function, control of resources, dependence, and power. In some cases, such as the relationship between a village middleman and a small holder, the difference may be small, and in others, such as the contractual relationship between a corporation and a wage labourer, the difference may be much greater; nevertheless, there is usually a distinct vertical cleavage, with the cultivating class almost always in a less advantageous position. In most rural social systems non-cultivating classes form the upper and cultivators the lower agricultural class.[22]

The significance of the class nature of commodity chains, which redounds to the disadvantages of the rural working class in Southern countries, is reinforced by Utsa Patnaik, who stresses the growing capacities of agribusinesses to transport previously perishable products to the North through logistic and technological advancements in transportation and storage. Patnaik claims:

> A study of history proves irrefutably that, far from benefiting both parties, trade in primary products entailed extremely heavy costs for the exporting country because it led to decline in the output and availability of basic food staples for its own population and in many cases even led to famine, with large-scale mortality. The inverse relation – between rising agricultural exports and falling domestic food grains [*sic*] availability – is repeatedly seen not only in colonial times but in every case of the trade liberalisation of a developing country.[23]

As such, Patnaik points out that the Southern working class is unaware of global North consumers' high level of dependency on commodities they produce in their regions. These products unequivocally increase the standard of living in rich countries. This system of subordination is maintained through the ideology of free trade, which justifies the undervaluing of the labour of global South agrarian and informal workers. Ironically, Patnaik argues that without agrarian and informal labour in the global South, the living standards of populations of the North would plunge.[24]

CONCLUSION

The vast majority of labourers in the global South, whether in urban settlements or rural regions, are employed under informal conditions with haphazard and irregular work hours and low wages. Workers in these regions produce a range of goods for the global commodity supply chain, whether in manufacturing, agriculture, or mining. They represent workers at the bottom of the economic ladder, but their work is crucial in creating profits for local, regional, and multinational extractive classes who are the recipients of surplus profits from their labour. The highest level of labour exploitation occurs in these regions, as producers commonly depend on the extraction of labour power as the major source of profit and surplus value rather than investing and subsuming capital into new more productive technology. Short of the capacity to extract this labour power, local, regional, and multinational capital is unable to accumulate the wealth. This process of production operates generally on the basis of value labour transfer, whereby Southern workers are deprived of gaining a small fraction of the inputs they contribute at the sale of the product in consumer markets in rich countries.

2

Workers' Movements in the South: Inequality, Poverty, and Enduring Relevance of Rural Proletariat and Informal Sector Workers

The expansion of the capitalist mode of production centre in Western Europe from the 1750s accelerated in the 1870s, and in the twentieth century and early twenty-first century has wiped out most vestiges of feudal political economies in Europe and throughout the world. In its place it has imposed capitalist relations of production, leading to the general subordination of indigenous peoples in Africa, Asia, the Americas, Oceania, and beyond to the metropolitan countries and Europe settler-colonial states.[1] This 250-year progression of capitalist development was both asymmetrical and uneven, but undeniably it profoundly reshaped economic change on a world scale. A distinctive factor in this development is that metropolitan and most settler-colonial states saw the emergence and expansion of capitalism that in a relatively short period satisfied basic human needs and provided social services and ubiquitous access to consumer goods and new technology. In contrast, by all historical accounts, most of the world's population experienced a dramatic decline in their standard of living as Western capitalism was imposed on the enduring social formations rooted in agrarian regions of the planet. In the twenty-first century, the world's working class is in its most dramatic stage of transformation since the origins of capitalism in the 1750s.

The decline of labour influence over the last half-century has shown the expanding difficulty for workers to establish influence through trade unions. This has led to efforts to devise new forms of representation and class action which diffuse working-class power and the development of a new body of labour research rooted in a nebulous form of autonomism of worker self-activity and rank and file action as a replacement for the large, bureaucratic, and unwieldy forms of organization that formerly exercised power on behalf of workers.[2] This critique tracks the labour studies literature which proliferated in the second half of the twentieth century to the present, and which generally identified the problem of trade union decline as rooted in bureaucracy and autocratic leaders, and championed oppositional factions within the ranks of labour unions.[3] Several labour observers today see the possibility of union revitalization occurring in the US through engaging directly with workers and mobilizing unorganized sectors of the economy.[4] Indeed, from the 1980s to 2000, the vast majority of labour literature focused on a critique of labour union leaders as complicit in the subordination of their own members. Trade union bureaucracies engaging in labour–management cooperation and concessionary bargaining did not represent members' best interests and sharply eroded the power of the rank and file working class, who, this argument goes, are far more militant than their union leaders. Though this argument may be true, opponents did not offer a new model of representation aside from championing factional opponents, who often went on to engage in the same practices as their predecessors.

The critique of conservative union leaders who defend their most privileged members certainly is valid, but there was no guarantee that alternatives would do any better in organizing new members. Moreover, this critique primarily approached unions as analogous to wayward socialist states which failed to deliver democracy or social and economic gains for their people. This 'rejectionist' school spent more time opposing leaders in power and supporting oppositionists than offering a comprehensive strategy for changing the inequities generated by neoliberal capitalism. Moreover, labour scholars have wholly ignored workers in the most impoverished regions of the world. Uncritically, there was little or no difference to opponents if the unionized workers were well-paid professionals or informal part-time labourers in the Third World.[5]

This was followed by a historical world-systems approach to labour protest, which asserted that working-class militancy reflects the expansion of capital throughout the world.

Beverly Silver's Political Economy of World Systems approach reveals a correspondence between industrial development and labour militancy through an examination of successive waves of working-class protest and unrest related to economic development throughout the expansion of capitalism in the eighteenth century. In the UK and Western Europe, the rapid development of capitalist economies was fed by the exploitation of inexpensive natural resources and agricultural commodities in Africa, Asia, and the Americas. As a result of the exploitation of the world economy, in a relatively short time period, capitalism had produced relatively high living standards in the core countries of Western Europe and North America. Due to the massive destruction caused by world war in the twentieth century, manufacturing production persisted into the twentieth century far longer, which, in turn, slowed the development of manufacturing alongside mining and agricultural commodity production. Even by the 1970s, commodity manufacturing for national markets was viewed by political economists as the road to development and prosperity. Accordingly, the expansion of global production, viewed by Political Economy of World Systems theorists as a stage of international capitalist economic development, transpired in a period of 50 years in the global South, from the 1970s to the present. Yet the process of development has taken on a different trajectory than in the capitalist centre, where the economic gains of imperialism have been inured to the benefit of most of the residents of rich countries. Lower-wage regions in Africa, Asia, and the Americas produce commodities for the rich countries for far less labour costs. In turn, the largest share of goods is sold in capitalist markets in the affluent countries. Even if goods produced in the South are sold in the South, due to the power of financial capital, profits and interests are repatriated in the leading capitalist hubs: New York, London, Tokyo, Frankfurt, Paris, and beyond.

Sociologist Beverly Silver contends that the relocation of industry is part of a system of global capitalist fixes, where money flows to the lowest-wage regions. Silver tracks this system of shifting production over the last 200 years, showing that major social unrest and strikes have occurred in regions where manufacturing was on the rise:

We found a cyclical pattern of labour militancy and Capital relocation – a kind of deja vu pattern in which strong labour movements emerged in each new favoured low-wage site to which the industry relocated. In other words, spatial fixes re-created similar working classes and class conflict wherever capital went.[6]

While labour militancy indisputably coincides with the flow of capital, the case studies in this book show that labour militancy also occurs in manufacturing, agriculture, and mining industries with low levels of capital subsumption. In this way, capital and also capitalist profits do not require spatial or technological fixes to generate profits, but rely solely on the super-exploitation of labour.

While this view shows that strikes concentrate where capital develops new industry, Silver's crucial analysis of the correlation between capital flows and worker unrest does not consider the capacity of labour-based organizations to consolidate worker militancy into durable movements and institutional regimes. Moreover, greater attention on the specific correlation between neoliberalism and the decline in working-class organizations is necessary to understand the capacity for institutional frameworks to maintain continuing power in the contemporary era (1970–present), where manufacturing has shifted to countries on the periphery, the locus of the highest level of surplus value extraction. In these regions, manufacturing has expanded along with the production of agricultural and mineral commodities, fuelling the growth of the global capitalist economy.

Witnessing the decline of the strike in the West, a number of labour observers maintain that working-class militancy has transformed in the twenty-first century from labour strikes to mass amorphous insurrections which have broken out in Western European and US cities (e.g. Baltimore and Ferguson in the USA, Tottenham in Britain, and Clichy-sous-Bois in France) by those who lack organizational representation. In this way, Joshua Clover observes contemporary trade unions as depleted social forces which lack relevance today as they are substituted by spontaneous non-institutionalized forms of mass insurgency without the need for organization.[7] Thus, the strike is just a break with the historical riot, and does not represent a challenge to capitalism, in contrast to Rosa Luxemburg's *mass strike* of the early twentieth century, which she observes as mass action unified by the political organization. While Luxemburg identifies working-class power springing from the interaction between political and economic social forces, it is the party's responsibility to organize and guide the working-class forces through the crucial moments of political struggle. Drawing on the Russian workers' movement of 1905, Luxemburg presents a sketch of the economic and political forces in the unfolding of the strike, maintaining the necessity of the political party in mobilizing, leading, and organizing the amorphous workers' movements:

> A consistent, resolute, progressive tactic on the part of the social democrats produces in the masses a feeling of security, self-confidence and desire for struggle; a vacillating weak tactic, based on an underestimation of the proletariat, has a crippling and confusing effect upon the masses. In the first case mass strikes break out 'of themselves' and 'opportunely'; in the second case they remain ineffective amidst direct summonses of the directing body to mass strikes. And of both the Russian Revolution affords striking examples.[8]

Whereas Luxemburg's focus on the popular nature of the strike is often invoked by contemporary scholars to exaggerate the autonomous mass movements which are pervasive throughout modern capitalist history, there is a tendency to neglect the magnitude of organization in rallying downtrodden workers to mass action. Devoid of organization ingrained in the struggles, workers continue to resist oppressors to unify and mobilize into mass action.

This view is reinforced by Lenin in 1923, writing on the significance of political organization. As global neoliberalism capitalism has expanded in the 50 years from 1970 to 2020, the absolute power of capital has grown *vis-à-vis* labour. Working-class organizations and trade unions have been unable to curb the absolute growth in corporate power on local, state, regional, and international levels. In turn, working-class organizations have eroded dramatically and have become marginal in most countries of the world. The consequences of the decline in working-class organization are far more deleterious for workers in poor countries of the South than in the wealthy metropolitan and settler states. At the height of capitalist development in Western Europe and North America, workers developed labour organizations to advance their material interests. Yet today, when working-class organization is severely lacking, Southern workers do not have the power to build defensive organizations to challenge a far more rapacious form of multinational capital. Thus, the disparity of wealth, wages, and income between North and South is expanding at a faster pace than at any time in the last

50 years. The decisive influence and significance of the global South to the world economy was predicted by Lenin in 1923 at a time when political and economic power was highly concentrated in the developed countries of the West:

> In the last analysis, the outcome of the struggle will be determined by the fact that Russia, India, China, etc., account for the overwhelming majority of the population of the globe. And during the past few years it is this majority that has been drawn into the struggle for emancipation with extraordinary rapidity, so that in this respect there cannot be the slightest doubt what the final outcome of the world struggle will be. In this sense, the complete victory of socialism is fully and absolutely assured.[9]

This book asserts that the deterioration of conditions of workers in the South is directly related to the decline in working-class organizations, many of which expanded during the period of decolonization from the 1940s to the 1970s. Labour unions, which formed and gained power in the era of decolonization, have been under relentless attack by the logic of capitalist profitability under neoliberalism and the modern state. Working-class organizations are eschewed by capital and the state as a constraint on profits and development. Thus, under neoliberalism, states which freely permit working-class organizations are bypassed in the commodity supply chains for products primarily for consumers in the rich countries. As labour unions' state social programmes complicate the production of low-cost consumer goods, states striving for integration into the global capitalist system view working-class organizations as anathema to development. Moreover, since foreign direct investments are likely to go to countries with the weakest social safety nets, even products sold for national consumption must abjure the formation of strong labour unions. Thus, even in states with robust labour and social protection, social programmes advocated by the UN, the International Labour Organization, and beyond are fiercely resisted by local capitalists and state regulatory bodies as capital mobility permits the freedom to invest and withdraw capital. States challenging the global neoliberal regime risk losing capital investments that are essential for economic expansion and growth. Yet, concomitantly, these very free market policies cause mass poverty and widespread misery.

GROWING ANTAGONISM IN CLASS MATERIAL
AND SOCIAL INTERESTS

Analysis and observation have been only recently reconsidered as a result of the regeneration of research on economic imperialism that examines the historical legacy of five centuries of colonization. Reconsideration of the enduring forces that remain stubbornly in place has taken on even more tenacious form in a global system that retains fundamental disparity between North and South. Indeed, this incongruity has deepened poverty and inequality in the Third World.

Neoliberalism and the Post-Cold War Era Consensus

Free market economics and privatization dominated by neoliberal free market governance came to a close in the second decade of the twenty-first century, in the aftermath of the 2008 Great Financial Recession. This system is characterized by the ascendency of free markets and the withdrawal of state controls and support for workers. Implemented on an international basis, labour and working-class parties and organizations have been unable to reverse or even control this trend. As a consequence, governments shifted to neoliberal policies which abandoned wage and social protections to workers from global and national markets. In the 1980s and 1990s, welfare states were replaced by free market policies benefiting investors who exploited the systematic privatization of national resources, industry, infrastructure, and investment. The concentration of wealth and intensification of economic divisions could not have been possible without the erosion and disappearance of political representation for workers, the poor, and peasants. A key failure of political movements is a pervasive view that desirable political movements and forces will grow stronger over time, and neglect for the unyielding power of capitalist and bourgeois forces which form and reform to challenge workers and oppressed classes. In particular, optimism about the resilience of forces of change eclipses critiques of the solidity and durability of the old order. Ever since the publication of the *Manifesto of the Communist Party*, classical Marxists have maintained a persistent suspicion of the old guard coming back and overthrowing the forces of social progress. To date, under capitalism, no socialist force and entity have successfully thwarted the intransigent challenges of the capitalist classes. Some social movements which have consolidated into organizations and institutions have been more successful in postponing or moderating the inevitable challenge from the capitalist class. As such, the classical Marxist maxim of dictatorship of the proletariat is so crucial to discerning how protest is transformed into lasting power. Organization is a prerequisite for working-class power.

ALTERNATIVE MODELS OF LABOUR REPRESENTATION AND NEW FORMS OF WORKER ORGANIZATION

The decline in existing unions has been accompanied by new models of worker representation. These new models have gained popularity among supporters of the traditional labour movement as well as Leftists who advocate new types of worker organization rooted in autonomism. In the first decade of the twenty-first century, the emergence of workers' centres was viewed as the antidote to union decline. Workers' centres were supposed to represent an alternative model for organizing the most oppressed workers in the global North.[10] Thus, several forms of worker organization emerged as the union movement declined and no traditional replacement emerged. The slogan 'from the ashes of the old' was invoked as a form of union renewal from the 1990s to 2000s to convey the view that fierce trade unions would re-emerge to replace outdated organizations formed in previous generations.

From Mobilization to Advocacy

As trade unions have become weaker and membership has declined from the 1990s to the present, human rights supporters of labour rights in the West have promoted hybrid forms of representation. In the USA, where migrant labourers are highly exploited in agricultural and food production, these new models of working-class representation have been formed mainly as legal entities to advance the cause of farm labourers in rural areas and food service and domestic workers in urban areas. These organizations are supported by private funders and philanthropists, and typically seek to bring working conditions up to code standard. In the 1990s and 2000s, migrant labourers employed in food services, transport, and domestic work or as day labourers often received a fraction of the federal minimum wage, and given the lack of labour law oversight, many were employed for 60–75 hours a week.

The model of workers' centres as a form of alternative labour representation has gained popularity among USA-born workers who have seen wages and prospects for decent employment decline significantly, for example in the e-commerce industry. As labour rights have eroded, the new organizational forms have come to be viewed as an alternative mechanism for representation. Meanwhile, as trade unions have lost members in traditional manufacturing sectors, some have sought to organize workers in growing service, retail, and transport industries in the gig economy. Most of these campaigns have failed to gain any traction in the West, due to fierce opposition from management and investors.[11]

NGOs and Migrant Labour in the USA: The Corporate Foundation Model of Worker Organization

In the 2010s, trade union density remained constant at around 10 per cent (5 per cent in the private sector). A high concentration of trade union organizing is in lower wage sectors of the economy, and efforts have focused on improving the lot for workers who are new entrants in the economy or in jobs that traditionally have lower wages; for example, the most prominent campaigns of the 1980s–2000s were among building maintenance workers, low-skilled hospital workers, and food service employees. Increasingly, unionization has expanded to contingent and unstable sectors of the economy where workers have no intention of spending a long time employed, for example graduate students, for-hire transport workers, security guards, cafeteria workers and other low-wage services. A large and growing unionization campaign involved migrant labourers, for example the Coalition of Immokalee Workers (CIW), essentially an NGO, directed a fair-food campaign educating consumers about the poor conditions among underpaid migrant labourers working for food processing companies and fast-food chains.[12] The organization, which serves workers in the fields, primarily relies on donations from middle- and upper-class consumers. The organization emphasizes membership involvement, but there is scant evidence of direct worker involvement. CIW is not a union of workers, but an NGO which considers itself a human rights organization conducting various campaigns claiming to be 'worker-driven', such as the Fair Food Program launched in 2011.

As we enter the 2020s, wages and conditions of migrant workers have only marginally improved. However, the number of migrant labourers in the urban sector of the economy has declined over the past 30 years. Some of the workers' centres have transformed their activities from direct representation to advocacy for better conditions. Consequently, migrant workers do not have direct representation, but their causes are supported through various corporate social responsibility (CSR) campaigns. Thus, for the most part, workers themselves do not participate actively in their own labour organizations, but rely on best practices established by these organizations. Devoid of direct representation, the leaders of these organizations, almost exclusively labour rights lawyers and advocates, have advanced the cause of changing the laws to protect migrant labourers, restaurant employees, and domestic workers. Consequently, CSR campaigns in the USA, as elsewhere, have evolved into promoting good practices and pose no risk to employers.

Thus, despite high hopes that workers' centres would become lodestones of organization for the lowest-waged and most oppressed workers who were not in traditional unions in the neoliberal era from the mid-1990s to 2010, the efficacy of these NGO-fashioned forms of representation in building working-class power has faltered badly. They have either hesitated, dissolved, or devolved into corporate-style advocacy organizations. A major reason for the dissolution of workers' centres has been demands rooted in reformism which did not actively engage rank and file workers in direct struggle. Set into motion by existing trade unions, anti-poverty coalitions, political coalitions, and NGOs, workers' centres set out to represent low-waged workers in a range of fields in the service sector: domestic workers, restaurant workers, for-hire vehicle drivers, the gig economy, and beyond. The coalitions were never organized as a challenge to the capitalist state, but mostly as legislative efforts to increase the minimum wage, improve working conditions, and incorporate migrant and informal labourers into the formal economy.

As neoliberalism expanded just-in-time production through offshoring production to the global South, industrial trade unions representing steel, electronics, and auto workers declined in the West as service and public sector unions also haemorrhaged membership. Concurrently, the new industrial proletariat in the global South did not have altruistic advocates in the rich countries, as they benefited from low-cost commodities. Thus, a strong correlation emerged between the rise of neoliberal economic policies and trade union decline in the West and intensified exploitation and oppression of Southern workers. Over the past 30 years, neoliberal capitalism has created greater precarity in the West through privatization and deregulation, which generates both greater wealth and higher rates of inequality. Whereas many have predicted a rise in militancy, no rank and file workers' movement has emerged to challenge the current system.

How do we account for the lack of activism and the organization of a working-class-based Left force in the West? Although Left labour platforms have been advanced by political opponents of neoliberalism, few organizations are firmly rooted in the working classes of the West. In many cases, the leading proponents are corporate foundations and the petit bourgeoisie. As a consequence, in new sectors of the 'gig' economy, low wages, job instability, and the erosion of labour standards for workers are more widespread. In the absence of working-class organization and/or the futility of organizational representation, new forms of worker organization (NFWOs) have emerged to represent workers in demanding or advocating elevation of the wage floor rather than of the ceiling. As they never demand the redistribution of income or jobs programmes, NFWOs tend to be organizationally weak and limited in scope. As a consequence, corporate and NGO-style NFWOs are fragmented and detached from broader working-class coalitions. Concomitantly, existing labour unions which had historically affiliated with social democratic parties have pursued transactional politics as they have declined, and have all but abandoned the broader working class to advance narrower industrial and sectoral interests and neglect the most vulnerable workers who lack job stability.

WORKING-CLASS SPONTANEITY, LABOUR ORGANIZATION, AND THE REVOLUTIONARY PATH

We will now assess emergence of chief organizational currents in the labour movement in the modern era. Over the past 125 years, with the rise of large corporations, organized labour has developed a range of distinct forms of representation and administration. The shape and configuration of these labour organizations have reproduced the nature of the political economic development of the capitalist mode of production, the constraints faced by the working-class organization, and the political currents which developed to challenge business, capital, and the state.

Syndicalism and the Industrial Workers of the World

Syndicalism reached its pinnacle in Western Europe, North America, South America, South Africa, and Australia from the 1890s to about 1920, primarily among European workers in metropolitan and settler-colonial states. The origins of what we can call NFWOs can be traced to the historical experiences of syndicalist movements that started in Europe around 1895 and expanded. Syndicalist unions viewed themselves as a revolutionary opposition to capitalism as mass industrial production was in the process of replacing craft industries. Syndicalists, as modern-day autonomists, placed the emphasis on direct worker action rather than delegating responsibility to union leaders as their representatives or intermediaries with employers. As the craft system was in the process of being replaced by large industrial enterprises, syndicalists filled a crucial gap, serving as a radical and rebellious organizational expression of workers who felt they were dispossessed of control over their own means of production. This early form of working-class organization is admired by contemporary syndicalists, who exemplify workers engaged in political struggle against capital without a defined organizational form – the bosses who exploited labour.

The suppression of spontaneity and insurrection is viewed as the critique of twentieth-century socialist organization. Sclerotic trade union organizations in the twentieth century have extinguished rank and file self-activity of the working class. Indeed, the last century demonstrates that union bureaucracy and cautiousness are major constraints on building a strong labour movement. Yet this book also argues that it is essential for anti-capitalist Marxist trade unions to capture working-class militancy in order for strong workers' organizations to emerge, which in the short term can build the power of the working class while aspiring to take state power from multinational capital. Indeed, new organizations are emerging today to challenge the ennui and torpor of existing trade union movements, which have frequently ceded power and control over workplaces, communities, and nation states to neoliberal capitalism.

As craft production shifted to industrial production, the Industrial Workers of the World (IWW) formed in 1905 as the expression of syndicalist labour organization, chiefly in the most advanced economies of Europe, North America, South Africa, and Australia. In the ensuing ten years, the IWW organized on a mass base against the American Federation of Labor (AFL) to be the dominant labour body representing workers. While the IWW did not approach a membership equivalent to the AFL's, it established inroads among industries, mines, and agricultural workers by organizing on a class-wide basis rather than on the basis of race, nationality, and gender.[13]

Objecting to the formation of a class-based political party, the IWW deemed the union organization sufficient, alone, in developing tactics and strategy leading to socialism. In isolation, the IWW took the idealistic view that the organization would engage in sabotage, direct action, and mass strikes and build international solidarity by itself without a political arm. The IWW's rejection of a militant working-class party ultimately led to the organization's demise, as it could not consolidate and strengthen militant yet fragile and insubstantial organizations into a strong force capable of extracting economic concessions from dispersed industries. Although the IWW built solidarity from workplace to community and neighbourhoods, an established organization did not materialize. Workers directed labour organizations in opposition to union officials and bureaucrats, and opposed collaboration with employers.

In the USA, as elsewhere, the IWW established the model for future working-class unionism which was to be adopted by the Congress of Industrial Organizations and the AFL, which competed for members in factories through organizing workers on a class rather than craft basis from the 1930s to 1955. But the IWW was vastly outflanked by established unions which were linked directly or indirectly to communist, social democratic, or labour-based parties. Though the IWW espoused the notion of 'One Big Union', the federation never established a strong central leadership which could win over workers as a representative of the industrial working class. IWW locals had frail ties to a strong central leadership with the capacity to mobilize workers beyond factories or city industrial zones. The IWW correctly criticized how the bourgeois political parties provided no option for empowering the working classes as they represented class fractions of capital. In this way, labour federations in Western Europe and the USA were operationally serving the organizational appendage of the ruling class.

However, the IWW did not represent a robust political organization representing the working class on a broader level. Thus, while militant workers mobilized and waged strikes, in every case any concessions from capital could not be preserved. In this way, in the absence of a political platform for workers, aside from perfunctory opposition to capitalism writ large, the IWW was an inchoate political force which would not attract workers seeking a strong organization capable of establishing and maintaining concrete gain. Like twenty-first-century autonomists, the IWW had no programme to challenge the capitalist state.

The autonomist IWW model had parallels with European trade unions forming from 1914 to 1918, particularly council communism, which reached a peak during this period. The council communist movement formed in Germany and the Netherlands among rank and file workers in opposition to sclerotic bureaucratic union leaders who had nebulous ties to members within the factories. Accordingly, rank and file shop stewards emerged to represent and reflect the aspirations of members against capitalist managers.[14] Unlike the IWW, council communists saw themselves as mobilizing the broader working class in factories who would construct proletarian revolution directly through workers' control over the shopfloor. In this way, council communists considered that the working class could directly appropriate the means of production and expand more widely into working-class communities surrounding factories. The leaders of the movement in Germany were the shop stewards, who would lead a democratic workers' movement in independent action, practically serving as parallel unions in resistance to the official union leadership and employers, and gaining the confidence and support of the working class as its legitimate and objective leaders.[15] While the movement was defeated in the German Revolution of 1918, future generations of council communists would emerge as shopfloor representatives of the working class when the bonds of existing union leaderships frayed and new leaders emerged directly out of the working class. Assuming new forms, council communists have emerged ever since 1918 to mobilize workers unrepresented by the established unions or disconnected from union members. Over the past century, on occasion, workers lacking vigorous representation in existing unions have detached themselves from their unions and formed new more militant unions. The question always remains whether these new more radical unions have the capacity to consolidate the militancy of workers and develop a comprehensive programme for social transformation. More often than not, the new union configurations have either failed to capture control of insurgent workers or formed independent organizations lacking in a political programme for social transformation. As such, the promise for workers' control over industrial enterprises is subordinated to reformist demands for higher wages and better working conditions within the context of a capitalist economy. Even if workers seize control of a factory, they remain subject to the profit-driven exigencies of commodity production within the capitalist market. Council communists and their successors may have had an immediate plan for seizing power, but have lacked the organizational capacity and programmatic resilience to surmount the demands of the logic of capitalist production, resorting to conventional unionism or being defeated along with their unions. In addition, they have often operated unsanctioned and unrecognized by the state under existing labour laws. Thus, if council communists are to succeed, they must shape a strategic plan to address the immediate needs of workers while developing a programme which does not lose sight of the workers' aspiration and hope for societal transformation.

Syndicalist and council communist autonomist models of labour representation were visibly outflanked by major social democratic union federations, often affiliated with the Second International, which did not maintain a revolutionary tradition. These mainstream labour federations operated within the constraints of the capitalist system and had a vision of a steady and gradual improvement of wages, working conditions, and labour protections. Yet these unions also adopted industrial union models to conform to mass organization of workers in the large enterprises which came to dominate the Western European and North American economies.

Simultaneously, the Russian Revolution and the rise of the Soviet Union in 1917 presented the world with a new model of worker representation rooted in socialism. Unmistakably, workers were emboldened to engage in mass action and strikes, and even seized control over factories such as the Putilov Mill in Petrograd in February 1916, along with other strikes at major industrial installations through to the end of 1917. The earliest representations of worker control emerged in the major factories through the creation of worker soviets in factories and town councils to defend and advance the interests of the working class. The trade unions abided by the notion of 'All Power to the Soviets' and opposition to competing bourgeois forms of labour representation. Certainly, opposition emerged to Bolshevik-led soviet trade unions from competing political forces among Mensheviks, social democrats, and monarchists. Indeed, Trotsky and other oppositionists called for the suppression of workers through the 'militarization of labour' to defend the Soviet State against the White Army and foreign aggressors.[16] But the consolidation of a workers' state in the ensuing years, and the Red Army's defeat of the White Army in 1922, granted workers a sense that they had taken power. Lenin called for the development of principled and competent labour union organizations represented by workers devoted to the service of building a communist state.[17]

The rise of the Soviet Union resonated throughout the world and was fiercely opposed by the major imperialist powers, which were also frightened by the rise of fierce labour movements in their own states and the chance that Soviet-style communism would gain appeal among the broader working class. For example, in the USA, the Communist Party expanded dramatically in the 1930s as new unions were formed in major industrial installations throughout the country. Worker occupations and sit-down strikes broke out in 1936 and 1937 in the automobile, electronics, and other manufacturing industries.[18] The formation of the Congress of Industrial Organizations in 1935 attracted the most militant and skilled labour activists and leaders from throughout the country into the Communist Party, which had also adopted an advanced platform, including women's rights, anti-racism, and industrial unionism.

Labour Unions and Fordism in the Global North

This book views Fordism as a model of labour relations as an interregnum which was confined principally to the West from around 1930 to 1975, and was not replicated in other eras or regions of the world. Fordism exemplifies the class compromise, a system whereby industrial workers consent to cooperate and collaborate with management to produce efficiently in exchange for stable and well-paying jobs. Fordism took root in Western Europe and North America in the era of mass production prior to the 1970s crisis of capitalism and the introduction of neoliberalism. In the metropolitan and settler-colonial states, Fordist unions typically were unified with social democratic and labour-based parties, where they had relatively formidable influence over organizational decisions influencing their industries. As strong sectoral-based unions in large industrial factories in steel, automobiles, and electronics, the parties customarily had high levels of membership participation, even if the end of the era was marked by speed-ups, intensification of labour productivity, and shopfloor dissent.[19] Global South Fordism was dominated by a small number of unions formed around state-owned public sector industrial manufacturing (e.g. steel, shipping, mining, electricity) dominated by strong, centralized Marxist and Left parties. In contrast to the global North, Southern Fordism encompassed a small segment of the urban industrial working class, while the vast majority of the population laboured in rural regions or in settlements surrounding urban areas (see the discussion of rural labour in Chapter 1).

The post-Fordist era which followed from 1975 is marked by the decline of social democratic parties and the attendant weakening and disappearance of trade unions in manufacturing industries. Even in those few areas with growing manufacturing, such as the US South, the United Auto Workers (UAW) and other industrial trade unions repeatedly failed to convince industrial workers to join their organizations. Over and over again, through the 2010s, workers rejected membership in new automobile plants where employers did not formally resist union organizing campaigns, such as Volkswagen's neutrality agreement with the UAW and its failure to convince workers to join the union in 2014 and 2019.[20] The failed organizing campaigns reveal that industrial workers in the US South who were generally satisfied with their relatively high wages did not view trade unions as a means to bring job security with what most viewed as excellent pay compared to workers in other sectors of the economy. In most instances, workers engaged in assembling parts in the global supply chain, parts which were manufactured in low-wage regions of the global South. US labour scholars often point to the sophisticated anti-union campaigns directed by public relations specialists and law firms as a reason for the failure to organize workers, but to most American industrial workers, trade union membership was not seen as appreciably improving relatively high wages compared to most jobs. Most significantly, by the 1960s, service and public service unions in education, healthcare, and beyond had surpassed manufacturing unions in membership and influence over the labour movement. Although a growing number of teachers and educators went on strike in the USA in

2018–19, the public sector is viewed as an essential service, in contrast to private sector work. Even though the teacher strikes were often unauthorized, they gained substantial public support. Consequently, manufacturing, service, and retail sector unions are typically far more cautious in taking job actions and strikes than public sector workers.[21] In this way, the demise of Fordist production from the 1980s to 2000s in North America and Europe and beyond has reduced the organizational power of labour and diluted the militancy of unionized workers.

Notably, under neoliberal capitalism, manufacturing is marked by global supply chains, where production is subcontracted to low-wage suppliers employing low-wage labour in smaller facilities and often sweatshops, where labour organizing is far more challenging than in the large factories of the Fordist era. Workers would have to be organized in hundreds of contractors and within working-class communities, instead of the large industrial plants. Thus, the neoliberal system of post-Fordism in the South took on a distinctly different form from in the West. In many countries of the South, trade union alliances with socialist and Left parties eroded dramatically as small facilities, often on the periphery of cities, replaced large installations where workers had higher levels of leverage *vis-à-vis* capital. While the industrial working class has grown dramatically in the South, state neoliberal development and employer anti-union policies have undermined the capacity of established organizing methods. In addition, the growth of Economic Processing Zones (EPZs) in exclusive industrial zones on the periphery of major cities has made it far more difficult to organize workers. At the same time, unorganized workers in EPZs have actively opposed rapacious employer practices which render workers redundant at an early age, dismiss workers who do not abide by rigorous and exacting changes in the labour process and work rules, or challenge employers through organizing campaigns.[22] The vast number of processing zones in Southern countries is evident in Table 2.1.

The dominant trend in globalized capitalism in the South is subcontracting work to low-cost producers who must produce goods and component parts at a defined cost, directly forcing down wages for the majority of workers who are employed in these sectors of the industrial economy. As workers in the global South are far more exploited, they have gained a high working-class militancy not found in the West.[23]

Table 2.1 Number of SEZs by region, 2019

	Total no. of SEZs	SEZs under development	Additional SEZs planned
World	5383	474	507
Developed economies	374	5	—
Europe	105	5	—
North America	262	—	—
Developing economies	4772	451	502
Asia	4046	371	419
East Asia	2645	13	—
China	2543	13	—
Southeast Asia	737	167	235
South Asia	456	167	184
India	373	142	61
West Asia	208	24	—
Africa	237	51	53
Latin America and Caribbean	486	28	24

Source: Derived from United Nations Conference on Trade and Development, 'Special Economic Zones', in *UNCTAD World Investment Report 2019* (Geneva, Switzerland: UNCTAD, 2019), pp. 128–206, https://unctad.org/en/PublicationChapters/WIR2019_CH4.pdf, accessed 30 June 2020.

Autonomist Workers' Movements: Theory and Practice

The fall and disappearance of most Fordist unions in the West has stimulated theorization about new forms of labour representation today. From about 1970 to the present, labour scholarship was dominated by critical accounts of trade unions, revisiting the bureaucratic, authoritarian, and mostly ineffective leaders who presided over weak and diminished organizations. Critics of the established labour movement supported assumed democratic opposition leaders who allegedly had the best interests of the rank and file members, and would activate a passive membership to militancy and strikes. As a result, a renewed labour movement would emerge and draw new members into its ranks. Others argued that unions had to devote greater resources to organizing and mobilizing. In both North and South, a significant segment of workers in existing ossified trade unions comprised racial minorities, women, and new immigrants.[24] In the 2010s, as union reform proved superficial in transforming existing trade unions, autonomism and syndicalism emerged as the main diagnostic critique of unions.

Autonomism represented a distinct form akin to syndicalism, as independent unions detached from the dominant unions. Workers are directly mobilized as independent unions without external sponsorship. Though proponents of autonomism have gained significant influence in the academy over the past two decades since 2000, the union form has expanded demonstrably in various regions since the late 1960s as a consequence of the defeat of large industrial unions in Continental Europe and the growth of the tertiary sector labourers. Notably, autonomism expanded in Europe in the late 1960s and early 1970s. The concept of *operaismo*, or workerism, introduced by Mario Tronti in 1966 has infused the autonomist movements throughout the world.[25] On a global scale, in the 2000s, autonomism has resulted in an array of organizations which have adopted tactics of opposition to large companies, the state, and existing unions which had deferred to state and capitalist domination.

Today, research on labour and class, rooted in autonomism, examines how new labour formations, as autonomist actors, respond to neoliberalism and the logic of austerity generated by the capitalist economic crisis. Autonomism has also gained a strong following among scholars in the global South.[26] As a rule, in the South, autonomist unions have opposed parliamentary-based and party-based unions, viewed as compliant to the logic of capitalist accumulation and the subordination of workers. Everywhere, autonomists have opposed the existing communist unions, which were also viewed by them as being just as servile to capital and the state as were social democratic unions. Autonomy, or independence, required a principled rejection of capitalism, political parties, and the state – a position which manifested itself differently throughout the world. For autonomists, the non-party union is viewed as the archetype of principled worker representation, a stance which also reduces their ideological sphere of influence and capacity to challenge the state and capital. No doubt, autonomism as a form of labour representation is an appealing and engaging viewpoint, as it rejects bureaucratic unionism, internal union reform, and the old Left. At last, autonomism encompasses the aspiration of a disillusioned Left through offering the reality of an alternative form of working-class organization, at best, with a patchy record of successfully forming durable organizations. Undoubtedly, existing unions have marginalized workers as subordinate third parties to employers and labour leaders. Critics correctly oppose traditional unions and bureaucratic hierarchy as well as concessions to capital and the state, which expose workers to the vicissitudes of the neoliberal market. However, do autonomist unions also relegate workers to a new heroic form of marginalization, one placing them all alone, deprived of a strong and resilient labour organization? Can autonomist unions challenge flexibility and compromise with capital?

Spontaneity: Strikes and Labour Militancy

A key dynamic is absent in debates about labour representation: the ubiquitous presence of working-class militancy, typically expressed as spontaneous struggle against management, capital, and the state. Contrary to prevailing wisdom found among labour analysts, we argue that the working class is always prepared to struggle against capitalist oppression, and the wave of unauthorized strikes across the world in the late 2010s reveals that workers are indeed engaged in spontaneous direct action against the neoliberal state and capital. We can expect this to continue. Spontaneous labour militancy and solidarity are essential elements in building a strong working class, and are what Lenin signified in *What Is to Be Done?* as necessary for building a democratic labour movement:

> There is much talk of spontaneity. But the spontaneous development of the working-class movement leads to its subordination to bourgeois ideology, to its development along the lines of the Credo programme; for the spontaneous working-class movement is trade-unionism, is *Nur-Gewerkschaftlerei* [union-only], and trade unionism means the ideological enslavement of the workers by the bourgeoisie. Hence, our task, the task of Social-Democracy, is to combat spontaneity, to divert the working-class movement from this spontaneous, trade-unionist striving to come under the wing of the bourgeoisie, and to bring it under the wing of revolutionary Social Democracy.[27]

Under capitalism, trade unions are necessarily economic organizations which seek reformist concessions from capital and the state. Crucial in this process is providing the organizational scaffolding for workers to engage in militant action to achieve concessions. According to Lenin, success requires sustenance from a class-conscious organization dedicated to revolution and a socialist future. Successful strikes often facilitate direct concessions from management. As such, contrary to Silver,[28] the number and intensity of strikes are not measures of capacity for the working class to build organizational economic and social power. In themselves, strikes do not consolidate the power of the working class. In the absence of a strong working-class organization, whether union or party, the inability to absorb the class-conscious working class and adopt the aspirations of workers in political decisions will not lead to short- or long-term success, as fetishizing the spontaneous strike is in reality a bourgeois construct.

Without doubt, a democratic, militant, and mobilized working class is indispensable for building strong labour unions, which can in turn consolidate and preserve working-class militancy of the past. However, trade unions which lack a transformative and revolutionary ideology, necessarily linked to a political party, are incapable of building lasting class-wide power and solidarity. Instead, labour unions will default into sectoral, geographic, racial, ethnic, and identity formations, dispensing with class solidarity.

For example, in the 2010s, spontaneous worker mobilizations among mineworkers in South Africa's platinum industry, which joined with an existing trade union, found themselves in an organization unwilling or unable to advance beyond immediate economic demands and build political capacity to advance working-class solidarity. In turn, the inability to build broader working-class solidarity reduced the union's ability to gain economic demands for members. Trade unions, alone, pursue narrower economic interests of members rather than improving the conditions of the wider working class. Thus, a political party is a necessity to express universal working-class interests and bridge the unavoidable development of self-interested objectives.

Constructing Working-class Solidarity under Neoliberal Capitalism

The primary contradiction for mobilizing and building working-class power today appears starkly as being due to the state of diminished and detached labour unions holding tenuous bonds to anaemic Left political parties. The frailty of political parties is a function of their inability to challenge neoliberal globalization and commodity supply chains coordinated by global multinational corporations which marginalize the working classes in poor countries which are distant from the final point of delivery and consumption of products. Since the 1990s, foreign direct investment has expanded significantly from the global North to manufacturers in the South, where wages and production costs are far lower. Accordingly, the industrial working class in the South expanded at an unprecedented pace from 1990 to 2020.

Governments in the global South compete for investment and foreign capital, and the availability of the lowest-cost labour. As the vast majority of commodities are produced by contractors, low wages and long hours speed up, and job insecurity at non-union contractors has defined global production in the contemporary era. As traditional unions are often incapable of representing informal sector workers in the global supply chain, a variety of autonomist unions have endeavoured to intervene in labour management disputes to seize on workers' militancy. Though some autonomist unions have succeeded in representing a small fragment of these workers, routinely these campaigns end in failure, or standoffs which contractors and multinationals outlast. In such cases, workers are defeated, both in achieving immediate economic objectives and in the long-term effort to mobilize into strong and enduring unions. Accordingly, globalized industrial production is ever more dominated by multinational corporations controlling costs through contractors and labour brokers in the informal production of commodities.

The Disappearance of Labour Unions under Globalized Production and Working-class Strategy

As more workers are proletarianized in rural areas, and as the informal sector has expanded in new urban zones of the South, the size of the global industrial proletariat grew dramatically in the period 1990–2020 (see Table 2.2). Today's global labour force is far larger than that during the height of industrialization in the mid-twentieth century. As a result, labour scholars must focus on organizing and mobilizing this highly exploited working class in the era of globalization. This era is marked by paradigm shifts in the *modus operandi* of capital and labour relations worldwide, in addition to the decline of Fordism and the rise of informal contract labour as the dominant system of production. The emergence of the so-called 'global assembly line' reveals the weakness of labour organization arrayed against rampant informalization, marginalization, invisiblization, and feminization of the working class, rendering once-strong labour movements ineffective. Particularly in the global South, the growth of the informal labour force uncovers the staggering challenges of labour mobilization of a workforce which, even today, bears no resemblance to the advanced economies of the global North. For example, in India, only 7 per cent of the labour force are employed permanently (see Table 2.2).[29]

Table 2.2 Informality and employment status, global and by country income group, 2016 and 2018

Country grouping		Informality		Wage and salaried workers
		Level in 2016 (%)	Level in 2018 (%)	Change, 2018–2023 (%)
World	Total	61.2	52.0	0.6
	Female	58.1	52.5	0.5
	Male	63.0	51.7	0.6
Low-income	Total	89.8	18.8	0.9
	Female	92.1	11.9	0.6
	Male	87.5	24.5	1.1
Lower-middle-income	Total	83.7	34.5	1.9
	Female	84.5	31.6	2.1
	Male	83.4	35.8	1.8
Upper-middle-income	Total	52.6	59.2	1.8
	Female	50.4	58.4	2.2
	Male	54.0	59.8	1.5
High-income	Total	18.3	87.2	0.2
	Female	17.6	89.7	0.2
	Male	18.9	85.2	0.2

Source: Derived from International Labour Organization, *ILOSTAT* (Geneva: ILO, 2020), https://ilostat.ilo.org/, accessed and calculated 24 March 2020.

Thus, imagining autonomism as a successful revolutionary programme for the broader working class is a utopian construct which proclaims the obvious and palpable militancy of industrial labour as a novel development, whereas the evidence of class struggle over 150 years plainly displays that labourers will always resist exploitation and oppression. However, this book argues that if workers form a strong revolutionary organizational force, that resistance will be sustained and far more successful. While it may be pleasing to proclaim autonomous resistance as tantamount to victory for the oppressed, contra John Holloway, we cannot change the world without taking power.[30] Undeniably, the historical record over the past century reveals that taking political and economic power (over the shopfloor, community, or state) has brought palpable gains for workers. Confirming that workers have the capacity to act is no more than the surrender of tangible power to capital and the state. Autonomism signifies an admission of defeat and a celebration of the capacity of workers to every so often disrupt capitalist exploitation and bourgeois state power with no viable organizational alternative with which to challenge neoliberalism.

Beyond doubt, the expression of autonomism and workerism over the past 50 years has played an important role in exposing the failure of existing working-class leaders and organizations. As we shall see in Chapters 3–5, workers can be empowered through alternative structures (e.g. social centres, workers' centres, advice offices, legal challenges, and even NGOs) seeking to encouraging corporate social responsibility. But these efforts are no substitute for a strong class-conscious labour union that is moored to a disciplined socialist party led by the working class. The rejection of organization is a major miscalculation which cedes power to capital and the persistence of divided labour in the global South.[31]

Global Production and Spontaneous Worker Organization

Even though the industrial working class in the South is far larger than that in the North, its organizational capacity is far more limited as global capitalism has shifted from post-Fordist forms of contracting in dispersed multiple units where labour is not directly employed by multinational firms. Rather than working directly for MNCs, workers are employed by contractors, subcontractors, labour brokers, and even worker cooperatives controlled by corporate suppliers. An exceptional case is India, where even when industrial workers are labouring in the very same facilities and often performing the same jobs, typically more than 80 per cent of all workers in the plant are informal workers who are unprotected by major labour unions. But labourers in Egypt, India, Indonesia, Malaysia, South Africa, and beyond are employed by subcontractors. Even if workers were to form their own small independent union of 100–500 labourers, the rise of global supply chains gives MNCs and large contractors the flexibility to shift production to other enterprises in order to prevent job actions and strikes.

The emergence of the labour broker industry in the global South has given producers even greater levels of flexibility through designing fixed-term contracts, reducing workers to temporary labourers. Even if workers are employed in large factories, they are employed on short-term temporary employment contracts that can be terminated at any time. Certainly, worker dissent and resistance at the plant level occur, but never rise to a level that exceeds spontaneous uprisings, which are unable to transform into sustained working-class struggle through sustained organizational and political action. Post-Fordist contractors rely on 'footloose' labour where it is far more difficult to successfully challenge and improve low wages and poor working conditions. Nevertheless, migrant and footloose labourers still engage in spontaneous job actions against employers, as evinced by mobilizations against employers who fail to pay wages and inflict harsh work rules on essential migrant workers employed in the electronics and other export-driven industries in Malaysia and Southeast Asia.[32]

Industrial workers labouring in the informal sectors of the global South often reside in the neighbourhoods where they work. Unlike developed countries, it is far more difficult to disperse workers living in slums, squatter camps, and unauthorized townships, as evinced by the case studies of India, the Philippines, and South Africa in Chapters 3–5. But organizing is certainly not impossible, as new means must be utilized in organizing and mobilizing workers.

Abhinav Sinha, the Indian scholar and activist, underscores the significance of community-based organizing, whereby organization of the informal working class is far more effective since workers are employed in a range of jobs in a given community. The existing trade unions dominating shrinking sectors of the economy have neither the intent nor the inclination to organize the unorganized. In such a scenario of informality, says Sinha:

> these workers are organizing themselves on their own. However, their raw forms of organization need to be studied, analyzed and refined. These are the workers who will be at the centre of the new resurgence of the working class movement.[33]

Essentially, this informal working class, which comprises the vast majority of the urban and rural population, is exploited by local capitalists and multinational capitalists, and will express itself eventually as anti-capitalism and anti-imperialism. Sinha continues: 'their relationship with Imperialism also is one of contradiction, though not yet an antagonistic one'. As such, if a class-conscious informal working class emerges, 'it is going to be anti-capitalist anti-imperialist, as the question of struggle against imperialism will be a question of immediate importance for the revolutionary working class movements' within these communities and within the Third World.[34]

Expansion of the Labour Aristocracy

Trade unions will habitually engage in economism and, in many instances, collaborate with management to diminish rank and file militancy and intensify the alienation of workers. But can we envision unions moving beyond addressing the immediate needs of workers and developing a programme for social transformation leading towards socialism? To do so, it is important to appraise Lenin's understanding of the trade union through expanding the intrinsic institution, composition, and performance as a working-class organization. To grasp the crucial tasks for revolutionary trade unions, Lenin directed criticism at their leaders, who, he maintained, shared a propensity to defend the economic interests of members, and rejected forming alliances with exploited and impoverished workers who were oppressed by imperialists. Lenin's *Critique of Trade Unionism and the Labor Aristocracy* examines their activity within the global system. In 1916, Lenin had identified a crucial convergence between the bourgeoisie and the labour aristocracy in imperialist countries in exploiting the masses of humanity on the periphery. In this case, Lenin viewed social democratic trade unions and political parties as collaborators in the imperialist wars against the rest of the world to ensure the continued extraction of profits.

Yet, for Lenin, this political convergence of the bourgeoisie and trade union leaders in imperialist core countries did not extend to the larger working-class masses in countries of the North. The merging of interests between capital and labour arises from material forces. Lenin predicted that the lower echelons of the working class would eventually rise up to oppose the corrupted, bureaucratic, and wayward leadership of trade unions and establish a class-conscious working-class opposition.[35] However, according to Eric Hobsbawm, following Lenin, the capacity for the working-class masses to contest and overthrow the exploitative power bloc unifying the labour aristocracy with the bourgeoisie is determined by their relations to the means of production. Most of the working classes of the global South are especially exploited in the global South and work under oppressive conditions. Thus, Lenin's critique of trade unions in colonial nations in furthering the misery of workers on the periphery is highly prescient, as privileged classes in rich countries engage in a fraction of the labour they had in previous generations:

> The non-propertied, but non-working, class is incapable of overthrowing the exploiters. Only the proletarian class, which maintains the whole of society, can bring about the social revolution. However, as a result of the extensive colonial policy, the European proletarian *partly* finds himself in a position when it is *not* his labour, but the labour of the practically enslaved natives in the colonies, that maintains the whole of society. The British bourgeoisie, for example, derives more profit from the many millions of the population of India and other colonies than from the British workers. In certain countries this provides the material and economic basis for infecting the proletariat with colonial chauvinism. Of course, this may be only a temporary phenomenon, but the evil must nonetheless be clearly realized and its causes understood in order to be able to rally the proletariat of all countries for the struggle against such opportunism. This struggle is bound to be victorious, since the 'privileged' nations are a diminishing faction of the capitalist nations.[36]

Accordingly, Hobsbawm finds that as the proletariat in the imperial core is farther removed from economic activity, it has a material and economic basis in maintaining the system and has a social susceptibility for social chauvinism toward oppressed peoples in the colonial world.[37] Without a principled trade union leadership, the working class resorts to self-interested organizational economism that has perilous consequences for working-class unity.[38] In this way, and following Marx, service sector workers and petit-bourgeois business owners, who comprise 80 per cent of all labourers in the USA, are not the main drivers of the global economy. Rather, workers and peasants in Indonesia and throughout the global South are directly subjected to the extraction of surplus value.

CONCLUSION: WORKERS, UNIONS, AND PARTY

The imposition of neoliberal policies since the 1980s has intensified the challenges for the labour movement of the global South. Not only must trade unions endlessly challenge capital to improve the conditions of workers, but on an immediate basis, the principled union directly engages in the unremitting labour struggles in opposition to state anti-labour policies that undermine existing standards of living by reducing wages, speeding up production, and replacing existing workers with even more exploited labourers to increase corporate profitability. A revolutionary union must both fulfil the immediate needs of workers and remain committed to ending the alienation of workers from the capitalist labour process through the establishment of a socialist society, which is a formidable task. Failure to resist the further erosion of wages and conditions on a practical level will invalidate the trade union's anti-capitalist programme. Time and again, the union and workers' organization must prove themselves to the worker. In this way, the union must be present within the daily struggles of the working class for sanitation, clean water, electricity, housing, and education, in addition to developing opposition against employers and the state. In the absence of a reliable and dependable working-class organization, workers will distrust organizers and refuse to accept the organization in leading a resistance and general mobilization against employers. In each case study in this book, workers respond to the ebb and flow of labour organizers. Sustained mass unrest will only come about where there is strong and determined labour organizational support. This tremendous task can only be achieved with the support of a detachment of the working class which is sympathetic to the needs and aspirations of workers, and which has the capacity and resources to wage a sustained organizing campaign, demanding improved conditions in the specific struggle while maintaining a programme for the empowerment of the working class. If we are to modernize Lenin's critique of working-class spontaneity and economism for the contemporary working class, unions and labour organizations must have a detailed revolutionary plan for overcoming the hegemony of capital and must build confidence by challenging oppressors every day.

As Lenin noted over a century ago, more and more unions and workers in the imperialist West do not share a common material interest with more than 85 per cent of the population in the global South. While precariousness has increased on a global level, more often than not, workers in rich countries benefit from the neoliberal order and global commodity supply chains which lower the cost of commodities.[39] As a result, workers in the North seek to maintain an unambiguous economic advantage over the South and are not predisposed to a common class interest with workers worldwide.

Labour scholars and socialists are far more comfortable perceiving the global working class as a cohesive unified force. Most prefer to blame declining living standards in the South on rapacious employers who are directed by compliant capitalist states, rather than drawing attention to the internal divisions within the working class, which essentially divide the world on the basis of most socio-economic indicators.

The global divide intensifies the importance of building a principled union leadership implanted within a revolutionary party, one which is attached to the broader working classes, including rural and informal workers. As this book will show, worker organizations assume a far more expansive character which links factories and plants to squatter settlements and the rural countryside. For that reason, it is important to conceive of the union as a mass organization of the proletariat rather than simply as representing sectoral workers. In addition, the new working-class organizations must go beyond serving as a reflexive expression of the immediate demands of segments of a decidedly unstable working class, which, following Pierre Bourdieu, is defined by the habitus that is circumscribed by the material conditions of capital. In the case of the vast majority of workers in the global South, workers are employed in informal and rural work, which shapes and delineates the probability of success.[40] This integral 'habitus' shapes the possibility of class contestation and the arena of possible engagement. While workers will unrelentingly protest against corporate and employer abuse and destabilization of working and living conditions, in the absence of a strong and revolutionary union, typically backed by a principled party, the autonomist and syndicalist activities of the workers will be squandered and lost. The union and party must establish deep roots in these communities to win over the workers and engage in campaigns to ameliorate and improve conditions. Workers' demands will be circumscribed by the habitus, but the calculus for transformation can change based on the revolutionary subjectivity of the working class.

On the Detachment of the Working Class

Beyond question, it is necessary that the workers should lead and actively participate in collective action. However, the spontaneous activity of the working class must not be the major force for change. To achieve tangible gains, workers must have discipline, knowledge of political economy, and an analytic grasp of revolutionary anti-capitalist theory. In this way, what has been referred to as an *advanced detachment* of the working class must lead and guide workers, rather than trail the disruptive spontaneous movements. This leadership must be situated within the working-class organization in advancing demands and inspiring workers to cast doubt on the capitalist system which exploits them. Without this leadership drawn from revolutionary leaders of the workers, the struggles will fail to meet their short- and long-term goals.

PART II

CASE STUDIES:
RURAL AND INFORMAL LABOUR STRUGGLES

3

Primitive Steel Manufacturing for the Global Consumer Market: Capital, Super-exploitation, and Surplus Value in Wazirpur, India

FROM AGRARIAN TO INFORMAL LABOUR: NEW PRODUCTION AND UNORGANIZED WORKERS

As the Indian economy has undertaken an unremitting neoliberal capitalist transformation over the past 30 years since the 1990 economic liberalization, a leading debate has focused on the nature of India's capitalism and the degree and intensity of the shift in social class relations.[1] Significantly, how has the balance of class forces shifted as the capacity of the peasantry to subsist in the countryside has diminished and informal workers have expanded in urban areas? The status of both workers and peasants is therefore cast into question as class forces are changing. While India's neoliberal reform has pushed agrarian labour into the teeming cities, giving rise to the vast expansion of the industrial working class, what is the capacity of workers to improve their socio-economic conditions?

Unquestionably, neoliberal reform has expanded India's urbanization, but the ambiguous capitalist development from 1990 to the present has not created large Fordist industry, but has had a propensity towards small and medium-sized enterprises (SMSEs), impeding unequivocal development of an industrial working class with a predisposition towards intense labour militancy comparable to the metropolitan and settler economic models of the nineteenth and twentieth centuries, or even late industrializing states. As political economist and activist Abhinav Sinha observes, 'capital has scattered the 93 percent portion of the working class in terms of the work place', and approximately 80 per cent of all industrial units in

India are SMSEs employing fewer than 50 workers. Job stability is not the norm in the 20 per cent of India's factories with more than 50 labourers, as the vast majority are employed on a contingent basis as contract workers for labour brokers.[2] The absence of job stability contributes to an increasingly volatile workforce, with little recourse to directly confront employers through durable, factory-based trade unions, according to Sinha:

> Even if such unions are somehow organized, their power is limited in most of the cases. With the labour laws becoming more and more flexible, their power has declined even further. In most of the factory struggles taking place in the last two decades, the working class has faced defeat in more cases than earlier. In many cases [...] even though the across-factory organization succeeded in bringing the State agencies to their knees, the issues on which the labour movement began remained more or less unsolved. In many cases, the factories whose issues were at the centre of the struggle either got closed down or the factory-owners closed them for some time and then restarted the production with an entirely new work force. Many a times such factory-owners shifted the factory from the old location to a new location with a new work force.[3]

Indisputably, India's urban working class is expanding as a consequence of urban migration, yet, at the same time, the rural peasantry endures as a salient socio-economic demographic force, as the country's population continues to grow, though at a slower pace, and a substantial share of the urban working class residing in slums return regularly to rural areas when regular work is unavailable, to till their small plots of land. Contrary to common outlooks promoted by global development organizations and scholars, the rural population is growing in the world, global South, and India. The major region which has experienced rural population decline is the developed states (see Figure 3.1).

Nevertheless, while the rural population continues to grow in India, so does the urban population. However, the densely crowded cities of India, as elsewhere in Southern countries, bear a resemblance to rural areas since they lack potable water, sanitation, electricity, and essential services. Most of the growth is driven by migration from rural areas where people are unable to subsist in the densely populated rural hinterland, where the landed feudal classes control most arable land, and where peasants holding small plots

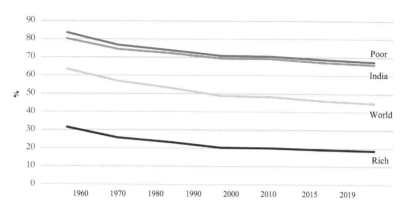

Figure 3.1   Rural population as a percentage of total population for India, the poor, the rich, and the world

Source: Derived from Word Bank DataBank, World Development Indicators, last updated 10 July 2019.

of land are unable to survive or are forced to pay exceedingly high rent to rural Junkers. As rural subsistence has grown more arduous in the 1980s, peasants have moved to destitute urban settlements areas to supplement their meagre rural incomes.

This chapter examines Wazirpur, a community that until the 1970s was on the northern fringes of the City of New Delhi, but in the 1980s was annexed as a subdivision. Initially planned as a hosiery manufacturing district, Wazirpur quickly became a major stainless steel production centre. In contrast to other 'developing countries' like the People's Republic of China, the Indian government has typically not invested capital in infrastructural projects to expand production, but has depended on a large reserve army of labour in manufacturing, where, as a rule, surplus value had been realized through their super-exploitation. In this way, the dominant strategy has been for SMSEs to compete through low wages, long hours, and poor and unsafe working conditions.

The Marxist view of the subsumption of capital seeks to expose how greater profitability is extracted from individual workers by virtue of investments. Thus, new investment in artificial intelligence and robotics has increased productivity in most industries, but is generally applied to logistics, telecommunications, biotechnology, e-commerce, aerospace, robotics, etc., where surplus value is significantly higher. While substantial surplus value can be realized through use of artificial intelligence and robotics in e-commerce, capital investment in new technology in basic industries (mining, steel, automobile, and electronics) has significantly increased corporate profits. But in many basic industries (mining, garments, stainless steel, furniture, construction, etc.), employers extract profits by the super-exploitation of labour. While new technology is often used alongside low-wage labour, a substantial share of global industrial production continues to rely primarily on the extraction of surplus directly from workers, with little new capital and technological investment.

FORMATION AND GROWTH OF AN URBAN INDUSTRIAL SLUM

Wazirpur exemplifies the rural–urban nexus in India, and the global South more generally, whereby the rural periphery and economic decay is situated in the centre of the major city.[4] Delhi and the surrounding region form a major region of manufacturing production, with leading production firms located in the National Capital Territory (NCT) of Delhi and surrounding cities of Gurugram (Gurgaon) Noida, Faridabad, and an industrial belt extending from nearby cities in Haryana to the west and Uttar Pradesh to the east. A fundamental feature in each industrial district is the absence of basic needs for survival: potable water, sanitation, electricity, and housing. As such, Delhi is a focal point of the contrasts between urban and rural life: capital investment versus lack of capital investment in production. A major feature of both advanced and backward sectors is the exploitation of informal and rural migrant labour. A dominant feature of production in Wazirpur is the proliferation of small industrial plants which are severely lacking in capital investment. Though the Wazirpur industrial zone lacks new technology and industrial investment, the site is a hub of production of steel plates and china for consumer use in India and throughout the world.

Wazirpur was formed as part of the Delhi metropolitan plan in 1962 as a 'Master Plan for Delhi' to restrain its haphazard growth and design the geographic, demographic, and economic expansion of the city and region in the post-independence era. Specific locations in the Delhi region were designated as industrial developments. While the plan was designed to ensure organized and systematic growth, it did not provide the funding for organized expansion nor did the government authorities regulate the labour and environmental standards of the businesses operating in industrial areas which were also populated by migrants from nearby states.[5] The passage of the Delhi Development Act of 1957 and its implementation in 1962 remained in force as the primary plan for the development of the city and territory, to be replaced in 1990 by the 'Master Plan for Delhi 2001'.[6] The master plans aim to ensure stable and balanced development and allocation of funds for housing, employment, infrastructure, commerce, and transport for the National Capital Territory of Delhi. The 1962 'Master Plan' recognized the significance of SMSEs for the industrial development of the region. It envisaged large-scale manufacturing units in the cities surrounding the NCT, and regarded the special industrial subdivisions within it as a means of serving the population's immediate needs for food and household products. S.C. Gupta and S.P. Bansal note:

> As regards location policy, small and medium size units were to be located more close [*sic*] to the centre of the city. Preference was to be given for establishing new units, which were essential for either feeding, servicing or maintaining Delhi's population. Delhi was not considered desirable to locate any new units within the Central city area creating problems of waste disposal, water pollution etc. Large manufacturing units were proposed in Ring Towns. Keeping in view these aspects, land for industries were identified at different locations for the estimated employment generation, based on the zoning regulations provided for different type of industries.[7]

It is astonishing, then, that most of the products produced in Wazirpur and many other industrial sites within Delhi do not serve the food and consumer needs of its population, but produce consumer goods and products for export, such as stainless steel utensils.

In 1966, as part of the New Delhi NCT expansion, regional planners designated Wazirpur's privately owned rural land for development into hundreds of small-scale industrial production units for hosiery and other specialized fabrics. In this way, Wazirpur was established by government authorities for small businesses with limited capital to produce consumer goods for the regional, national, and international markets. However, by the late 1980s, the development of Wazirpur as a hub for hosiery production in

New Delhi never took shape as the location unmistakably became a primary focal point for stainless steel production.

The Wazirpur Industrial Area (WIA) is a 85-hectare (210-acre) subdivision in the district of Chandni Chowk of the NCT of Delhi. Wazirpur, a rural village, was officially established as the WIA in 1966 as part of the capital's expansion plan into New Delhi's surrounding agrarian hinterland, which now forms the NCT. At first, urban planners designated Wazirpur as an industrial zone for plastic, hosiery, and electronic production, but according to authoritative accounts by documentary observers and interviewees, by the mid-1980s, the steel industry had emerged as the dominant industry here and a leading steel manufacturing centre in the world. The zone has three unique features: a vast number of workers employed in a relatively small area, a large number of small producers, and an urban slum lacking basic housing, transport, and healthcare facilities. In all, about 60,000 workers are employed in the area's industries. Wazirpur has about 1,000 SMSEs, employing workers who are primarily integrated into the production of stainless steel kitchen utensils. According to sociologist Moueshri Vyas, approximately two thirds of the factories, or about 600–650 units, employ workers directly involved in the production and fabrication of steel and steel utensils. The average factory has fewer than 50 workers, though some steel plants employ more than 100 workers. About 90 per cent of all the workers are employed in some aspect of steel production, including rickshaw and handcart pullers.[8]

Rickshaw pullers and other transport workers are integral to the production of steel as they move products in various stages of completion from one factory to another. The working conditions of rickshaw pullers are dangerous. Several workers interviewed revealed that the main risk was the loading and unloading of thin metal sheets from hot-rolling, cold-rolling, polishing, and finishing factories. Several rickshaw pullers sustained major injuries as a result of accidents related to falling plates of metal; in some cases, when steel cut through major arteries, the delivery workers perished. A large proportion of workers in all components of the industry, especially polishing, are young boys of 15 years of age and exposed to noxious chemicals. After a 12-hour day, at around 6–6:30 pm in the polishing factory, these boys can be seen leaving work with black and grey covering their faces and all their clothing (interviews and observations in July and August 2016, and January 2017).

Additionally, women who are residents of Wazirpur work as copper and other scrap collectors of discarded computer and electronics parts within the industrial area. These workers are highly visible as most of the labour is performed outside in the empty lots where computer parts are dumped for the purpose of picking. In this way, there is a high degree of integration of the Wazirpur slum's residential workforce into the global supply chain, as recycled copper and other valuable metals re-enter production industries.

Wazirpur is also a residential area for most of the workers and their families. Most of the workers in Wazirpur have been employed for at least five to ten years and live in the neighbouring slums that are typically on the same street as the factories dispersed throughout the area and Delhi, known as *jhuggi basti*, or squatter settlements. *Jhuggi basti* have expanded adjacent to industrial and commercial developments in Delhi and other cities in India. In Wazirpur, generations of workers from surrounding states have lived in the neighbourhood, where the concept of upward mobility is largely a fiction. From interviews with the most educated children of workers, who are also tutored by activists working with the dominant independent union in the area, it was learned that the students were mostly interested in government jobs. In one instance, a 16-year-old student said he wanted to go to post-secondary school and become a factory inspector to improve conditions in the community's local factories.

Vyas notes that local residents in Wazirpur comprise a significant share of the workers in the vicinity:

Most of the workers are tenants here and share a room and the rent of about INR 1500–2000 per month.[9] Water and electricity facilities are available, but sanitation and solid waste management facilities are inadequate, resulting in water overflowing into the streets. Health conditions of workers are poor because of twelve-hour working days, congested surroundings, polluted environment, and lack of health facilities. Two or three major, and eight to ten minor accidents occur each day, with death of four or five workers every year due to accidents.[10]

On recent visits to the housing units in the summer of 2016 and winter of 2017, I found most of the residents in Wazirpur living in one-room housing units of 5–14 square metres (53–151 square feet) situated above shops vending food and other supplies. Enter a housing block, and you will encounter women and children coming and going through unlit corridors which turn day into night, open drainage systems, and an unexpectedly tidy and organized milieu where residents seem to work together in a ramshackle location that is uninhabitable to *any* Westerner. As most of the housing units are situated above the ground floor, residents must climb makeshift ladders to reach home. Taking into consideration the general absence of lighting and poor egress to and from one's home, it is virtually impossible to go out after dusk or before dawn. But given that the stainless steel factories operate two 12-hour shifts, workers do come and go at all hours of the day. The residential area is inhabited by workers who share dwellings on the basis of their work shift, as well as men and women raising children.

The production of stainless steel kitchen utensils and supplies is made possible by the presence of highly exploited stainless steel utensil workers who primarily reside in the slums of the area. However, a large proportion of workers earn far less than steelworkers of the area, working in the informal economy of day labour, domestic work, and other tertiary jobs. Most noteworthy is the scale of industrial production. In the more than 30 years from 1987 to 2020, the WIA has relied on the presence of about 600 independent and individually owned small factories producing stainless steel utensils for the national and international markets. The steel-based businesses include hot-rolling mills, cold-rolling mills, stainless steel polishing factories, and utensil pressing and packaging factories. In addition, the private businesses of Wazirpur also engage in essential support services for the factories, especially rickshaw pullers, who are responsible for transporting steel products in various stages of fabrication to and from the hundreds of small factories, employing on average 50 or fewer workers. Typically, Wazirpur is bustling with activity 24 hours a day to produce kitchen utensils for national and international markets, especially stainless steel plates and serving trays in various forms. Wazirpur's products are often found in leading South Asian and other restaurants in major metropolitan areas of North America and Western Europe. Unknown to restaurant customers in London and New York, as well as Delhi, is the fact that these essential products are produced by highly exploited labourers who are exposed to dangerous conditions on a daily basis.[11]

According to historical accounts, Wazirpur was quickly marked by the contrast between rich and poor, opulent and squalid conditions, as numerous illegal steel fabrication units dominated the area. In 1989, writing just before the implementation of India's liberalization, Bharat Dogra wrote in *Economic and Political Weekly*:

> The imposing roadside mansions, including a luxury restaurant, on the stretch of Delhi's ever-busy Ring Road around the Shalimar Bagh bus stop give the impression of prosperity. Turn to the road towards the railway crossing and you will see shop after shop of glittering steel utensils. This is Wazirpur, a big centre of steel utensil manufacture. Move into one of the roadside lanes, however, and you will come face-to-face with the stark reality of a huge, sprawling industrial slum. Here there are huge piles of iron and steel scrap (or scrap-like sheets) and cart-pullers carrying these sheets on their ramshackle carts. And there are the sheds where these sheets undergo numerous industrial processes before emerging as the glittering steel utensils that decorate the shops. There are children with their bodies and faces blackened in the process of polishing the utensils. Women inhale toxic fumes as they work with acidic solutions. And if it is one of those bad days which are becoming quite frequent, one may also see a profusely bleeding worker, the victim of an industrial accident, being rushed to one of the medical shops that pass as nursing homes. The predominant feature of the Wazirpur steel units is the unauthorized or illegal nature of most of the work. Most of the units are unregistered and are functioning in premises which were meant to house some other units.[12]

This same general account of Wazirpur conditions for workers and residents depicted by Dogra is starkly analogous to an appraisal of the subdivision as we enter the 2020s. Thirty years on, neoliberal economic reform has permitted Indian businesses and capitalists to dodge legal liability to improve conditions and protect the rights of workers and residents. The stark conditions of blight and danger are all-encompassing in visits to the neighbourhood. Though changes may have been mandated by law as a consequence of a series of militant worker uprisings organized by political activists, over the 30-year period working conditions bear a remarkable similarity to those prevailing in 1989.

On the whole, workers continue to work 12 hours a day, six days a week. Labourers work very long days, on average 12 hours, six or seven days a week. Whereas some workers in hot-rolling mills have achieved a modest reduction in hours, nearly every small business circumvents the restrictions on the work day and has maintained two 12-hour work shifts. The approximately 600 hot- and cold-rolling mills operate 24 hours a day, seven days a week. The author interviewed labourers during break times, after work, and for those who had one day off, on Wednesdays at meetings in the Wazirpur public park. Even if workers in the hot-rolling mills work eight-hour days, they are unable to survive. Thus, even if the employers' association conceded to allow mill labourers a shorter work day of eight hours, factory owners would reduce workers' wages by one third, largely defeating the purpose of the strike or actions that have been advanced by organizers and workers. This demonstrates the inadequacy of contracts and legal conventions to enforce workers' rights.

What makes Wazirpur so oppressive and terrifying for workers is not only the long work days, but the exhausting, strenuous, and dangerous working conditions imposed on all labourers in the vicinity: hot-rolling mills, cold-rolling mills, steel polishing factories, stainless steel utensil fabricators, and transport. In each of these factories, which resemble penal workhouses, employers have not invested in new equipment to reduce the need for gruelling labour. Thus, employers profit from the absence of investment, rather than new outlays of capital to reduce labour time. Profit is extracted from the absence of capital investment in new labour-saving technology, rather than drawing out surplus labour directly from the workers themselves, without reinvesting profits in new equipment and technology. The norm for capitalist enterprises is to reinvest in more profitable businesses where surplus extraction is higher. However, Wazirpur is the exception to the propensity of productivity extraction through capital investment.

The factory owners of Wazirpur may be investing in new capital that contributes to labour redundancy and extracts even higher rates of worker productivity in other industries outside stainless steel, but do not invest in new technology which would improve the conditions of workers. Thus, they rely on a high rate of 'living labour power' in situ. The low rate of capital investment in technology does not diminish surplus labour as mill owners expand profitability through the super-extraction of surplus from workers. In the same way as factory owners in early to mid-nineteenth-century Britain, when factory owners depended on highly exploited Irish labour to increase productivity and profits, the Indian stainless steel industry derives profits from highly exploited labour rather than investing in labour-saving technology. New technology investments in Wazirpur's stainless steel industry would wreck the business model rooted in a very low organic composition of capital that relies on the intensification of labour, and would thus shift production to new sites. The significance of the composition of capital in industry is analysed by Marx as the proportion of value which is determined by the means of production (constant capital) and labour power (variable capital).[13] The distinctiveness of Wazirpur is that it demonstrates how, in the contemporary era, capitalism continues to rely significantly on a high proportion of labour relative to capital to create value in the global economy. Stainless steel production in Wazirpur defies the standard paradigm advanced by political economists that the labour share is declining everywhere. Undeniably, Wazirpur in India, metropolitan Johannesburg in South Africa, and Mindanao in the Philippines are crucial sites of capitalist extraction through primary reliance on labour, or variable capital.

The remarkably low composition of capital in Wazirpur redounds negatively upon the workers, among whom serious injury and even death are highly prevalent and a daily occurrence. In the hot- and cold-rolling mills, workers are exposed every day to dangerous work conditions due to heat exhaustion. It is common to see workers with burned, bruised, and missing fingers, and bodies pierced by shrapnel resulting from the production of steel. On a visit to Wazirpur in the summer of 2018, *Indian Express* reporter Somya Lakhani interviewed a labourer applying for work at a machine shop who was seeking to conceal his missing fingers so he could find employment:

At 9:20 am, Naresh landed at the Aarah Machine Chowk in Wazirpur industrial area, in one of the two oversized full-sleeve shirts he owns. The 33-year-old looked sharp, his hair neatly parted, shirt tucked in and shoelaces tightly knotted around his ankles. [...] But the unbuttoned long sleeves of his shirt gave him away. 'I am trying to hide my hands by wearing long-sleeve shirts. I don't have three-and-a-half fingers, so I don't get picked for factory work [...]. A day at the steel factories here earns Rs 400, but if I don't get that, I end up taking odd jobs all day and return home with less than half,' he said.[14]

In Wazirpur, industrial labourers with lost fingers are not scarce, due to lack of safety equipment protocols, as well as under-maintained and obsolete machinery, along with inescapable miscommunication or lapses that occur regularly and are factored into the stainless steel production process. But lost fingers are not the worst that can happen to a worker. The coroner at a local morgue has witnessed deaths of workers employed in the cold-rolling mills. As sheets of steel cool, due to the poor quality and impurity of the steel, steel pellets frequently burst through like bullets and pierce the bodies of machine workers. If the workers are not equipped with protective gear, they may easily be killed. The steel particles shoot into their torsos and limbs. The more fortunate will have the pellet enter and exit their arms or hands. The less fortunate are seriously injured, or more often killed, when the pellets crash into their torsos and hit major organs and arteries.

Industrial deaths in Wazirpur are not accidental, but a routine occurrence that employers consider a cost of the production process. Coroners are essential to the operation of Wazirpur's stainless steel industry. When a worker dies, which occurs frequently, it is the coroner's responsibility to file reports to determine the cause of death. Police investigations of the cause of death often result in no punishment. If there is a complaint from a family member, payments are arranged in the order of US$500, or less than three months' pay, to spouses and family members back home in the villages of Bihar and Uttar Pradesh. Such close kin do not have the money to travel to Delhi to oversee an investigation, and even if they do, the probability of the employers being held to account is so low that the long trip is not even feasible.[15]

Interviews were conducted in 2016 and 2017 with a coroner who had worked for six years in the nearby morgue. This morgue is required to report workers' causes to the police department, but not one determination of steel mill owner or employer responsibility had led to an arrest for the death of a worker during his tenure in Wazirpur (interviews with Wazirpur coroner, 11 January 2017 and 24 July 2019). In late July 2016, workers in Wazirpur's mills became alarmed by an unusual rise in the number of deaths by shooting pellets. In response, incensed workers reported the accidents to the main local union in which they had most confidence: Bigul Mazdoor Dasta ('Workers' Bugle'). When several deaths occur within a week, workers typically appeal to the union, which lodges legal complaints and organizes meetings in Wazirpur and outside the offices of the High Commissioner of Delhi. Legal action is a slow process, and usually culminates in an agreement with the worker and his family.

In India today, it is illegal to pay workers below minimum wage, and employers are required to provide workers with the protective equipment and gear to prevent major injury and death. Following a sequence of worker strikes in Wazirpur and other locations in Delhi, where workers labour for exceedingly low wages, workers are required to take breaks from the work in the hot-rolling mills.[16] However, despite these wage and government legal protections, over the past 30 years workers' wages and conditions have remained relatively the same. Today, as in 1987, the Wazirpur business model is to draw as much surplus value directly from the worker as possible, rather than to invest in new equipment and worker training.

Walking through Wazirpur today, the conditions prevailing in Dogra's description 30 years ago remain pervasive. Without exaggeration, Wazirpur conjures impressions of what it may have been like as an industrial worker in Manchester, London, or Birmingham in mid-nineteenth-century England. In the same way as the Irish or rural English worker Frederick Engels describes in *The Condition of the English Working Class* of 1844 or a figure in a Charles Dickens novel, in full view one immediately encounters numerous ramshackle small-scale steel mills on dusty roads with young men pulling rickshaws piled with dozens of sheets of flattened steel from a small hot-rolling mill to a cold-rolling mill, or from a cold-rolling mill to a utensil fabricator.[17] Today, as 30 years ago, illegality prevails. While the area is known as a stainless steel utensil producer, many of the mills and operations operate illegally or in open violation of all laws intended to protect labour rights and prevent the abuse of workers.

Who are the workers of Wazirpur, and why are they important? The workers are almost entirely migrant labourers from the nearby states in northern India (Uttar Pradesh and Bihar) who have been forced to relocate to New Delhi due to economic despair and the deteriorating living conditions in their rural villages, to which they send home remittances to family members unable to survive without such support. Marx's distinction of Britain's labouring population into three sectors (well paid, badly paid, and the 'nomadic population') is especially apt in conceptualizing the status of the industrial workers of Wazirpur:

> We turn now to a class of people whose origin is agricultural, but whose occupation is in great part industrial. They are the light infantry of capital, thrown by it, according to its needs, now to this point, now to that. When

they are not on the march, they 'camp'. Nomad labour is used for various operations of building and draining, brick-making, lime-burning, railway-making, etc. A flying column of pestilence, it carries into the places in whose neighbourhood it pitches its camp, small-pox, typhus, cholera, scarlet fever, etc. In undertakings that involve much capital outlay, such as railways, etc., the contractor himself generally provides his army with wooden huts and the like, thus improvising villages without any sanitary provisions, outside the control of the local boards, very profitable to the contractor, who exploits the labourers in two-fold fashion – as soldiers of industry and as tenants.[18]

EVERYDAY WORK IN WAZIRPUR: SURVIVAL, AND ENDURING CLASS CONFLICT

Over the past 30 years, workers in Wazirpur's steel mills have consistently engaged in industrial conflict to improve their wages and working conditions. These workers' uprisings have arisen spontaneously in response to the unrelenting exploitation. As in many class conflicts, workers' conflict emerges through autonomous action and organizations. However, though autonomous action has broken out, workers do not have the capacity to challenge the employers' associations which dominate Wazirpur. Employers also factor in the possibility of sporadic worker tooldowns and strikes in their business operations. Workers alone do not have the power to overcome the power of the employers, who are supported by public officials and the police. Among workers in Wazirpur, as elsewhere, autonomy signifies a lack of broader popular and organizational support capable of challenging employers and capital. In the first two decades of this century, as trade unions and labour organizations have weakened or become increasingly removed from the workplace, labour scholarship has shifted toward analysing organizational forms within the sphere of work, inferring that rank and file and workplace action alone reveal the power of workers. In fact, these everyday forms of resistance and self-organization have been a feature of class conflict since the emergence of industrial capitalism and were popularized by the IWW in the early twentieth century as it sought to galvanize this rank and file activity into one big union (see Chapter 2 for discussion of the IWW and syndicalism).

A century later, analogous though more nebulous forms of direct worker (and in some cases, community) organization have emerged that bear a resemblance to the IWW. In most cases, these organizations are far weaker than the IWW was a century earlier, as they lack a broader national and cross-national identity. Thus, contemporary independent unions and workers' centres are sustained by external funding and campaigns, often through NGOs; in some cases they are funded by foreign foundations and governments. The concept is that workers are incapable of advancing their interests and must depend on external support to shift workers out of poverty. In India, during the period of economic liberalization from 1990 to the present, NGOs have formed and become recipients of foreign funding for the purposes of advancing worker rights and human rights: for example, the Self Employed Women's Association (SEWA).[19] While perhaps well meaning, these organizations have the propensity to diminish the power of organized workers. What workers in Wazirpur and beyond require is strong labour organization and powerful political parties. Yet Western and a growing number of Indian NGOs and some political fronts on the Left oppose strong organizations that are backed by Marxist and revolutionary party organizations. Notwithstanding substantial differences among these organizations in terms of a strong commitment to principles of advancing the cause of the mobilized workers, local Leftists often oppose strong organizations, positing that workers in Wazirpur and other industrial areas of India will in some way or another advance their interests through amorphous rank and file activity. Western and Indian social scientists advocating the benefit of workers' autonomous activity romanticize the undefined organization of humanity that is advanced through some ethereal forces lacking definition or specific description.

MAJOR WORKER MOVEMENTS AND UPRISINGS, 1987–2019

We will next examine two major strike waves in the stainless steel utensil industry in Wazirpur: the seven-day strike of 1988 and a major strike wave in 2014. In both cases, workers sought to achieve improved wages and conditions. In each case, these conditions were improved, but not nearly far enough. Terms of employment were only improved marginally, and the major dynamic has been the weakness of social organization.

Rise of Small-scale Production and the 1987 and 1988 Strike Wave

For most of its history as an independent country, the Indian economy has always been dominated by small-scale enterprises. In 1988, industrial workers employed in small and medium-sized enterprises waged the first major strike in India's history, led by the Centre of Indian Trade Unions (CITU), one of India's leading trade unions affiliated with the Communist Party of India Marxist (CPI[M]) and the mass strikes of 2014 organized by Mazdoor Dasta, an independent Marxist organization which, despite limited resources, successfully mobilized the disparate workers of Wazirpur to improve wages and working conditions. In each case, the workers' conditions improved, yet the contours of the system of oppression were unchanged.

Indian industrial relations had been dominated by the political party-affiliated trade unions that had for 40 years participated in a system of collective bargaining relations with the major state and private corporations. Labourers in India's trade unions commanded wages and pensions which had ensured higher standards of living for a small sliver of the industrial working class. In the period 1949–90, most labourers were in non-union jobs in the Indian semi-feudal economy as the vast majority of the country's population resided and worked in agrarian regions.

The shift to a flexible labour market by policymakers began in the 1980s. The programme of liberalization did not directly challenge India's capitalist class, but rather those small and limited institutions where state policies shielding labour could be eroded piecemeal. As political economist Vivek Chibber explains, the Indian state's failure to gain a broad consensus on reform and industrial development in the 1960s set the stage for neoliberal reforms of the 1980s and 1990s which were directed against state-linked industries.[20] Liberalization demanded concessions from a small and weak working class to relinquish labour protections in large state-dominated industries to attract capital investment, and to restrain India's large but circumscribed trade unions from defending the burgeoning workforce in newly developing domestic industries. Under neoliberalism, domestic industries linked to the global supply chain had far lower rates of capital development, while in some other industries (e.g. high technology, business services, automobiles, electronics), foreign capitalists joined national capitalists. A central aspect of this programme was labour law reforms, which ostensibly would achieve higher levels of industrial growth and accountability by creating a more flexible labour force. India's proclivity has been toward taking the low road to industrialization: extracting as much surplus value as possible from labour rather than new technological productivity. Thus, labour flexibilization and de-unionization did not necessarily lead to greater investments. Economist Alakh Sharma observes:

> As long as a firm can continue competing on the basis of low wages and bad working conditions, there is no motivation to innovate for improving productivity. Only when the path to competition on the basis of low wages and bad working conditions is barred by providing a floor of labour standards, the firms can become enterprising and invest in technological and organizational innovation, which, in turn, leads to better wages and working conditions. In fact, the absence of a minimum floor of labour standards would inevitably ensnare the industrial economy in the syndrome of low wage and low productivity.[21]

Yet this would erode union membership in established sectors and undermine labour unions' ability to organize new sectors. Those workers who would encounter the pressures of market flexibilization would be new entrants to the labour market rather than existing workers, notably rural migrants from agricultural regions.

INDIA'S LIBERAL REFORMS

Wazirpur was one of four major industrial zones of organized and unorganized worker uprisings in 1988. As Mazumdar observes, the 1988 seven-day strike was decisive as it represented the first major uprising among workers in SMSEs which exemplified the nature of capital investment in India. Liberalization did not significantly transform India's economy at once, as the dominant form was small-scale capitalist investment. Only a small share of capital was dominated by a large share of capitalist investments. In addition, it represented the first of two major attempts by a party and union to challenge neoliberalism through labour mobilization.

The Centre of Indian Trade Unions, a trade union federation affiliated with the Communist Party of India (Marxist), mobilized the rank and file dissent in four key industrial areas of Delhi (the National Capital Territory which subsumes New Delhi): Wazirpur in the northwest, Mayapuri in west Delhi, Okhla in south Delhi, and Shahdara Jhimil-Friends Colony in the east-central sector of the NCT. CPI(M) was founded in 1964 as a breakaway from the Communist Party of India (CPI), initially in opposition to the latter's submission to working with the Congress Party, which had allied with the USSR, and in recognition that acknowledging India's agrarian peasant majority over the urban working class was a prerequisite for social transformation and revolution. The CPI(M)'s support for workers in rural regions in anticipation of the development of a revolutionary movement was reflected in major factions that immediately developed in the aftermath of 1964, most notably in West Bengal with the Naxalbari Uprising of 1964 (which also gained the official support of the People's Republic of China). While major splits emerged on a regional, tactical, and ideological basis, major strands of the CPI(M) were committed to advancing the revolutionary aspirations of the peasants and urban poor.

Indrani Muzamdar, a researcher of migrant labourers, conducted a wide-ranging and detailed analysis of the strike wave in New Delhi's unorganized industrial sector, providing detailed historical accounts drawn from key organizational documents and interviews.[22] In the 1980s, the characteristics of the Indian industrial working class shifted dramatically from the organized to the unorganized sector due to the implementation of neoliberal policies which allowed for the development of factory zones in Delhi and other cities, each employing 50 or fewer workers and dominated by the production of specialized commodities. Indeed, low wages and poor conditions, lack of government oversight, and general blight comprised a policy implemented by the Indian state and the municipal authorities. This is not representative of post-industrial small-scale development, which is often depicted by Western scholars as showing that informal workers are expanding in the global South just as in the global North. In fact, Delhi's development of industrial zones represents a sanctioned system of disarray that is intended to extract labour power from the Indian industrial working class. Muzamdar portrays conditions that are far more analogous to early industrialization than to what is regularly described as informalization:

> there lie thousands of almost identical tales of individual workers or for that matter individual factories which upon scrutiny, reveal in shocking vividness, the sweated conditions of industrial workers, and the shifting

continuum between industrial work and the multifarious uses that the metropolis can put any cheap labour to – in the form of informal relations. It was only a fraction which ended up in secure jobs with minimal facilities in the medium sized factories. All that was required to ignite this tinder-box was to convince the workers that something could be done about the key issue of wages and organize/direct the anger.[23]

It is important to stress the dynamic of labour mobilization in India and among workers everywhere. A sustained job action is the outcome of workers' rank and file spontaneous activities, but to have a modicum of success to change conditions a priori requires organization, strategy, and tactical guidance. Conditions of extreme despair or the erosion of labour standards, as found in India and elsewhere, will often lead to dissent and rank and file opposition. In India, as elsewhere, the key question is how to channel unrest into concerted activity to build organizational power. In 1988, unorganized workers in Wazirpur in north Delhi and three other burgeoning industrial subdivisions were ready to oppose oppressive conditions with the support of a formidable and devoted organizational force committed to the working class. In 1988, CITU was in position and willing to mobilize industrial workers in Wazirpur, which culminated in the mass seven-day strike across hundreds of industrial SMSEs in Delhi. Competing unions and major labour federations in India did not support CITU's mobilization of Wazirpur's working class to improve conditions for the workers. In this way, commentators argue that the 1988 seven-day strike represented the first strike among unorganized workers in India, a strike which required significant planning to mobilize workers across the four major industrial locations.

In Delhi, the implementation of neoliberal reforms in industry involved a concerted plan to abolish the power of workers in the manufacturing sector. From the 1950s to the 1970s, most of Delhi's textile workers were employed in large enterprises that had successfully mobilized workers into three leading trade union federations: All India Trade Union Congress, Indian National Trade Union Congress, and CITU. Workers' unions typically formed in the large textile factories, but the introduction of new technology eroded the power of textile workers' unions in the 1970s and 1980s, culminating in the 114-day strike of 1986 against the closure of weaving departments, poorer wages and conditions, and the decline of textile workers in the city. In the 1980s, small-scale industries mainly served by unorganized workers came to dominate the industrial sector in Delhi. While public sector workers employed in administrative jobs or state-owned enterprises continued to benefit from membership of trade unions by the 1980s and 1990s, the composition of Delhi's workforce began to shift to employment in small-scale commercial manufacturing in districts (estates) of the city devoted to individual forms of production. In the 1980s, with a dearth of capital investment, locating industry in a particular industrial zone increased economies of scale, permitting businesses to gain advantage by proximity to other producers building components of specific products. The proliferation of small-scale production in a single zone facilitated specialization in products such as stainless steel which required several stages of fabrication and distribution with a stable workforce residing in the *jhuggis* (slum dwellings) that would provide housing and a constant flow of labour.

In the late 1980s, CITU focused on the organization of workers in the small-scale enterprises by promulgating a minimum wage plan which would cover all employers throughout the industrial estates. The organization involved setting up union offices in each area, where organizers would distribute flyers and union literature and speak with workers, then holding meetings and marches through the communities. In August 1987, CITU's successful organization of workers directed a major 72-hour strike to raise the minimum wage, demonstrating an ability to mobilize workers dispersed among hundreds of factories. As CITU gained a greater foothold in the four industrial areas through daily picketing at the major road entering Wazirpur, holding processions and demonstrations of organizers and workers for improved wages, and the capacity to defend workers' from arbitrary employer actions, workers gradually gained confidence in the union's capacity to confront the employers. Together, plans were developed to take more significant actions. More than a year later, workers had become a major force of dissent, and joined meetings and picket lines with the union to demand that the government recognize them and certify CITU as their representative. Steel workers in Wazirpur had become increasingly emboldened during their public campaign to improve wages and workplace safety through membership of a union. One year later, a plan was made for a seven-day strike in November 1988 to demand higher wages and government recognition that the union could be certified across the industrial area of Wazirpur as representative of all workers.[24]

According to Muzamdar's account of the seven-day strike, the Wazirpur (and extended Karnal Road) subdivision was the best-organized of CITU's four industrial locations. The major reason for the extensive labour support for unionization was that most of the workers lived in the *jhuggis* within the community in a subdivision which was geographically contiguous. The area was also the site of two large former textile mills, which contributed to a strong memory of the benefits of union membership and a location where unionized and non-unionized workers mingled and socialized. Still, as the textile factories closed, Wazirpur was dominated by unorganized workers employed in small factories. This history of labour militancy in Wazirpur gave rise to a greater knowledge and confidence in the union as a means to project the collective interests and power of the workers.

The workers mobilized across the small shops in each of the industrial areas of Delhi, directing demands to the government for higher wages and the end of the contract labour system. The strike was the first major industrial action of unorganized labourers. The industrial action extended for one week in the four sites in Delhi, from 22 to 30 November. They called on government leaders to raise the minimum wage from Rs 562 (US$43) to Rs 1,050 (US$81) per week, and to regularize the workers as employees recognized by the state. CITU mobilized over 100,000 workers to strike in the four major industrial sites in Delhi, and Wazirpur became the focal point of unrest and demands for higher wages and improved working conditions.[25] Workers also demanded the provision of the Dearness Allowance (cost of living adjustments typically paid to government employees). During the strike, employers raised their wage offer of Rs 601 (US$46) per week. The size and intensity of the strike surprised even union and party leaders. S.B. Bhardwaj, CITU's Delhi State General Secretary, said: 'We were frankly overwhelmed by the response.'[26] CITU did not gain the support of India's other major federations, which were accustomed to sectoral or large-scale plant-level tooldowns.

Most labour federations, unfamiliar with the nature of the strike or opposed to a potential major gain for CITU, distanced themselves from or even opposed the strike. The press was not sympathetic to the demands and actions of unorganized workers, and their reporting favoured the police and law enforcement. According to accounts of the strikes, there were 13 *lathi* charges against the workers,[27] and 521 workers were arrested and faced criminal charges.[28] On 30 November, the last day of the strike, 10,000 workers marched from each industrial district to the Labour Office and the Old Secretariat building where the governor and Cabinet were situated.

The unorganized industrial workers in Delhi waged an unprecedented challenge for higher wages and ending the contract labour system, but were unsuccessful in achieving immediate wage gains upon completion of their strike. CITU leaders and workers maintained their pressure into 1989, when 12,000 workers mobilized on the streets and held a rally demanding a wage increase and regularization, otherwise the struggle would be escalated. In April 1989, the government acceded to an unprecedented 33 per cent increase in the minimum wage from Rs 562 to Rs 750 (US$58 at the time). In addition, the government agreed to give minimum-wage workers an increase of 85 per cent of the biannual increase in the consumer price index.[29] CITU's efforts to register as an independent union were unsuccessful, and over the years the union federation withdrew its organizational presence in the four districts. One year later, in 1990, India's liberalization reforms were implemented, and over the following three decades wages have declined to 1987 levels. While weekly wages increased dramatically in 1989, over the next 30 years minimum weekly wages have barely kept up with inflation. In 2017, the minimum wage hovered at US$45 per week, and in many cases, given that employers are often unregistered with the government, many workers do not even earn the minimum wage. Many unregistered employers failed to pay workers even the mandated minimum wage. Despite the failure to maintain and expand wages and workplace rights in the ensuing years, the 1987 strike is a testament to the capacity of workers in the *jhuggis* and squatter settlements to mobilize across shops in a single action. CITU did not have the power to transform the conditions of these slums, but workers recognized that mass mobilization with the support of allies could lead to improved conditions. Periodic efforts have been waged over the decades since by workers and Left political organizations, most notably in the worker insurgency of 2013–14 led by Bigul Mazdoor Dasta, an independent Marxist Leninist organization that has the dominant presence in Wazirpur and has organized unions among contract labourers throughout Delhi and beyond.[30]

Erosion of Trade Unions and Militant Worker Organizing: 2013 and 2014 Strike Wave

It was not until June 2014 that a new generation of workers would mobilize and strike for improved conditions. This time, the workers' mobilization was confined to Wazirpur Industrial Area and focused on demands that were analogous to those of the late 1980s. The erosion of the minimum wage was a crucial issue for workers, but by 2010 many employers were not even paying workers the mandated minimum wage; hence, enforcing local employers' payment to their workers of the minimum wage was the major worker demand. In addition to demanding the minimum wage, the People's Union for Democratic Rights, a Delhi-based organization committed to advancing civil liberties and democratic rights, reveals the deterioration of working conditions in Wazirpur since 1989:

> Today, more than a month later, the workers continue to struggle for basic work conditions. In complete defiance of labour department's instructions and outright violation of all norms, the factory owners have shown complete indifference to workers' demands. They have also been unresponsive to the labour officials' call for interventions. As a result, the workers are still struggling to reclaim their rights.[31]

In the early 2010s, many workers employed in the stainless steel mills and tertiary factories and operations were organized into a union: Garam Rolla Mazdoor Ekta Samiti (GRMES). This union was affiliated with Bigul Mazdoor Dasta, a national network of militant unions situated in eight Indian states, which had developed a presence in Wazirpur and throughout Delhi.[32]

Through establishing a base of worker mobilization amongst the workers neglected by other unions, GRMES became the major union in Wazirpur, waging strikes to increase the minimum wage and ensure payment of it. These strikes and worker mobilizations began in 2012 and extend to the present day, revealing Bigul Mazdoor Dasta's long-term and sustained commitment to workers in Wazirpur. The initial strikes in 2012 and 2013, demanding workers receive a guarantee of basic rights and wage increases of Rs 1,500 (about US$23 a month/US$6 a week) and one day off every Wednesday for all workers, were successful in improving the living conditions. However, as in the past in Wazirpur, the moment the collective bargaining agreement is reached, the major task is to ensure that owners abide by the terms. Even with the wage increase, workers in Wazirpur were not paid the legal minimum for the NCT of Delhi:

> The workers are paid less than the minimum wages as prescribed by the latest order dated 28 March 2014 of the Labour department of the Government of NCT of Delhi. Rs. 8,000 is paid to the unskilled labourers for a 12 hour work shift as against the prescribed wage of Rs. 8554 for an 8–9 hour daily work shift excluding rest intervals. Rs. 9,000 is paid to the semi-skilled workers as against the prescribed minimum of Rs.9438. Similarly Rs. 10,000 is paid to the skilled labourers for a 12 hour work shift as against the prescribed minimum of Rs. 10,374 for an 8–9 hour daily work shift. It should be noted that the cost saving for the factory owner occurs not just in the forms of absolute difference between prescribed minimum and actual wages paid. It also occurs in the form of the extra or unpaid work hours that are put in by the worker. Again, whether the minimum wage itself is an adequate measure for a dignified standard of living is also another question that needs to be probed.[33]

One year later, due to the failure of many owners to meet the terms of agreements, it was recognized that striking to enforce employer compliance is a major element in achieving and sustaining gains. On 6 June 2014, GRMES led over 1,000 workers at 23 Wazirpur hot-rolling plants in striking to demand that the factory owners pay workers the minimum wage. Worker organizers were dismissed in the strike's aftermath, after which organizers formally submitted demands to factory owners. A letter was sent to the Labour Inspector at the District Labour Court itemizing the demands, which was completely ignored by the factory owners. When a labour official and health inspector raided 23 hot-rolling mills in Wazirpur on 16 and 17 June 2014, many of the factory owners had locked their gates as the government officers seized the records at some of the factories. In the aftermath, a factory owners' association formed to negotiate with the workers, who requested that all negotiations be held at the office of the Delhi Labour Commissioner (DLC). A widespread practice among employers is to pay off local gangsters posing as union representatives each time a worker insurrection takes place. It was only because of the GRMES' involvement that the

DLC forced 23 factory owners to respond to investigations and legal notices. Over a period of several months, GRMES and the workers built an escalating campaign to demand employer compliance with minimum wage laws.[34]

What is remarkable is that the contract labour system had become even more entrenched, and many workers were not even listed on the records of the steel mills as being employees. Without the record of employment, workers could not demand wage and working condition improvements. Thus, in addition to enforcing the minimum wage, GRMES workers sought overtime payment, appointment letters, worker identity cards, salary slips, Employees' State Insurance, Provident Fund, bonuses, the implementation of safety measures, vacation for government holidays, and payment of wages in the first week of each month.

OUTCOMES AND IMPLICATIONS OF STRIKES

The mobilization and strike of workers in 2014 are reflective of the major strategies which inflect labour disputes today, and the ensuing divisions on the Left between autonomists and advocates of strong unions. GRMES' mobilization of workers to defend their rights and its organizational presence to enforce the rights of workers remain crucial in enabling workers in Wazirpur to defend themselves against local factory owners. The union has maintained an organizational capacity in Wazirpur by filing legal claims on behalf of workers, mobilizing dissent against rapacious factory owners when workers are injured or die on the job, holding regular meetings with workers, and carrying on mass mobilization efforts to increase and honour the minimum wage. In the absence of the organizational force of GRMES and Bigul Mazdoor Dasta, Wazirpur workers would remain engaged in dissent on a daily basis without the capacity to marshal their rank and file activity through a clear voice and labour organization. As many labour organizations have turned to NGOs, non-profits, cooperatives, and autonomous, non-binding forms of representation, a growing number of labour activists and scholars suggest that autonomous labour action with external support and NGO leadership is the primary means of expanding worker power. Moreover, others in India and beyond believe workers do not require organization, but we can only hope for the periodic expression of dissent without organization, which always tends to bureaucracy and ossification. Some seek to take down existing organizations to enforce supposedly democratic terms.[35] But there is no path to power through promoting weak and feeble unions that may have a modicum of democracy among an ever-dwindling membership. The answer to the weakening of established unions is not turning to syndicalist formations without any means to apply power, especially in the Third World.

The political and labour organization Bharat Mukti Dal (BMD) mobilizes among workers most unions have disregarded beyond Wazirpur. The union's major affiliates in the NCT of Delhi are: (1) domestic workers, (2) cleaners and service workers employed as subcontractors for the Delhi Metro, which began operation in December 2002, and (3) informal auto workers who lack job security in the hub of Gurugram, southwest of New Delhi. Significantly, Bigul Mazdoor Dasta engages in direct organizing among each community of workers to build an organic relationship of trust and confidence. Organizers in each community educate members in practical scientific knowledge: for example, theories of evolution, the humanities, music, and art. Most importantly, Bigul Mazdoor Dasta introduces members and their families to political education, focusing on the classical works of Marx, Engels, Lenin, and Mao Zedong to build class-consciousness grounded in scientific socialism. This method has educated the workers and their families while establishing an organizational base in each community, serving the function of galvanizing the power of workers. Notably, unlike many other organizations, BMD does not accept money from NGOs, and thus does not have the taint of other NGOs and labour-based organizations such as the New Trade Union Initiative (NTUI) and SEWA.[36] All three organizations (BMD, NTUI, and SEWA) have recognized the significance of organizing among impoverished workers in the informal economy. Timothy Kerswell and Surendra Pratep, in *Worker Cooperatives in India*, have characterized SEWA as an extension of 'imperialist funding agencies'. In contrast, BMD is among the very few Indian labour organizations which maintains autonomy from foreign NGOs and is untarnished within working-class communities. In this way, BMD retains strong ties to communities and workers without outside interference. In Wazirpur, workers have publicly stated their confidence in BMD, which maintains a long-term presence within working-class communities based on a highly focused and clear materialist understanding of the significance of workers within specific communities that are linchpins to the Indian political economy.

In Wazirpur, it is clear that workers will remain in continuous struggle against local employers and the state for higher wages, regularization of employment conditions, upgrading workplace conditions to prevent major injuries and death, and meeting the housing and service needs of workers. The struggle is not just for achieving trade union rights or for higher wages, and employers will always seek to chip away at any victories. Unlike the trade union or NGO model, the workers' struggle does not come to an end with recognition of a union, the latest wage gain, or even the emergence of a new system, but according to BMD, must continue under any political and economic system.

CONCLUSION: SPONTANEITY, DISRUPTION, AUTONOMY, OR CONSOLIDATING POWER

In India, the implementation of neoliberal policies and erosion of traditional labour unions and federations raises the question of practical strategy for working-class empowerment. Even in those sectors where trade unions remain strong, their power has been seriously eroded as multi-tier systems have replaced the wage and pension systems in previous generations. Thus, as in many other countries, there is an informalization occurring within the erstwhile formal and public sectors. Concomitantly, most workers entering India's labour market in the early twenty-first century are employed in the non-unionized informal sectors of the economy, where low wages and harsh conditions prevail unlike anywhere in the First World. The NGO and cooperative models of empowerment are contingent on meeting the goals and objectives of foreign imperialist organizations, and do not provide an alternative to the existing system of trade unions.

Over the last three decades, existing Indian trade union federations have declined due to the imposition of neoliberal policies and the conversion of permanent state employees into non-permanent non-union labourers, often performing much the same labour as full-time workers. In some cases, successor unions have agreed upon concessionary contracts that do not provide guarantees for continuous employment. However, most frequently, manufacturing workers are employed in jobs that require long work hours without job guarantees, permitting employers to dismiss them when the work is completed.

In response to the restructuring of labour, a growing number of labour organizations have emerged to represent workers through independent workers' unions, often known as autonomist labour organizations. These organizations are promoted by labour entrepreneurs who oppose both established and emergent unions which seek to represent workers. These organizations promote the concept of 'workerism', a form of syndicalism where industrial workers do not have organizational representation. Eschewing supporters of these ephemeral labour organizations, advocates of worker autonomy take solace in encouraging workers to take matters into their own hands through syndicalist rank and file action, such as tooldowns, strikes, general strikes, and the development of independent organizations.[37] In the NCT of Delhi, the most prominent advocate of workerism is *Faridabad Majdoor Samachar* (FMS, 'Faridabad Workers Newspaper'), which has distributed newspapers to workers in the industrial zones in the region. While FMS began publishing in 1982, claiming an initial distribution of 1,000 newspapers in Faridabad, the organization gradually extended circulation to new industrial areas. Today, FMS claims a distribution of 7,000 newspapers in Faridabad, Okhla, Udyog Vihar, and Gurugram (Gurgaon), industrial areas where some 2.5 million factory workers are employed.[38]

Each newspaper provides news and updates on the status of a range of labour struggles in the industrial area. Certainly, FMS has an impressive outreach to industrial workers, but it would be surprising if even a small fraction of workers have read it. Even if they have, most do not have the organizational wherewithal to build independent campaigns capable of challenging a rapacious capitalist class. While celebrating worker autonomy and self-activity, the FMS has a small administrative staff, recruiting outside supporters and partisans, especially among academics who embrace this tautological model of organizing that does nothing beyond reporting on workers' opposition and struggle against management without making any effective demands for employers to improve workers' conditions. This model takes succour in the acts of protests without recognition of the reality that workers are always engaged in class struggle against employers. The genuine conundrum is how syndicalist activities of workers can solidify the organizational power to transform these struggles into concrete gains over time. In fact, class struggle is inevitable, but working-class power requires the strength of organization of a union and political party to advance and consolidate its interests. The critique by FMS of the propensity towards bureaucratic caution and lethargy among existing trade unions is valid, but this does not imply that workers are better off without organization. Clearly, as the Wazirpur steel utensil workers' case suggests, the decline of trade unions, working-class organizations, and Marxist-based parties has severely undermined the power of all workers in India. The culmination of worker collective power in Wazirpur is not in the absence of organization, but when the workers have a common ally and vanguard capable of defending and advancing their interests by mobilizing workers into organized collective actions, challenging employers and capital directly and placing demands on the state.

4
The Enduring System of Global Agricultural Commodity Production and First World Commodity Extraction: The Case of Mindanao, the Philippines

THE PERSEVERANCE OF RURAL LABOUR EXPLOITATION IN MINDANAO

The Philippines is an anomaly in Southeast Asia and the world as a dependent capitalist country which is reliant on the extraction of natural resources, agricultural commodities, and human migrant labourers for national economic development and growth. Unlike other countries in Southeast Asia and population centres in the global South, the Philippines is not developing a large manufacturing sector, but depends largely on exports of agricultural products, natural resources, and foreign remittances from skilled, semi-skilled, and unskilled migrants who work primarily outside the region. Poverty and underdevelopment are especially prominent in the southern island of Mindanao, where the economy is the primary supplier of unprocessed primary products, minerals, and food for export into the global commodity supply chain for natural resources.[1] For more than a century, with the support of American and Philippine military forces, foreign capital developed mines and plantations, and devastated a natural habitat that had supplied subsistence for indigenous peoples.

Today, Mindanao's agricultural and mineral products are crucial for the development of global commodity chains. Resting at the bottom of the chain, the Philippines is the primary source and producer of commodities. However, due to the Philippines' subordinate position in the global commodity chain, the value of the products is transferred to destination regions in the rich countries of Europe, North America, Japan, and beyond.

The vast majority of the Philippines' population resides in agrarian regions where surplus is extracted from the land and people by comprador oligarchs and multinational corporations for the benefit of multinational corporations. The extraction of the land and labour of the Philippines by a privileged oligarchy, with the support of foreign MNCs, has endured from the era of Spanish and US colonization, through independence, and has continued even after the 1986 popular protests which dislodged the dictator Ferdinand Marcos from power.

This chapter examines the exploitative organization of rural workers in the Philippines' southernmost state of Mindanao. It documents the persistence of poverty and destitution through control of the land and natural resources by MNCs and oligarchs, with the unwavering support of the Philippines state legal and security apparatus. The chapter documents how, even after the land reforms of the 1980s and 1990s, the rural proletariat has remained highly marginalized by a fraudulent land reform policy which has pushed landless workers into precarious working conditions through the institutionalization of a system of labour contracting. Through a case study of the Sumifru strike of 2018–19, the chapter demonstrates that banana workers on plantations and in packing houses have lost their status as regular workers and have been shifted into labour contracting through a duplicitous worker cooperative system. Worker cooperatives in Mindanao exploit labour for MNCs by avoiding labour laws, safe working conditions, and pensions while also obliging workers to pay for the right to join their organizations. Rural worker cooperatives in Mindanao are even more exploitative than the corporate farms they replaced in the early 2000s, while remaining obsequious to the demands of MNCs. On fertile land that could potentially be cultivated to provide food and sustenance for the Philippines' population of 110 million, workers labour to produce bananas, pineapples, mangos, and other exotic tropical fruits to conform to the latest culinary tastes of First World populations.

As a corollary, the chapter demonstrates that with the mobilization and organization of restless rural workers by the militant anti-imperialist union Kilusang Mayo Uno (KMU; 'May First Movement'), founded on 1 May 1980, the potential remains for the development of a broad and commanding movement of the rural proletariat in the Philippines capable of challenging the oligarchs and foreign exploiters.[2]

103

PEOPLE'S POWER, REFORM, AND NEOLIBERALISM

The expectations among some of the People's Power Revolution of February 1986 as a transformational moment for Filipino peasants and workers have faded away and disappeared as repression, poverty, and inequality have deepened for the popular majority.

Unlike other countries in the global South, the Philippines is not a major destination of foreign direct investment, but has been mired in a system of resource extraction, and entrenched as a semi-colony attending to the financial interests of international capitalists and the populations of metropolitan and settler states. In this sense, comprador and venture capitalists serve as a parasitical national class which facilitates the exploitation and plunder of Filipinos for the benefit of foreign MNCs and consumers.[3]

The Philippines is a prototype of an extractive economy which is highly dependent on a rural proletariat and agrarian class. As the rural population declines as a share of national population in other countries, in the Philippines, after a precipitous decline from 1960 to 1990 (from 70 per cent to 53 per cent), the rural population grew marginally during 1990–2018 from 53.0 per cent to 53.1 per cent (see Figure 4.1).[4] However, relying on percentages to depict the rural sector disguises the real growth in the Philip-

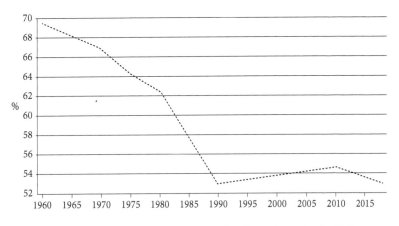

Figure 4.1   Rural population as a percentage of total population in the Philippines

Source: World Bank staff estimates based on the United Nations Population Division's World Urbanization Prospects, 2018 Revision.

pines' rural population, which expanded by nearly 25 million (57.9 per cent) over the same three decades, from 32,229,656 in 1988 to 56,624,705 of the country's 109,577,036 population in 2018.[5]

The People's Power Movement which formed in the Philippines in the mid-1980s and burst into the People's Power Revolution from 22 to 25 February 1986 was a broad expression of dissent against the authoritarian and fascist government of Ferdinand Marcos. The extensive popular expression of dissent was the culmination of two decades of organizing by the Maoist movement, which established a broad United Front against the fascist dictatorship. The strategy of the Maoist National Democratic Front (NDF) was to build a broad popular alliance to expel the Marcos dictatorship and lay the base for a broader movement of land reform and socialist transformation. The mass movement formed in 1964 by the NDF was the first stage in a broader strategy of socialist revolution which initially comprised church groups, and agrarian labourers along with urban workers, professionals, and students in Metro Manila. Its aim was to overthrow the dictatorship, which had intensified popular repression with the support of the comprador oligarchy and the USA.[6] The People's Power Revolution was instrumental in overthrowing Marcos through a broad popular alliance that forced the USA to withdraw its support for his regime.

The promise of the People's Power Movement to democratize Philippine society through redistribution of land and resources to the broad masses of peasants and urban poor was thwarted by powerful national capitalists and foreign imperialists. The alignment of domestic and international capital, and the abiding power of the USA, forced the government of Corazon Aquino, elected on principles of democracy and redistribution of resources, to withdraw plans to implement a programme to ameliorate the destitute plight of rural agrarian workers and the urban working classes. While People Power was technically a revolutionary movement, by calling on the International Monetary Fund to cancel foreign debt Aquino and her successors did not challenge international financial institutions, and remained under the economic, political, and military domination of the USA.

Less than a year after the People Power Revolution, on 22 January 1987, Philippines state security forces fired on 20,000 farmers protesting for land reform on Mendiola Street outside the president's Malacañang Palace residence. In the massacre, riot police fired on unarmed peasant protesters, killing 19 and injuring about 100 others. As Timberman notes: 'To some, the

Mendiola massacre was bloody proof that the Aquino government was just as brutal and reactionary as its predecessor.'[7] The NDF, for example, used the incident to justify the abandonment of peace talks with the government. The Mendiola massacre marked the end of any pretext that the government, oligarchs, and multinational capital would tolerate social transformation in the Philippines, and regenerated popular movements in the rural regions for authentic redistribution to landless peasants.

After land reform, Mindanao banana workers have continued to experience poverty conditions and high levels of exploitation. Key struggles between workers, the KMU, and the banana industry continued through the first two decades of the twenty-first century.[8] Labour leaders and activists often faced death threats from employers, police, and their allies.[9] These conditions were exacerbated by the declaration of the third extension of Martial Law in Mindanao by Filipino president Rodrigo Duterte on 23 May 2017 through to the end of 2019. Superficially, this was a counter-terrorism operation against Muslim militants, but it was also directed at the KMU and rural workers who were seeking to improve their standards of living by challenging the system of labour contracting in island.[10] To be sure, Mindanao's rural workers endured the most significant impact of the police state restrictions on labour rights, as they were severely restricted within agricultural communities and workplaces in Mindanao. On 14 December 2018, Sharon Burrow, General Secretary of the International Trade Union Confederation, stated:

> Extending martial law is akin to treating the symptoms while ignoring the root cause of the instability. The culture of impunity has worsened since the anti-narcotics campaign. You cannot achieve sustainable peace by razing peoples' rights. Building social consensus takes commitment to social dialogue. A prerequisite to that is ensuring that workers' rights are respected.[11]

In view of the harsh restrictions imposed by martial law in Mindanao, union leaders, activists, and supporters faced corporate and state repression, violence, and death for organizing strikes. Martial law was extended to the KMU, which is sometimes viewed by right-wing government officials as an arm of the New People's Army. As the rise of the banana workers' movement severely obstructed the union campaign to improve workers' conditions in Mindanao plantations and packing houses, its leaders had to take their campaign over 1,600 kilometres (1,000 miles) northwest to Luzon and Metro Manila, where they would have the right to organize and engage in protests.

The focus of this chapter is an examination of the political economy of agricultural extraction in the Philippines and the struggle of the banana workers in Mindanao employed as subcontractors of multinational corporations for improved conditions during the rule of martial law during 2018–19.

MINDANAO'S POLITICAL ECONOMY OF IMPERIAL PLUNDER

A vast proportion of the land in Mindanao was controlled by indigenous peoples who comprised a majority of the population of the southern island. In three centuries of Spanish colonial rule and feudal land tenure systems, the local populations of Luzon and the Visayas were largely displaced by large colonial settlements. The Americans purchased all of the Philippines from the Spaniards in the Treaty of Paris of December 1898, and the US colonial administrators gained control over the entire island chain, which included lands which were not subjugated by the Spanish authorities. Indigenous lands were seized and expropriated, and the habitat was destroyed through logging, mining, and the establishment of plantations. Historical sociologist Arnold Alamon writes:

> Hungry for the profit to be given by timber, pastureland for cattle ranches, and the potential rich agricultural land of logged-over areas that the island had to offer, the Americans were finally able to achieve what the Spaniards for three hundred years failed to attain – the subjugation of the island of Mindanao and its people. This was secured through a ruthless military campaign of the new colonial authorities which decimated whole populations of a gallant Moro resistance.[12]

In the subsequent half-century of US colonial rule, a violent military offensive was waged against the indigenous people of Mindanao. These constituted a majority of the island's population, especially the Lumads and

Moros. Their lands were nearly entirely confiscated by the violent expropriation and resettlement of impoverished migrants from Luzon and the
Visayas, who became a landless peasantry in an exploitative feudal system.
While much of the indigenous population was defeated in US military
campaigns and their land expropriated and turned over to commercial
interests, landless migrants from Luzon and the Visayas were forced to work
on plantations for their very survival. Alamon continues:

> Ultimately, it was the same desire for profits which was behind American
> presence in the province and not really the expressed objective of eman-
> cipating the natives from their backwardness. In hindsight, regardless of
> how the Americans saw themselves, they were not unlike the lowland
> traders out to make a killing from indigenous land, labor, and resources.
> Soon, a powerful landlord class would take over from the colonial author-
> ities and reign over both the business and politics of the province.[13]

The descendants of these migrants remained impoverished throughout US colonial rule, and the comprador Philippine state as the system of
land tenure remained under the control of rural oligarchs. In 1964, a mere
18 years after the Philippines' independence from the USA, indigenous
ancestral lands stolen from the Lumad and Moro peoples were transformed
into Del Monte and Dole plantations to produce palm oil, bananas, pineapples, and tropical fruits for export to rich markets in North America and
Europe. Western enterprises destroyed the landscape through the clear-cut-
ting of forests, mining, and the creation of plantations for export to Western
markets. The Philippines is the second largest exporter of bananas in the
world, trailing only Ecuador in exports (see Table 4.1).[14] Control of the
banana industry is dominated by four global North multinational corporations: ChiquitaFyffes (Ireland), Dole Food Company (USA), Fresh Del
Monte Produce (USA), and Grupo Noboa S.A., Sumifru (Japanese subsidiary of Sumitomo Corporation), the largest exporter of Philippines
bananas.[15] Today, as tropical crops and rich mineral reserves are discovered
in Mindanao and foreign concessions are established, the land is owned
and controlled by multinationals and oligarchs who mine among the most
extensive reserves of gold, nickel, and chromite in the world. Indigenous
peoples continue to struggle for the return of their land and are countered
by the rapacious Philippine military and paramilitary forces.

Table 4.1   World's largest exporters of bananas, 2019

	Country	Exports (US$)	% of global exports
1.	Ecuador	3.3 billion	22.6
2.	Philippines	1.9 billion	13.2
3.	Colombia	1.6 billion	11.0
4.	Costa Rica	999.7 million	6.8
5.	Guatemala	944.5 million	6.4
6.	Netherlands	790.6 million	5.4
7.	Belgium	782.1 million	5.3
8.	United States	450.3 million	3.1
9.	Dominican Republic	432.7 million	3.0
10.	Panama	379.1 million	2.6
11.	Ivory Coast	339.7 million	2.3
12.	Honduras	302.7 million	2.1
13.	Mexico	269.5 million	1.8
14.	Cameroon	256.4 million	1.7
15.	Germany	242.1 million	1.7

Note: Belgium, the Netherlands, the United States, and Germany import bananas for re-export to third countries.

Source: Daniel Workman, 'Bananas Exports by Country', *World's Top Exports*, 25 March 2020, www.worldstopexports.com/bananas-exports-country/, accessed 17 April 2020.

Mindanao's Demography and Population Dynamics

In 2015, the population of the southern Philippines island of Mindanao was 24,135,800, comprising 23.968 per cent of the total national population. Based on population growth estimates of 1.9 per cent per year, equivalent to the period 2010–15, in 2019 Mindanao's population would comprise 26,022,863 of the nation's estimated 110,000,000 people.[16] With a land area of 10 million hectares (247 million acres), Mindanao encompasses approximately one-third of the country. Approximately 30 per cent of the population is indigenous, comprising Moro and Lumad peoples who had lived on the island before Spanish colonization and the Spanish–American War of 1898. Subsequently, US colonial authorities and the independent government of the Philippines sponsored a settlement plan by settlers, chiefly from Luzon and the Visayas, the two other primary island groups. The settlers now form about 70 per cent of Mindanao's population.[17]

Poverty in Mindanao

The incidence of poverty is far more extensive in Mindanao, as the per capita income is lower than the Philippine national average (see Table 4.2).[18] Poverty is concentrated in rural agricultural regions where a large proportion of the population live below subsistence levels. In particular, poverty is concentrated in regions where export agricultural and natural resource production are situated. These regions have higher proportions of indigenous Moro and Lumad peoples who have been forced off their ancestral lands. Development sociologist Eduardo Climaco Tadem observes that:

> The extensive monocropping patterns of agribusiness corporations dependent on high levels of chemical applications deplete soil nutrients. In the case of the banana and pineapple industries, it is feared that once their operations cease, the badly damaged soil would not be able to sustain any other crop for many years.[19]

As Mindanao's economy primarily produces agricultural products and natural resources, the vast majority of the industries on the island are highly dependent on exports and the swings in the prices of international commodity markets, determined by investors in the global North. In addition, as Mindanao does not engage in the fabrication and production of natural resources and agricultural commodities, the economy and population do not benefit from the value added which is realized in the rich countries. As a result, the expansion of the export sector for natural resources and agriculture contributes to the further economic destitution of peasants and low-income residents unable to afford subsistence products on the local market. Indeed, the highest-quality tropical fruits produced in plantations are reserved for foreign export, and are unobtainable on the market in Mindanao and the Philippines as a whole.

Due to its abundance of fertile land and natural resources, the island of Mindanao is a crucial producer of foreign exchange for the Philippine economy, especially as a primary source of agricultural and mining production for foreign export. Mindanao's economy is concentrated in the production of primary products in global commodity chains, thus the extraction of surplus from agriculture and mining is highly extensive. The

Table 4.2   Philippines population and poverty rate by region, 2015

	Per capita GDP indices (at 2000 prices)			% of population in poverty, 2015
	2010	2016	2018	
Luzon				
National Capital Region	279.3	295.8	294.0	3.9
Cordillera Administrative Region	120.1	95.8	101.6	19.7
Ilocos	61.6	62.9	63.0	13.1
Cagayan Valley	50.0	50.0	49.1	15.8
Central Luzon	82.1	87.2	90.3	11.2
Calabarzon	128.8	120.5	121.2	9.1
Mimaropa	60.9	50.6	50.6	24.4
Bicol	34.7	33.9	34.0	36.0
Visayas				
Western	51.4	52.6	53.8	22.4
Central	80.9	88.1	88.0	27.6
Eastern	59.0	47.2	44.7	38.7
Mindanao				
Zamboranga	56.8	54.7	52.4	33.9
Northern	79.8	81.0	81.0	36.6
Davao	78.2	83.8	88.4	22.0
Soccsksargen	59.5	57.8	58.6	37.3
Caraga	41.8	45.5	42.4	39.1
Autonomous Region in Muslim Mindanao	22.7	17.0	17.0	53.7

Source: Derived from the Philippine Statistics Authority. See also Rolando T. Dy, 'Which Philippine Regions Are Advancing and Lagging?', *Business World Online*, 1 July 2019, www.bworldonline.com/which-philippine-regions-are-advancing-and-lagging/, accessed 4 July 2019.

extraction of surplus redounds to more prosperous regions in the Philippines. As Tadem found:

> Lured by vast reserves of natural resources, businesses have … generated enormous profits for their owners and executives. But the resulting wealth and incomes have not benefited the greater majority. Poverty and other social indicators point to a more distressed condition for Mindanao than

for the nation as a whole. [...] In the Mindanao case, this enigma is exacerbated by the effects of internal colonialism – the transfer of wealth from the southern regions to the nucleus of economic and political power in the north.[20]

But the vast majority of profits are extracted by foreign MNCs for the benefit of the rich economies in the global North. As Tadem concludes: 'as a result of the dominant role of transnational corporations in virtually every aspect of the various industries in Mindanao, wealth and resource transfers also occur in the direction of the developed economies of the world'.[21]

Mindanao's 3.73 million hectares (9.2 million acres) of agricultural farmland constitute 38 per cent of all agricultural production in the Philippines, focusing on commercial and agricultural crops for foreign export. In 2012, Tadem found that more than half of Mindanao's farm areas produced export crops, including bananas, coconuts, tobacco, rubber, sugar, palm oil, coffee, abaca, and fruits. This is a share that has consistently grown during the decade as the government prioritized export over domestic agriculture. The region is also rich in mineral deposits, including gold, copper, nickel, chromite, coal, silver, zinc, and lead, controlled by US, British, and Japanese firms. The world's largest nickel reserves are in Mindanao, and are mined by major multinational corporations, including Sumitomo Metal Mining Company.[22]

MINDANAO: HISTORY AND EPICENTRE OF GLOBAL AGRARIAN STRUGGLE

The significance of imperialism and exploitation of rural workers has endured from the US conquest of the island after the Spanish–American War in 1898, and in the subsequent years under Philippine independence class oppression of indigenous peoples and rural peasants has escalated through war and the confiscation of lands and natural resources.

The Spanish colonization of the Philippines from 1521 to 1898 did not conquer the southern island of Mindanao, which remained relatively autonomous until the Americans gained colonial control of the archipelago. The practical isolation of Mindanao and tenuous penetration by the Spanish is widely established in historical accounts of the island. In contrast to Luzon and the Visayas, historian Onofre Corpuz maintains that the lack of jurisdiction over the island is demonstrated by Spanish colonizers' lack of historical records for the Mindanao economy; the 1897 census could count only 50 per cent of its population.[23] Consequently, it was only after the US defeat of the Spanish that relentless armed campaigns were waged against the indigenous population of Mindanao, policies which included war against the local population of Lumads and Moros, expropriation of land by the US colonial occupiers, and immigration of a workforce of landless peasants from Luzon and the Visayas. Arnold Alamon, historical sociologist and author of *Wars of Extinction*, examining the onslaught against the Lumad indigenous people in Mindanao, observes that over the subsequent century, military conquest and class subjugation transformed the Mindanao economy from subsistence agriculture to capitalist extraction:

> The entry of these capitalist relations under the benevolent patronage of the American masters transformed the local economy and further sutured the local indigenous population into the workings of the new economic order as it responded to the demand for cheap raw materials for their industries such as corn and timber, and rice for the local food supply.[24]

In the province of Bukidnon, hundreds of thousands of hectares of ancestral forest lands of the indigenous people were expropriated by Del Monte and Dole for the creation of plantations to grow and process pineapples for export to US and Western markets. For over a century, lands were expropriated for logging despite the Lumad and Moro populations' resistance.

The discovery of rich mineral reserves in Mindanao has amplified imperialist MNC competition for mining concessions, as the island holds an abundance of mineral deposits. Philippines ranks second in the world to Indonesia in nickel deposits, which accounted for 55.8 billion pesos (US$1.1 billion) in revenue in 2018, of which 75–80 per cent is located in Mindanao's northern Caraga Region. In addition, Davao Region in south-central Mindanao is a leading site of gold reserves and extraction and processing.[25] Mineral prospecting poses a serious threat to the remaining habitats of Mindanao's indigenous people.

Inequitable land tenure is the defining political-economic form of conflict in the Philippines, from the Commonwealth period, through independence in 1946, to the People Power Movement in 1986 which toppled

Marcos. Given the lack of significant redistribution in the ensuing 30 years, landlessness and rural poverty have remained the central economic crisis up to the present day. In the aftermath of the People Power Movement, which portended a more equitable distribution of the Philippines' wealth, the landed oligarchy and foreign tropical fruit companies have unified in dominating the most profitable foreign export market by controlling the commodity chains for tropical fruits and natural resources.

In the aftermath of Marcos's reign, the promise of land reform was not directed through the state, but carried out via a market-driven corporate land reform policy in the rural sector by distributing small plots of land to landless peasants. De los Reyes and Pelupessy contend that the 1980s land reform in the Philippines following the People's Power Revolution did not visibly confer economic resources to landless workers in the countryside, but instead instituted new forms of exploitative practices by forming a system of rural contract labour:

> The agrarian reform of the 1980s made land workers the owners of their land, supported the establishment of cooperatives and introduced contract agriculture for the export markets. In this way the new banana smallholders could have access to the export channels of their former multinational or national landowners.[26]

However, landless peasants typically received too little land in remote locations to be able to sell fruits in the domestic and international markets. Most remained dependent on state authorities, large plantation landowners, and national and multinational fruit companies to assist in growing standardized fruit for sale in the domestic and international markets. The chain of command over the production and marketing of bananas and other tropical fruit made it impossible for almost all agrarian workers with small plots of land to survive. To mitigate the economic isolation of smallholding peasants, a cooperative system was established with the intention of pooling small plots of land into larger units to sell products to plantations. But this system of collective ownership was dominated by corporations and plantation owners who had access to capital to purchase the technology, pesticides, and other resources necessary to operate larger estates and sell government- and corporate-certified products to the national and international market. Often the cooperative farms are now dominated by managers who negotiate and collaborate with multinational and domestic fruit companies. Cooperatives commonly lease lands to plantation owners who rely on agrarian workers to produce bananas, pineapples, and other tropical fruit.[27]

BANANAS AND THE GLOBAL COMMODITY CHAIN

The Philippines is firmly integrated in the global commodity chain (GCC) as a producer of agricultural products and natural resources. Beneficiaries are the major corporate firms, oligarchical families, and trading companies that control the production, supply, and markets for banana exports to consumers in the metropolitan and settler states. The production and distribution chain that provides commodities to consumers in the rich countries begins with growing and harvesting of tropical fruits in the Philippines, Central America, and South America, where the soil and temperature are conducive to the cultivation of what are known as wet fruit. The GCC is highly dependent on the availability of a large reserve army of labour in the countryside to maintain, harvest, package, preserve, and transport tropical fruit to retail consumers in food markets in the rich countries. At each stage in the production process, surplus value is extracted from labourers and the highest rate of profits is realized by the multinational corporations controlling the retail food markets in the destination countries. The majority of workers in this value chain are employed in the plantations, packaging houses, and distribution centres in the Third World countries where the products are harvested, packaged, labelled, and shipped to major markets. Once the tropical fruit reach the destination countries, fewer workers are necessary and higher profits are realized.

Multinational corporations dominate the GCC for agricultural products by preserving a system of unequal exchange. By this means, firms in the rich countries retain the distribution of profits by extracting super-profits from Third World labourers. This is achieved by keeping wages very low among workers, choosing between hiring workers at the firm level or outsourcing production to contractors who employ workers at fixed costs rather than paying them directly. For example, by governing the global value for bananas, multinational food companies indirectly control the production and distribution of tropical fruit, secure high levels of returns, and retain the incentive to constantly reduce wages and production costs.[28] Since the 1990s, MNCs have dominated GCCs in the Philippines and throughout the global South through the outsourcing of labour further down the value chain in the countries of origin rather than directly employing and supervising workers. In the global North, closer to the point of consumption, MNCs more often directly employ workers at retail outlets. In the system of agricultural commodity production, rural workers in the Third World are most likely subordinated and exploited by processes and practices in the global value chain for bananas and other tropical fruit. Thus, the standard terminology in political economy of a commodity chain as a group of organizational *networks* with non-hierarchical relationships advancing mutual and common interests fails to address the entrenched inequity. As Jennifer Bair notes:

> networks are unlike either markets or hierarchies because they generate mutual expectations and relations of trust, which arise from repeated exchanges that become 'overlaid with social content' [...]. The benefits of networks relative to other organizational forms derive in large measure from the kind of interactive and collaborative learning that trust is presumed to enable.[29]

In the context of the Philippines' tropical fruit industry, not only do MNCs and Filipino oligarchs benefit from the GCC, but consumers in the rich countries who are recipients of agricultural products also benefit from broad access to relatively inexpensive high-quality commodities through value transfer from the expropriation of rich cultivated land and low-wage labour in Mindanao.

UNCERTAIN LAND REFORM AND CORPORATE CONTROL

The notion was to give land to farm workers through the Agrarian Reform Beneficiary (ARB) programme. The process took on a trajectory which shifted ownership over small plots of land to farmers who did not have the capital nor capacity and networks to benefit from holding agrarian land as the GCC for bananas and other tropical fruit is a unified network controlled by retailers, large plantation owners, foreign-owned agribusiness, and capitalist states. Contrary to conventional interpretations, banana growers holding small plots of land cannot possibly influence the export of products to affluent markets and do not benefit from the system, and if their lands are pooled under cooperatives, rural workers are still necessary for the labour-intensive production process.[30]

Consequently, the banana GCC is a hierarchical network dominated by the MNC agribusinesses which establish and preserve consumer markets and thrive by controlling and regulating production and distribution. MNCs garnered significant advantage through the partial land reform of the 1980s–2000s by shifting accountability from business to labourers. The need for economies of scale in a capitalist commodity chain forces farmers to rely on the costly resources and supplies of MNCs to produce and coordinate the distribution of bananas through the network. Even rural cooperatives rely on MNCs for these means of production and distribution. Thus, in a capitalist supply chain dominated by MNCs, landless peasants must work in the fields and packaging plants, where surplus labour is extracted from workers and the largest share of value transfer occurs, but value added is concentrated by the MNCs at the point of consumption in the global North. The suggestion by economists that formerly landless peasants with small plots of land can thrive in this process is illusory.

It is not a matter of improving the conditions of farmers with small plots. Improving these conditions without a socialist collectivization is illusory. The rural working class in the Philippines does not have the resources nor capacity to respond to market demands in destination countries. Lacking capital, they are unable to even respond to the changing market demands and recommendations from NGOs and government agencies. Only large plantation owners and MNCs controlling large tracts of land have the resources to respond to market demands.[31]

Control of the banana industry is established through the major firms governing the production process and ensuring that bananas are grown at the lowest possible cost. The highest levels of profitability require maintaining control over all three processes: production, distribution, and markets.

In production, the corporate distributors must ensure that the cost of growing and packaging bananas is kept to a bare minimum. Low-cost production is achieved through the subcontracting of the production process to local growers. It is unnecessary to directly control the managerial system of production. By withdrawing from the direct ownership of plantations and packing houses which employ agrarian workers in the fields and packing houses, fruit companies gain advantages by detaching themselves from the production process. Instead, producers must ensure that production costs are reduced by setting wholesale prices, which direct producers must accept and secure if they are to gain access to the markets. Thus, the primary focus of corporate banana, pineapple, and papaya companies is the sourcing, direct and indirect production, shipment, and sale of fruit in affluent overseas markets.

The system of production is legitimized by providing perfunctory control over rich agricultural lands to private and cooperative local producers who must retain low-cost agrarian workers to maintain, harvest, and package bananas and other fruit. Thus, the arduous and dangerous conditions of work are not ameliorated by control and ownership by local growers. Meeting quotas and controlling product quality compels workers to endure labour under extremely harsh working conditions, long hours of work, and exposure to chemicals and pesticides which are mandated by the consumer markets in the rich countries.

In the Philippines, the major growers have maintained firm control over banana production and marketing by forcing the growers to pay low wages to workers. Fruit trading companies operate similarly to other natural resource companies. Controlling the use of land or minerals is essential to the production of bananas and other fruits, just as mining companies seek to exploit lands with rich mineral deposits. Thus, in most instances, peasant farmers have little to gain through maintaining direct ownership of small plots of land. Rather, retaining the right to determine land use and ensure labour exploitation is far more consequential to guaranteeing profitability.

Rentier Capitalism

Corporate control over the banana industry is equivalent to other natural resource extraction industries, yet the global supply chain degrades the benefit accruing to the Philippines. The Philippine state receives little in return for allowing multinational fruit companies to operate the tropical fruit plantations which dominate Mindanao and exploit its rural working class. Mineral industries require local and regional workforces to extract precious metals and ore from the earth. The petroleum industry requires even fewer workers than extraction of precious metals and ore, and in some cases relies on foreign (e.g. Middle Eastern and North African) workers. Continuous technological innovation and advancement have diminished dependency on labour supply through deep-sea drilling and new advancements in storage and transport. However, equivalent technological advances have not reduced labour demand in the growing and harvesting of agricultural commodities such as bananas, pineapples, mangos, and other tropical fruit. Labour dependency endures as primary in the production of cash crops in tropical zones, and the inability to produce labour-saving technology generates greater demands for capital to extract surplus labour directly from workers themselves. As Prabhat Patnaik observes, in the contemporary stage of capitalism multinational agribusiness companies, through the global supply chain in cash crops, deflate income for peasant workers by dominating both production and markets:

> and hence a larger share of the value added along this chain [is] going to them, rather than to the peasant producers and petty traders. Above all, however, these mechanisms include a substantial increase in income inequalities in these peripheral economies; since the total consumption of food grains [...] as a proportion of income is higher for the lower income groups than for the rich, an increase in income inequalities has the effect of restricting or curtailing overall food grain demand, and hence making other agricultural goods produced by the tropical land mass, which are demanded by the metropolis, available to it at non-increasing prices.[32]

The process of production forecloses successful agricultural output through land redistribution and egalitarian landownership, and collectivization in the countryside, which 'can enable the proletariat to advance [...] towards socialism, all these needs are greater today than ever before'.[33] In this way, the rural catastrophe of unemployment, impoverishment, and destitution growing out of marginal employment is exacerbated. In the case of global South countries, rural populations are on the border of survival and often dependent on the nexus of migration to urban areas, where the informal sector produces unsteady employment, joblessness, and rampant poverty. Without a significant transition to authentic land redistribution and collectivization, the rural population of the Philippines and beyond will grow ever more desperate. Furthermore, MNC domination of the GCC for tropical fruit and agricultural commodities undermines food security by shifting production away from essential grains and food crops for the rural and urban populations.[34]

THE PHILIPPINES AS A COMPRADOR STATE IN
THE GLOBAL BANANA SUPPLY CHAIN

The position of agrarian farmers and rural workers at the bottom of the production chain marginalizes them further. Their power and room for manoeuvre to influence the global supply chain for fruits are severely restricted. Direct workers in the fields and packing houses have little recourse aside from protesting and withholding their work to demand improvement in their wages, working conditions, and safety measures. Yet the powerful corporations which dominate the production process have little incentive to improve the lot of workers. Striking workers in the packing houses can be replaced by the subcontractors who manage the banana plantations and packing houses. The recurrence of the process of protest throughout the major banana and pineapple production regions of Mindanao is symptomatic of the rural workers' abiding efforts to transform the dynamic of power which confers it to the corporate fruit companies while limiting the influence of the direct producers. Thus, there is no shortage of protest and insurrection in the industrial plantations and packing facilities. The key factor in building rural worker power is the presence of organized and effective worker representatives. In this way, workers will continue to protest, and do not require the mobilization of labour and political representatives. What they require is the capacity of representatives and organizers to channel the dissent into effective action. As such, the significance of organizational discipline and effective representation is fundamental to the success of workers. Even if workers are represented by local labour unions, they require the support of the independent oppositional bodies: the KMU and the forces of the democratic popular resistance against the Philippines government. Without the support of the organizational and political movements, the worker campaigns will fail to force the multinational firms to improve wages and conditions and ensure the region is safe for workers. Thus, the government and its military and police operations regularly seek to terrorize leaders of the opposition union and movement.

The rural labourers and producers in banana plantations, packing plants, and transport are paid the bare minimum for social reproduction. Corporate farmers seek to restrict remuneration to workers in order to maximize profits. Workers frequently challenge the overwhelming economic and market power of the corporate fruit companies. For instance, in 2015, rural packing house workers challenged the piece rate system imposed by Sumifru Philippines Corporation, the Japanese multinational distributor of bananas.[35] The Philippines' banana industry produces for the domestic and international market. Banana production for the international market is controlled by the three major MNCs: Dolefil, Sumifru, and Del Monte. The Philippines produces high-quality fruit for consumption in affluent markets. Domestic bananas are grown by individual farmers on small plots, and are of inferior quality to those for the export market.[36]

Production for the export market is highly centralized by major MNCs and family oligarchs through an elaborate system of control. Thus, the narrow system of land reform which transferred land to local peasants did not include a mechanism to collectivize agriculture. Inferior-quality bananas are grown by small landowners and consumed in the Philippine market, while high-quality Cavendish bananas are grown under the control of agricultural MNCs under meticulous standards.[37] Individual farmers do not have the capital and resources to grow Cavendish bananas and are forced to join ARB cooperatives through lease agreements known as Agribusiness Venture Arrangements. The MNCs then dominate the industry through their financial resources and access to rudimentary inputs (fertilizer and pesticides) to grow bananas for consumers in foreign markets. Collectivization is a means to mobilize the labour, technology, and distribution to meet the quality standards required by produce retailers overseas. As a result, MNCs are able to exploit agrarian labour and lands in the Philippines, and to deliver remarkably low-cost bananas and tropical fruit to foreign consumers all the year round.[38]

MINDANAO AS A TROPICAL FRUIT PRODUCTION AND DISTRIBUTION CENTRE IN THE PHILIPPINES

Transnational banana corporations control the production and distribution of bananas on the largest plantations of Mindanao in the most arable lands with highest yields. Mindanao is the site of the largest share and most highly concentrated source of Cavendish banana production, while Lakatan bananas for domestic consumption are mostly grown on other islands.

The proximity of the Davao Region and adjacent areas in southern Mindanao to the strategic port of Davao City has amplified its significance as a key logistic staging ground for the growing, packaging, and distribution of bananas and tropical fruit to foreign markets. These areas include Region 11, encompassing the key tropical fruit production areas of Davao Oriental, Davao del Norte, and Compostela Valley. In these regions, MNCs and large plantation owners dominate the production of bananas by controlling cooperatives established after the market-driven land reform.[39]

Philippines Agrarian Reform: MNC Profits Resulting in Poverty and Inequality

In the 1980s and 1990s, the Philippines embarked on a comprehensive system of land reform to provide sustenance for the Philippines' population of rural dwellers. In the Philippines, urbanization has not occurred as swiftly as in other emerging economies, and 55.7 per cent of the country's population reside in rural areas where agriculture is the major source of income. As some countries in Southeast Asia have shifted to manufacturing and tertiary services, the Philippines is an anomaly as it continues to rely on agricultural production for both domestic Gross Domestic Product and international trade.

Before the Comprehensive Agrarian Reform Programme (CARP) was signed into law by Corazon Aquino, large plantations producing lucrative tropical fruit crops for export were owned by a small number of rich families. This system of oligarchical control did not change following CARP as the lands of rich families were not expropriated by the state and redistributed to landless workers. As a substitute, large foreign-owned MNCs which controlled GCCs redistributed small parcels of land from large plantations to landless workers. However, these plots were generally too small to grow the substantial crops necessary for exports; smallholding farmers were typically on lands which supplied domestic rather than foreign consumers. Rural peasants with new plots also lacked the capital to operate small farms. They simply did not have the capital or supply linkages to support farming independently. Therefore, rural agricultural workers with small parcels were forced to lease the land back to MNCs and large landholders, which remained in control over the land and reinforced their control and authority over agrarian workers.

CARP has not improved the living conditions of peasant workers in the Compostela Valley countryside. Instead, it has led to the erosion of their ability to survive, because almost all peasants were dismissed as direct employees for MNC multinationals and hired as contract labourers through cooperative associations serving as labour brokers.[40]

From the 1990s to the present MNCs have developed growing agreements under CARP, the Philippine land redistribution system initially planned for introduction in 1987. But CARP was delayed for more than a decade to 1998, and did not fulfil its promise to meaningfully redistribute land for Filipino peasants and rural workers. The plan conferred small plots to some rural dwellers, while the plantations and contiguous farms remained under the control of large landholders who held close ties to MNCs. Thus, the landless farm workers who were the recipients of land as Agrarian Reform Beneficiaries (ARBs) benefited minimally from the land reform. CARP was highly dependent on employing local workers in the Compostela Valley region as growers, packers, and in distribution for export, and also on the continuation of control over the plantations by MNCs and wealthy Filipino families.

Under the CARP system, small farmers have plots of 5 hectares (12 acres) or less and produce Latakian bananas for domestic consumers. Most peasant workers were not granted land at all. Large plantations of 20 hectares (50 acres) or more produced Cavendish bananas for export to foreign rich consumer markets. Under the ARB system, comprehensive land reform has not occurred: farm labourers remain highly dependent on the MNCs for their income. Following CARP, MNCs and large landholders remained in control of the banana production system by controlling the contracting of rural labour. Workers now typically lease their land at minimal cost to MNCs, or pool resources through cooperatives which charge farmers high fees for growing and maintaining banana crops. Landholders with small plots of land have little choice but to join cooperatives, which are ordinarily viewed as a means of sharing resources, but in the Philippines context are extractive agents which work closely with the MNCs through deductions, charges for basic services, and ensuring that rural workers comply with the demands of the export firms. Thus, the advantages of land reform through income derived from leasing land to MNCs or through membership of cooperatives have limited impact on rural workers.[41]

Large landholders were not required to transfer parcels from their plantations to landless farmers, and were able to maintain their agricultural links to MNCs. Some banana farmers with small parcels of land joined ARB cooperatives as an alternative to leasing land back to MNCs. However, the cooperatives were controlled by managers who served as agents for MNCs rather than representatives of small farmers. By joining together plots of land, cooperatives could conceivably gain a capacity to enter the far more lucrative international markets. But due to cooperative charges and deductions, the agrarian reform intensified the challenges faced by rural workers in surviving on the income they were able to earn in the process, and many became contract workers for the MNCs.

COOPERATIVES: DECEPTIVE INSTRUMENTS FOR CORPORATE CONTRACTING AND EXPLOITATION

Typically envisioned by proponents as a means to empower workers and the poor through collective ownership, the Philippine banana cooperatives are the agents of exploitation and oppression of the rural working class. Agrarian cooperatives do not confer collective ownership and worker control, but conceal a system of hierarchical control by MNCs, disguising the everyday reality that rural workers remain beholden to the GCC controlled by MNCs in the metropolitan and settler economies. The elusive cooperative system established by CARP and ARBs provides rural workers with little or no means of social protection to improve their plight as precarious and contingent labourers, thus the rural poor have no means to lift themselves out of systemic poverty. In effect, members of the cooperative are even more beholden to the MNCs and large domestic plantation owners as they must rely on the cost structures which are regulated by foreign companies and consumers in rich countries.[42] These costs are typically not variable, but fixed, thus, under the neoliberal system of capitalism, workers in the cooperatives must participate in all phases of production, from propagating banana plants to growing, packing, and shipping. In addition, shareholders of cooperatives are responsible for paying for all the inputs: seeds, fertilizer, harvesting machinery, pesticides, cleaning supplies, boxes for packaging in corporate packing houses and trucking to cold storage warehouses, and rapid cold shipping and distribution of bananas to container ports for overseas consumer markets. Participation in the global commodity chain for bananas has reduced the capacity of rural workers to survive, and has increased dependence on MNCs. As the rich farmlands of Mindanao have been appropriated for export crops, food and grain production for the domestic economy has eroded.

The condition of agrarian workers in the Philippines has been degraded, and as contract and cooperative labourers, their capacity to resist the MNC agribusinesses is diminished. Under greater pressure to survive, rural workers have increasingly mobilized to improve their standard of living against MNCs and the oligarchs who control the industry by forming independent trade unions and supporting the broader struggles for a legitimate redistribution of the Philippines' agrarian land. Workers organizing against MNC agribusinesses and plantation oligarchs for higher wages and improved conditions have gained support from the KMU, a coalition of revolutionary organizations which forms part of the National Democratic Front. The New People's Army (NPA) is dedicated to an authentic popular redistribution of land and natural resources extending well beyond the post-People's Movement Revolution market-driven land reform policies of the 1980s to the 2000s. The NPA seeks the transfer and redirection of all lands and resources to collective ownership and control, and the creation of a new socialist society.[43]

Cooperatives do not have the capital nor expertise to ship Cavendish bananas to these markets, which requires inspection, foreign export licences, and purchasing agreements with wholesale importers for eventual sale to food product retailers. Thus, workers and members of cooperatives in the Philippines are under significant pressure to produce for the global commodity chain. On the contrary, the 1980s–2000s land reform in the Philippines has pressed agrarian workers into greater dependence on MNCs, which dominate agribusiness for their survival without improving wages and living conditions in the rural regions where the majority of the population live.

Labour cooperatives are deemed by their proponents to be agencies of worker self-management and collective ownership and a significant component of socio-economic redistribution from owners to workers. Rather than employers owning and exploiting labour, cooperatives are viewed by supporters of workers' rights as a way to exercise control over their economic livelihood and wellbeing. But in the Philippines, cooperatives are used by MNCs to control labour. This system of exploitation through cooperatives is elucidated by a comprehensive study of cooperatives in Philippine agriculture, which regards the system of corporate and oligopolistic control as a form of 'imperialist plunder'.[44] The ultimate aim of the agribusiness transnational corporations (TNCs) is to extract super-profits by reducing lease payments to ARBs and small landowners, purchasing produce at cheap prices, heaping debts on growers, keeping wages to the barest minimum, imposing stringent quota systems, and hiring workers on subcontracts via labour cooperatives to escape accountability.[45]

The labour contracting system through cooperatives conceals the system of labour oppression established to defend and expand the interests of MNCs, oligarchs, and state officials to extract surplus profit from rural workers, known as Agrarian Reform Beneficiaries. Through the ARB cooperative system, MNCs are replaced by labour contractors which do not have conventional labour–management obligations to workers and are not obligated in the same way as conventional businesses to comply with state labour laws, including minimum wages or state-mandated benefits. In addition, because workers are required to join cooperatives, they must pay deductions that can amount to nearly 50 per cent of their wages.

SUMIFRU AND MULTINATIONAL CAPITAL CONTROL OVER MINDANAO

The international banana commodity chain and tropical fruit industry are operated on a global and regional basis. Accordingly, transporting tropical fruits shorter distances ensures that fresh produce reaches affluent markets in East Asia, Europe, and North America. As such, the Philippines exports primarily to Asian markets and not North America or Europe, while Ecuador and Guatemala export to North American and Western European and not Asian regional consumer markets. The Sumifru Philippines Corporation (Sumifru), a Japanese fruit producer affiliated with Sumitomo, a leading Japanese investment firm, has entered the Philippines as a source of tropical fruits for consumer markets in Japan, Korea, China, Arab Gulf States, and New Zealand.[46] The tropical fruit company identifies regions to grow and produce Cavendish bananas, pineapples, and papayas, then transports and markets them in rich countries, reaping enormous profits through the value transfer of these commodities produced at a meagre proportion of the sale price.[47] In the Philippines state of Mindanao, Sumifru operates over 12,000 hectares (29,000 acres) of plantations where it contracts labour to grow, produce and truck bananas to shipping ports. In the municipality of Compostela, it cultivates Cavendish bananas on 2,200 hectares (5,436 acres) and operates nine packing plants which produced 7 million boxes of bananas in 2018, valued at US$135.2 million in revenue.[48]

In the Compostela Valley, situated 160 kilometres (100 miles) northeast of Davao del Sur, the capital of Mindanao Province, Sumifru has an enormous capacity to extract and exploit labour through contractors and cooperatives the company indirectly controls. In 2018, about 4,700 workers were employed through contracting schemes in the plantations and at packing plants controlled by Sumifru. By subcontracting growing and production, the company circuitously evades responsibility for the exploitation of impoverished rural workers in Compostela Valley. Even though Sumifru controls the production process, the company fully disowns any obligations to pay workers' wages and pensions while profiting from the enormous surplus value it realizes upon sale in rich foreign markets. The vast majority of Sumifru's workers are employed on fixed-term contracts for contractors and cooperatives which grow Cavendish bananas, including 1,700 workers subcontracted by the packing plants.

A crucial demographic characteristic of the rural population in Mindanao from the People's Power Revolution in 1986 to the present has been the reconstitution and intensification of the exploitation of rural labour through the creation of new institutional structures under an inequitable and anaemic land reform which fortified the privileged position of the rural oligarchy and the reorganization of corporate power dominated by MNCs domiciled in rich countries.

The incomplete and inequitable land reform which commenced in the 1990s granted rights to small plots of land to some rural workers while failing to break apart the large tropical fruit plantations owned by rural oligarchs who predominantly served MNCs and foreign markets. Most land parcels allocated to rural workers were small, remote, and often situated on lands with poor cultivation. Thus, the corporate-dominated land reform did not confer on rural workers sufficient farmland to produce crops and ensure survival. Rather, most rural labourers in Mindanao were forced to work for contractors which served the interests of foreign-dominated corporations that controlled and dominated GCCs for tropical fruits. Contractors typically operated under the guise of rural cooperatives, providing a patina of communal control. In reality, the cooperatives were established by MNCs to benefit a thin layer of rich peasants who employed rural workers at minimum and sub-minimum wages under dangerous conditions in the plantations and packing plants controlled by Sumifru. As a result, those peasants who were allocated small parcels rented the land back to cooperative contractors and earned a fraction of the income necessary for survival. They were forced by economic necessity to work in the plantations, packing plants, or tropical fruit transport.

RURAL WORKER SPONTANEITY AND ORGANIZATIONAL MOBILIZATION: 2000–PRESENT

The CARP and ARB systems that were implemented by the Philippine state authorities in support of plantation oligarchs and MNCs from about 2000 to the present demonstrated that land reform and ownership of small parcels of land are not synonymous with equity and control. While many advocate cooperatives as the answer to building working-class and peasant power, cooperatives under capitalism are instruments for oppression as they are used by MNCs to advance the process of surplus and natural resource extraction from the poorest populations. In addition, cooperatives are viewed as a means to collective shared and communal ownership. But in reality, cooperatives are an ideological and concrete distortion and fiction used to justify the further expropriation of work and land from peasants and indigenous populations. Indeed, in the banana plantations of Mindanao, the system of cooperatives which came into existence in the 1990s has been used as a means to extort from the poor and enable agencies to deflect the social and stakeholder obligations that corporations would otherwise have under capitalism. Thus, cooperatives are not agencies and institutions for redistribution of wealth, but an ideological apparatus which legitimizes and legalizes a system of production, and intensifies the oppression of the poor in the global South while benefiting corporations and their customers in the rich countries of the global North. How is this process carried out?

The touchstone of oppression is the system of ideological control which legitimizes a system of corporate and imperial control. The cooperative system in the Philippines, instituted during the 1990s–2000s, is a primary instrument for multinational fruit companies to guarantee the continuous exploitation of peasants and workers in the plantations and packing plants of Mindanao.

THE WORKERS UNION AND SOCIAL MOVEMENTS:
THE KMU AND NAMASUFA-NAFLU

Rural worker resistance against the US colonial authorities and then the Philippine state in the Compostela Valley of Mindanao has been ongoing for more than a century since the USA gained administration over the colony after its victory in the Spanish–American War in 1898. For nearly half a century of colonial rule, the US colonial authorities and corporations expanded their reach into Mindanao, the Philippines' southernmost major island, which was not exploited by the Spanish colonialists on an equivalent basis to the two other major island groups, Luzon and the Visayas archipelago.

The KMU and the Rural Working Class

The colonial conquest of Mindanao and the establishment of a rentier state for foreign capital remains a contentious issue for indigenous populations and the rural working class. The vast majority of them continue to be impoverished and destitute as a consequence of the operation of the island as essentially a foreign concession state for the benefit of TNCs and local oligarchs. The stark inequality throughout the Philippines contributed to the development of an organized rebellion in the 1970s and 1980s aimed at regaining the lands from the foreign and local expropriators, a movement which continues today and has gained the support of a large segment of the urban and rural poor. The Philippines represents an anomaly in the Third World, as rarely do trade union organizations support the poor and indigenous people against foreign imperialists. While urban and rural workers in the Philippines have waged spontaneous opposition to the system of imperialist control and local exploitation, the system cannot change without an organized and dedicated organizational opposition to the comprador classes which control the society.

In the Philippines, the KMU formed as a labour union on 1 May 1980 in opposition to the stark inequality and widespread poverty among the country's urban and rural poor, viewed as rooted in the maintenance of a system of imperialist control over the land and natural resources. A remarkable feature of the KMU is its bond and devotion to the National Democratic movement, which seeks to expel foreign control from the Philippines and establish an equitable society. The enduring goal for the KMU and its allied organizations is the establishment of an independent state which benefits the people of the Philippines and is not beholden to foreign capital. As such, the KMU is dedicated to the liberation of the society. In the interim, the KMU supports struggles against predatory capitalists who engage in super-exploitation of workers. The KMU represents a labour-based organizational force which supports both labour and broader popular struggles to improve the conditions of the poor and working class. These struggles are principally engaged in opposition to foreign capital.

As most trade unions train their organizing and mobilizing efforts toward the urban working classes, the KMU is also distinctive in its recognition of the significance of rural labour. In contrast to practically all other trade unions in the Philippines, Southeast Asia, and the world, the KMU considers agricultural workers in the countryside as a focal point of its organizing campaign.

In extensive discussions between the author and KMU leader Elmer Labog and other organizers in February 2019, there was a clear emphasis on the centrality of defending and advancing the conditions of the most exploited workers and communities in Filipino society. In most major trade unions of the global South, organizing is typically directed at those workers who are employed in the most profitable and technologically advanced industries. Labour mobilization campaigns are most frequent in large factories and manufacturing enterprises and in the remnants of state-owned sectors where workers often tend to have higher wages and skills than those in the agrarian regions. In contrast, the KMU expresses its dedication to building a broad front among workers across all sectors of the Philippine working class, especially those in the rural areas. KMU's policy is unique and unusual in trade unions, where often a thin layer of workers in the most productive industries is protected, and the majority of highly exploited workers and communities are ignored.

In view of the domination of the Philippines by MNCs in the global North, the KMU's political platform identifies foreign capital and local comprador agents as the primary adversaries which must be challenged if wages and living conditions are to be improved. By taking on the MNCs, which profit mainly from unequal exchange, the KMU can materially improve conditions of the working class and confront the inequitable system of trade which suppresses local workers' and producers' wages.

In interviews, workers expressed confidence that the KMU and its affiliates in Mindanao were committed to defending their material and class interests. While the rural workers in the tropical fruit industry are eager to challenge capital routinely, they do not have the resources or power the KMU can bring to bear to counter the large multinationals and the highly repressive Philippine state.

The KMU has been willing to provide sustenance to organizing campaigns and labour strikes against private enterprise. It has emboldened workers to oppose the oppressive system which defends the powerful classes and had not actually granted land reform in the 1990s, but reinforced a system of power by establishing a system of corporate-dominated land reform that has consigned rural workers to a life of precariousness and poverty.

Background: Banana Multinationals, the KMU, and Formation of Agrarian Unions in Mindanao

The restructuring of the banana industry following the land reform reveals how the KMU has maintained steadfast support for rural workers against MNCs and contractors. During the 1990s, in the fertile Compostela Valley, workers in the banana packing plants were either non-union or were represented by the employer-dominated ('yellow') unions the Alliance of Labour Unions and its successor, the National Federation of Labour, which sought to suppress all worker demands for higher wages and improved conditions. The fledgling KMU had organized in several packing plants but established authentic union organization in only one of them. As land reform took hold in Mindanao during the 1990s, the foreign MNCs recognized that higher profits could be achieved by contracting banana production rather than supplying peasant banana producers with fertilizer, pesticides, and other inputs.

In 2000, in Mindanao, an incomplete and limited land reform was established. Stanfilco (Standard Philippine Fruit Company), a unit of the US MNC Dole Company, relinquished its relationship with workers who were employed directly through the company and abandoned agreements with peasants who held small plots of land. In the place of purchasing product from peasant growers and employing workers in packing houses directly, Stanfilco terminated their contracts and set up agreements directly with cooperatives, which supposedly would represent the interests of growers and workers. The workers in all the packing plants were in effect fired and replaced by the cooperatives, which were provided with supplies to grow and pack bananas. Workers lost their rights as employees of the Dole subsidiary, and were forced to join the cooperatives. Under the new system, known as Freight on Board, Stanfilco was no longer responsible for providing banana workers' wages, pensions, and benefits. In the Compostela Valley, the transition from employees of Stanfilco to cooperative members was completed by 2002 as nearly all banana farms were incorporated into the cooperatives. By bringing the direct employment relationship to an end and shifting responsibility to local cooperatives, Stanfilco obscured the real objective of providing a patina of ownership and self-management to workers while eliminating responsibility for all wages, benefits, pensions, and other obligations. The cooperatives mainly served the interests of managers, who do not offer workers equivalent wages, benefits, and obligations.

The yellow unions which dominated most packing plants in the region were dismantled, with the exception of Packing Plant 98, where workers were members of the KMU. Labourers in the plant refused to join the cooperative system, and as a result maintained their rights as workers and received higher daily wages, overtime pay, sick leave, vacations, and other benefits. The only workers to resist the arrangement were members of the KMU, and the union defended their interests as employees of Stanfilco. In view of the better wages and working conditions at the KMU packing plant, workers in the other facilities sought to join the union. In the ensuing years 2002–2006, workers at other packing plants joined KMU-affiliated unions throughout the Compostela Valley. The KMU represented workers in grievances over underpayment of wages, violations of labour standards, management harassment, and intimidation from politicians and the military. According to two fact-finding missions in 2006, the Armed Forces of the Philippines (AFP) directly intervened in union affairs and sought to suppress the exposure of the violations of labour rights and the cooperative scheme developed by Stanfilco which violated the rights of packing plant workers through the subcontracting scheme. Subsequently, government authorities had consistently sought to establish phoney unions that opposed increasing wages for workers. Frequently, the KMU and its affiliates were red-baited as communist labour organizations to instil fear in workers who feared police and military targeting.[49] That same year, Stanfilco was sold to the Japanese multinational Sumitomo Fruit (Philippines) Corporation and AJMR Holdings Company, which became known as Sumifru.

The new firm did not seek to reconcile the differences with workers, and refused to negotiate with KMU. Instead, it intensified the conflict through union-busting schemes aimed at dividing workers, including expanding the number of contractors in the Compostela Valley as it also sought to expand its network of banana production and shipping in the region. KMU sought to certify Nagkahiusang Mamumuo sa Suyapa Farm (NAMASUFA) as the exclusive bargaining agent of the workers, but Sumifru continuously claimed that it was not the employer of the workers. In February 2010, after the Philippine Department of Labour and Employment (DOLE) in the Compostela Valley declared Sumifru to be the employer of the workers in the packing plants, the Japanese multinational appealed the decision, but this was denied by the Court of Appeals. Subsequently, the MNCs and plantation owners continued to depend on the armed forces to intervene in disputes with workers, gaining the support of the AFP and appealing to the legal apparatus of the state to suppress rural workers in 2013.[50] Sumifru repeatedly appealed to the Philippine courts, delaying resolution of its status as employer for seven years, even after 2017, when the Philippine Supreme Court ruled that Sumifru, not its contractor, was the employer of record.

Striking workers were repeatedly prevented from travelling from the Compostela Valley to Davao City, where the police chief claimed that the union members were aligned with communists, and others claimed they were members of the NPA. In the weeks before and after the strike, union leaders were killed by gunmen who were never identified by the authorities.[51] The perpetrators of the crimes against union organizers and workers operated under the pretext of martial law in Mindanao. Thus, workers had to take extreme precautions to protest and make their demands in the region. Concomitantly, despite the intimidation and violence, the workers had broad support among most residents throughout the Compostela Valley. With the support of the KMU leadership, the workers continued to press their campaign from Mindanao to Manila, and then on to Tokyo.

UNFOLDING OF THE STRIKE:
UNION MILITANCY–WORKER MILITANCY

In the wake of the Supreme Court decision, eight local KMU unions joined together as a single representative of the workers: Nagkahiusang Mamumuo sa Suyapa Farm-National Federation of Labor Unions-Kilusang Mayo Uno

(NAMASUFA-NAFLU-KMU) was registered by the DOLE in August 2018. In spite of the Philippines' legal decisions that the workers were employees of Sumifru, the multinational refused to bargain with the KMU affiliate, setting the stage for KMU's strike on 10 October 2018, a labour dispute which was to last for ten months. The demands of the striking workers are recounted by KMU organizer Paul John Dizon, who says the strike focused on the precarious status of the workers, and unambiguously claims that KMU went on strike to end the contractual system of employment and demand regularization as employees: 'The striking workers were employed at seven packaging plants of SUMIFRU and at the plantation, and were represented by KMU affiliate NAMASUFA-NAFLU-KMU in the Compostela Region of Mindanao.'[52] While the courts ruled that the packing plant workers were employees of Sumifru, the strikers were violently dispersed and physically assaulted at protest sites in the presence of the Philippine National Police and the AFP in the weeks following the tooldown. In the days following the strike on 10 October 2018, threats and violence against strikers, activists, and union members escalated, culminating in the murder on 31 October of a prominent union activist of the NAMASUFA workers' union by a death squad.[53]

The ten-month strike was concentrated in the packing plants owned by Sumifru located near the banana plantations of Compostela Valley. In the packing houses, workers clean and package Cavendish bananas for export by Sumifru to markets in Japan, Korea, China, New Zealand, and the Gulf States. Paul John Dizon, president of NAMASUFA-NAFLU-KMU, stresses that the packing house workers enthusiastically went on strike to gain recognition from Sumifru as regular employees of the company, and to achieve a collective bargaining agreement with the company as regular employees rather than as subcontractors. Dizon asserts the significance of union recognition in improving the workers' conditions in the banana packing houses:

> Recognition of the workers as employees would mandate that workers could bargain directly with the company with regards to their wages and benefits. They would have security of tenure because they could not be terminated immediately because they would have security of tenure. Now they are hired by agencies and labour cooperatives to supply manpower to Sumifru. Under the present arrangement, workers in the packing houses work for different labour agencies and can be terminated at any time.[54]

In an extensive interview, Dizon points out that the cooperatives are set up as a ploy to pretend that workers have a direct stake in the production and distribution process when, in reality, the cooperatives are labour brokers providing non-union workers to the MNCs:

> Contractors and cooperative administrators are entitled to a minimum of 10 per cent of the total amount of the labour contract as administrative fees. In name they are cooperatives, but they are used by Sumifru to circumvent the labour law. Under Philippine law, if you are a member of a cooperative, you do not have to join a union because you are the owner of the cooperative. But before the workers could get a job with Sumifru, they were obligated to have a capital share of the cooperative. Since most workers do not have the capital, they borrow the funds from the cooperative managers, who operate as labour brokers.[55]

In effect, the worker cooperative model in the Philippines abolishes worker rights. At the same time, workers must join these labour cooperatives, which are the only agencies permitted to secure labour to work in the Sumifru banana packing plants. In addition to the fees rural workers must pay cooperatives for the right to work at Sumifru, they must pay other fees for insurance and other requirements. Any workers who do not join the cooperative are detached from the GCC for bananas. Dizon explained that Sumifru is directly responsible for organizing the labour cooperatives and contracting their principal leaders. These principals enlist workers both in the plantations and packing plants of the Compostela Valley. As labour brokers, multinational banana firms only supply cooperative managers with fertilizer, chemicals, bagging materials, and packing materials necessary for harvesting and shipping bananas. Dizon notes: 'NAMASUFA views the cooperative managers as contractors for Sumifru in the same way as labour agencies secure labour for large firms. In this case, the labour cooperative managers do not operate any differently from the principal company.'[56]

Typically viewed as a means to empower workers as owners, cooperatives in Mindanao have instead harassed rural workers. Ebenezer Chibo Tan, KMU vice chair for Mindanao, observes that progressives often point to the advantages of cooperatives in building worker power and control. But the cooperatives are labour brokers that are plainly 'the employers of workers'. Accordingly, the KMU encourages workers to withdraw their shares of capital investments in the cooperatives, which are in fact fees that brokers expropriate from rural labourers. Tan explains that the cooperatives are viewed as schemes to defraud workers, which benefit labour brokers, and mostly the banana multinationals.[57]

On 9 August, the conflict was suspended when NAMASUFA-NAFLU-KMU, representing workers at five packing plants, and Sumifru in the banana plantations of the Compostela Valley agreed to abide by the judgment of the National Labour Relation Commission. Under the terms of the agreement, Sumifru was to reinstate workers it had illegally terminated in October 2018 at Packing Plant 220. According to the agreement: 'All parties agreed, through the cordial intervention of SUMIFRU officers, to wait for the final resolution of the case before action for reinstatement will be executed,' while 'officers of NAMASUFA-NAFLU-KMU agreed to suspend the pickets at the packing plants, and the packing operations resumed immediately thereafter'. The agreement included a plan to assist the 450 workers displaced in the strike.[58]

Rural Worker Uprising and Aftermath of the Strike

A remarkable attribute of the Sumifru strike was the ability of workers to economically sustain a ten-month strike. More often than not, when employers resist union demands, workers are forced to return to their jobs to pay living expenses. According to workers and union officials, the job action was sustained by the determination of a core of the workers and peasants and the organizational support of the KMU. While most strikes include a majority of workers, only 700 of the 2,700 workers across 11 packing plants in the Compostela Valley joined the labour action. Most of the 2,000 workers who chose not to join the strike were concerned that Sumifru would retrench or close down rather than settle and agree to granting all workers employee status. According to Tan, some of those who stayed and continued to work also trusted management's pledge that they would be granted regular work, known as 'regularization of employment'.[59] In view of the high level of unemployment, rural workers are endlessly seeking job guarantees for survival in a region where many cannot find work. To persuade and support workers to go on strike, the KMU had to take extraordinary measures to wage a proactive campaign, making the most of the support of peasants in the Compostela Valley as well as allies across the country. An often-used tactic of the government against striking workers was known as 'red tagging', claiming that the workers engaged in the job action were communists and terrorists. According to Tan, the management sought to use martial law to its advantage as a means of harassing and threatening workers on strike:

> Charging us as terrorists, leftists, and that this is part of the martial law that was implemented in Mindanao. This is a big factor in red tagging [...] they are using this language because this is part of the rebellion. The state forces can gather our names which are part of the labor organization and force us to sign waivers to quit the union and the labour centre; the main union, KMU. The government is trying to push the workers to quit the union because the KMU are red, destabilizing, and are trying to destroy the government. They are all mere allegations, baseless allegations.[60]

Moreover, activists and striking workers also faced severe repression from the police and military during a period of martial law across the region. Striking risked the lives of workers and their families, who could be arrested, assaulted, or killed. Thus, the KMU labour centre and organizational allies across the Philippines were necessary to support and sustain the strike by providing alternative employment and supporting and financing the long trek of workers from Mindanao to Quezon City to escape police and military authorities and publicize the exploitative and abusive conditions prevailing at Sumifru more widely without the threat of martial law. In all, 350 Sumifru striking workers travelled by land and boat from Compostela Valley to Quezon City, and a core group of 40 workers stayed on in an encampment for the duration of the strike. KMU sought to bring the striking workers to Quezon City to pressure Sumifru and the government to accept them as employees and appeal to the adjudication bodies, especially the Philippines Department of Labour Relations. The striking workers were especially eager to continue the struggle as about 30 per cent had worked in the packing plants for 15–20 years, were approaching retirement age, and required recognition as employees to collect pensions which the cooperatives operated by Sumifru could not pay.

Sumitomo Sells Its Stake in Sumifru: June 2019

As the strike reached nine months, KMU strike organizers increased public awareness of the strike by sending a delegation to Tokyo in June 2019, where

Sumitomo, the holding company of Sumifru, was publicly disparaged for its treatment of rural workers in Mindanao. Paul John Dizon, chairman of NAMASUFA-NAFLU-KMU, held a press conference revealing that workers earned minimum wages under the contract labour system operated by Sumifru and were exposed to severe occupational health hazards from exposure to hazardous chemicals.[61] The health hazards included lack of protective equipment or garments, skin rashes and allergies, and daily exposure to chemicals.[62]

In the aftermath of the damaging publicity about Sumifru's labour practices in Mindanao, Sumitomo sold its stake in the production operations to distance itself from any obligation, while continuing to secure profits by indirectly controlling the GCC. On 18 June 2019, Sumitomo, Sumifru's parent company, relinquished the 49 per cent stake it had held in the Philippine operations of the joint venture since 2003 to Thornton Venture Limited, which owned a 51 per cent majority stake of the banana operations in the Philippines. The sale took place as the KMU expanded its campaign to demand that the MNC 'regularize' the workers by directly employing them and ending the subcontracting relationships with cooperatives. The sale of Sumifru, which had operated in the Philippines since 1970, occurred only two-and-a-half years after Sumitomo purchased Fyffes, the Irish tropical food corporation which produces bananas and tropical fruits in Central and South America, as the Japanese multinational corporation sought to expand into the Western European and North American markets.[63] Rather than complying with the Philippine Supreme Court order to recognize KMU NAMASUFA as the union representative and bargaining agent of the workers, Sumitomo opted to distance itself from the direct production of bananas and control the supply chain in the major markets of East Asia and Oceania. Under the agreement, Sumitomo would continue to rely on exploitative subcontractors for the vast cultivation and extraction of bananas by rural workers in the plantations and packing houses of Mindanao.[64]

Notably, KMU's mobilization of 700 packing plant workers has had a significant impact on the GCC for bananas, and disrupted the plans and operations of a leading global MNC. But in similar circumstances, MNCs facing major strikes seek to sell direct ownership to corporations while maintaining control over the supply chain of the commodities. By relinquishing direct ownership and control, the dominant MNCs like Sumifru and local rural capitalists preserve their vast control over the banana-growing commodity supply chain. Meanwhile, local Filipino landowners and rural capitalists have emerged to compete with major growers, which largely serves to increase profits by driving down wages and working conditions for rural workers.[65] As value transfer of commodities produced in the South is secured by MNCs in metropolitan and settler states, direct ownership is not a measure of the capacity to improve rural workers' standards of living. As demonstrated in Southern regions and this study of organized workers' unrest and militancy in Mindanao's Compostela Valley, MNCs and consumers in the North gain at the expense of workers and peasants. The KMU performs the crucial function of providing organizational support for the struggles of rural workers in the Philippines.

Labour, Community, and Popular Support for Strikers in Mindanao and Throughout the Philippines

The KMU is the Philippines' largest independent national labour federation, representing highly exploited workers throughout the country by advocating militant class-struggle unionism. Established on 1 May 1980 during the Marcos government, KMU has taken the Tagalog name of the date of its formation ('May First Movement Labour Centre') to represent workers' organizations in the country that advocated National Democratic struggle, especially the end of US imperialism. KMU endures and has expanded as a growing workers' movement which views foreign imperialism as a major opponent. As the Philippines is dominated by foreign MNCs which extract natural resources and agricultural products, and exploit the country's labour force with the willing and compliant support of national capitalists and a rural oligarchy, anti-imperialism is a central concern in advancing the conditions and rights of the country's working class. The union opposes the dominant form of class-collaborationist unionism advocated by Western capitalists, and advances a unionism rooted in collective struggle to defend workers and democratic rights of the people. KMU has an estimated membership of 115,000 workers employed in the manufacturing, service, and agribusiness sectors and operating in the Philippines' major regions: Luzon, Visayas, and Mindanao.

The official position of the KMU is to protect and promote workers' right to employment, wage, humane working conditions, and their right to form unions, bargain collectively and strike; and to heighten workers' political awareness and class consciousness through massive education, organizing and mobilization in and out of the workplace.[66]

The Sumifru Strike Ends

On 18 August, the ten-month strike came to an end. University of the Philippines sociologist Sarah Raymundo notes:

> while it is good news, it remains to be seen how many workers the reconstituted company will absorb back as regularized employees. Under the agreement, the workers face no penalties. This is not the end as the workers are not getting any raise, just their jobs back after almost more than ten months of striking. Imagine all those workers who went on strike and were kicked out and replaced, protesting and travelling all the way to Manila. I think by now the workers have progressed beyond unionism into a cohesive social movement.[67]

The KMU and NAMASUFA remain committed to advancing a nationwide campaign to end the labour contracting system, and to regularize and increase compensation for low-wage workers in the private and public sectors through the restoration of the minimum wage. Elmer Labog, KMU chairman, argues that the KMU is staunchly opposed to neoliberal government policies that generate informality among low-wage workers, and seeks to increase job security and secure the right to organize into trade unions to advance workplace rights, improve health and safety conditions, provide living wages, and to mobilize informal labourers to fight for broader worker rights in urban and rural sectors of the economy:[68]

> We view neoliberalism as a central feature of imperialism and the national implementation of deregulation, privatization, and liberalization are policies advanced by multinational companies and finance capital in the imperialist countries which deepen poverty and repression of urban and rural workers in the Philippines.[69]

He continues that the KMU opposes the World Trade Organization, which severely reduces wages, erodes working conditions, and marginalizes the

Philippines as a region for the production and exploitation of agricultural goods, natural resources for export to the rich developed countries in the global North. In this way, the Philippines' ruling class colludes with MNCs to exploit the Philippine people.

A crucial component of the subordination of the Philippines is the rural agricultural sector. As such, the union is steadfastly committed to improving the conditions of the Philippine peasantry, who, according to the KMU, 'compose the majority of the population'. The KMU argues that the land reform initiatives in the aftermath of the People's Power Revolution from the late 1980s to the present have not only decreased the standard of living for the majority, but eroded the wages and living conditions of most rural workers in the country. Because of this, the KMU advocates a far-reaching socialist policy of nationalizing all land and industry. In the rural sector, the KMU advocates the redistribution of all land to the peasant population and the nationalization of electricity, water, petroleum, and all basic and strategic industries. Labog and the KMU believe that only through nationalization can the Philippines advance in the interest of urban and rural workers and provide an industrialized and developed economy for the majority of the population who remain neglected by the large landowners and foreign capitalists who control the natural resources of the country.[70]

On 1 October 2019, workers who were members of NAMASUFA-NAFLU-KMU decided to stop their operations and installed makeshift barricades in seven Sumifru Packing Plants, including (PP) 370 in Barangay Pilar Babag, PP 98 and PP 340 in Barangay Osmena, PP 92 in Barangay Alegria, PP 90 in Barangay Gabi, PP 99 in Barangay San Miguel, and PP 115 in Barangay Maparat. These workers were members of the local unions Nagkahiusang Mamumuo sa Os-miguel, Nagkahiusang Mamumuo sa San Jose, Nagkahiusang Mamumuo sa Suyapa Farm, Packing Plant 92 Workers Union, Packing Plant 340 Workers Union, San Miguel Workers Union, Maparat-Montevista Workers Union, and Nagkahiusang Mamumuo sa Pilar-Mangayon. Of the total number of 931 workers who were union members, 540 were women.

Many of the union members have worked for Sumifru for more than a decade, but remained contract workers despite a recent pronouncement by President Rodrigo Duterte to end the system in the country. According to Labog, the flexible labour practices have produced mass joblessness for about 10 million Filipinos, and have buttressed the status of the country as an underdeveloped semi-colony. In most instances, unemployment is engendered by the contractual labour system, which remains a strong spur for labour unrest and strikes in both informal urban and rural regions. 'Workers are going on strike because they want to fight for regular work, because their jobs, their very source of livelihood is under threat,' said Labog.[71] As the struggle at Sumifru shows, the KMU has taken a principled stance against the labour contractor system, where members of the union, fired for going on strike to establish a system of regularization, continue to seek status as workers, and a greater share of the profits generated in the GCC for bananas.

CONCLUSION: TRADE UNIONS, PARTY, AND DEMOCRATIC REVOLUTIONARY MOVEMENT

This chapter has shown that the Philippines' economy remains distorted by economic reliance on agricultural and human exports into the GCC for agriculture, natural resources, and migrant workers. The state primarily serves the interest of a comprador bourgeoisie to advance the interest of multinational corporations.

The central objective of this chapter has been to bring to life the significance of rural labourers in the national economy of the Philippines, and to highlight these workers' strategic position in the generation of profits for MNCs and the local comprador bourgeoisie. In accentuating the crucial importance of rural informal workers in the Philippines, the chapter has striven to revitalize research on this highly neglected sector of the global population. In his work, Lenin contended that the rural proletariat was crucial in the generation of surplus profits for imperialists in the early twentieth century and comprised a vital sector of the modern working class. Likewise, today, more than 100 years later, rural workers in the Philippines validate the far-reaching significance of the rural working class.

In addition, this chapter has established that rural workers in the banana plantations and packing houses require a disciplined working-class organization to advance their collective interest to confront a rapacious state which serves the interests of imperial MNCs which benefit from the organization of land into plantations for the production and distribution of commodities for consumption in the North and the extraction of surplus value from a rural working class. In the absence of a strong working-class organization like the KMU, workers would have continued to rebel against corporate abuses but would have lacked the organizational capacity to resist the oppression and begin to transform conditions in Mindanao, a region which serves the interests of multinational capital without benefiting the majority of the population of the island. The KMU has applied an ecumenical strategy of allying with sympathizers the world over while maintaining a principled commitment to the nationalization of all lands and the development of Mindanao for the local population, free of imperialist interference.

5

Global Capitalism: Corporate Restructuring, Labour Brokering, and Working-class Mobilization in South Africa

The vast majority of the literature on South Africa's post-apartheid era is duplicative and mostly indistinguishable, with a sobering narrative proclaiming that the end of apartheid has not addressed the pervasive poverty and inequality in this society.

From the emergence of a post-apartheid state, South Africa has remained stubbornly recognized by demographers as the largest economically unequal country in the world, with the highest Gini coefficient ratio in income, far exceeding comparable countries (Figure 5.1). Over nearly three decades since 1993, inequality has not contracted, but has widened, along with high rates of poverty.[1] The high rate of inequality is principally due to the hybrid nature of the post-apartheid state, which has continued to confer most private economic resources and benefits on the white minority at the expense of the majority of black South African citizens.

While income inequality has principally divided black and white populations, the end of the apartheid state in 1994 bestowed economic benefits on the black elite, which prospered as a consequence of ties to state institutions and corporations, while passing over the black South African majority. Paltry social benefits were conferred on the black working class, informal workers, and peasant labourers, but the major economic objectives demanded by the South African anti-apartheid movement (the Freedom Charter) and institutions of the tripartite black-led government in 1994, such as the Growth, Employment and Redistribution (GEAR) programme, were

144

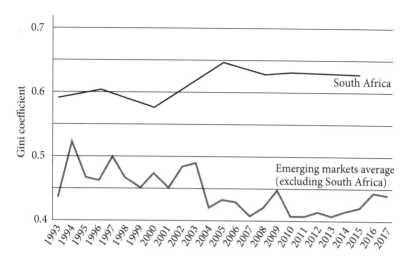

Figure 5.1   Increasingly unequal South Africa, 1993–2017

Note: Index scaled. 0–1.

Source: Derived by International Monetary Fund from World Development Indicators. See 'Six Charts Explain South Africa's Inequality', *IMF Country Focus*, 30 January 2020, www.imf.org/en/News/Articles/2020/01/29/na012820six-charts-on-south-africas-persistent-and-multi-faceted-inequality, accessed 22 April 2020.

never seriously pursued.[2] Though inequality and poverty have persisted, and despite popular challenges from workers and social movements, an entrenched capitalist class in the dominant private sector and multinational corporate control over extractive and financial institutions have expanded and persisted through the 2010s with the support of the Tripartite Alliance. Social movements have formed among the working classes, impoverished communities in settlements, rural movements, and university students. These have challenged state officials' and elites' failure to confront the persistence of poverty, poor services, and inequality in what has become known as the Rebellion of the Poor.[3] A transition to a socialist and equitable system of income and wealth distribution in South Africa is constrained by an economically advantaged white population, multinational corporations, and a compliant black state leadership which supports neoliberal capitalism.

This failure to challenge dominant economic institutions stems from both domestic and international factors. Though South Africa's economy has shifted from manufacturing to services, it has been further integrated into the global capitalist economy and financial system. State economic elites have remained steadfastly supportive of the institution of informal and precarious labour conditions, including the contracting of work to third parties, and the rise of the labour broking industry throughout the economy to secure greater domestic and international corporate profits at the expense of debasing general labour conditions and undermining labour unions.[4]

GROWTH AND INTENSIFICATION OF CONTRACT AND TEMPORARY LABOUR IN SOUTH AFRICA

Popular discontent punctuates the period from the formation of a post-apartheid South Africa in 1994 to the present, as the new majority government has failed to accomplish major policy goals in fashioning a state built on multiracial equality and participatory democracy. Following the formation of the post-apartheid state, the government enacted crucial legislation to achieve greater inclusion among the dispossessed black South African majority, including the 1995 Labour Relations Act. This aimed to ensure that workplace labour organizing rights were extended to workers of all races, especially the dispossessed black majority working in all sectors of the economy. It was intended to allow mining, manufacturing, transport, service, public sector, domestic, and farm labourers to form unions and have the right to collective activity.[5] The labour law and new constitution were a far cry from the demands of the Freedom Charter of 1955, written by the African National Congress and allied anti-apartheid organizations committed to the end of a white-dominated society. In addition to demanding an end to the white racial hierarchy, the Freedom Charter had called for nationalization and socialization of industry, and multiracial control of all natural resources, wealth, land reform, housing and security, labour rights, cultural diversity, and democracy. It became the unifying document for opponents of the apartheid state.[6]

Since the establishment of the post-apartheid state in 1994, new initiatives have been enacted to end the abject poverty confronting the black South African majority through creating economic growth, employment, and social inclusion of the black majority. Yet, these new initiatives – the Reconstruction and Development Programme, GEAR, and the Accelerated and Shared Growth Initiative – were pretentious, ineffectual, and ultimately not carried out as government policy.[7]

Thus, the principal social objectives of the Freedom Charter to stimulate a just post-apartheid transition in South Africa failed and were aborted and repeatedly amended as popular recognition of and disillusionment with the fundamental demands for equality and economic rights amounted to no more than rhetoric. Ultimately, they were neglected, only to be summoned again by popular aspirational demands. In this way, the post-apartheid era presents a stark disjuncture with the Freedom Charter and recurrent failures of the popular majority to push the privileged middle and upper classes of South Africa to establish a new society based on equality and prosperity for all. By 2012, in the wake of the Marikana Massacre of platinum miners by South African State Police, it was clear that the Tripartite Alliance of the African National Congress (ANC), South African Communist Party (SACP), and the Confederation of South African Trade Unions (COSATU) would not push for social transformation, but defiantly protect the dominant capitalist neoliberal order. Marikana defined the limits of the post-apartheid state and its commitment to capitalist development rather than labour law, and its commitment to pursue neoliberal policies to sustain informalization of the labour market. In league with international capital and consulting agencies, subcontracting informal and temporary labour would be advanced through support of the labour brokerage and temporary employment services, representing a refutation of the principles of multiracial equality.

The mainspring of the post-apartheid state was to support the development of a compliant workforce for maximum capitalist profitability across every sector of the labour market. To accomplish these goals, the South African ruling class would have to ally itself with global and international capital to restructure its labour market by integrating its economy into the international supply chain and enacting neoliberal policies which extracted surplus labour from workers while subordinating and pacifying widespread trade union militancy that reached its height in the 1980s and early 1990s.

South Africa's Labour Brokerage Industry and Temporary Employment Services: Labourers' Life and Work in the Johannesburg Region

The rise of the labour brokerage industry illuminates the neoliberal shift that beleaguered the South African working class by weakening and harming the reputation of trade unions among the working class. As the South African economy diversified, temporary employment services (TES) encompassing tertiary work in the retail sector and the gig economy have captured a larger share of jobs in South Africa, replacing jobs that once constituted stable work and standardized employment. A study by Bhorat, Cassim, and Yu estimates that the TES subsector created 6.4 per cent of all new South African employment in 2013, more than agriculture (5.1 per cent), utilities (0.9 per cent), and even mining (3.1 per cent).[8] On the whole, unskilled and semi-skilled African workers have been unable to find regular employment in the formal sector of the economy. The rise of informal labour results directly from the denial of living-wage and stable employment to the black workforce and a growing reliance on rural informal labourers, in some cases workers migrating from Mozambique, Malawi, Zimbabwe, Eswatini, and Lesotho, as well as internal South African migrants. These jobs consign black South African workers to a marginal existence where employment is conventionally scarce and unreliable. In some cases, employers directly recruit workers from abroad, and in other instances workers are provided by labour brokers. The process was well under way in the late 1990s. As sociologist Franco Barcheisi observes:

> corporate outsourcing and subcontracting provided alternatives in myriads of non-union small and micro enterprises that operated along an increasingly uncertain boundary between formal and informal. Equally important in the decentralization of production was the shift of labor recruitment towards temporary employment agencies [...]. Under the impulse of labor brokerage, casual, fixed-term, part-time, and 'homework' arrangements are on the rise across the whole occupational spectrum, as shown by studies that also emphasize the disparities between temporary and permanent workers in wages, benefits, and working conditions.[9]

Barcheisi's study shows how previously stable employment is converted into informal job arrangements. In the East Rand industrial region of Gauteng Province, he documents the reduction of the workforce at Union Carriage & Wagon (UCW), a manufacturer of railroad transport equipment, from 800 to 150 through the loss of contracts abroad and the government's general neglect of public transport, thereby cutting the number of workers at a key manufacturer. UCW was also able to cut its workforce by hiring labour brokers to become the direct employees, averting any responsibility for employment, health insurance, or guarantees for employment beyond three-month fixed-term contracts. The proliferation of temporary service jobs contributes to widespread job insecurity and weaker ties to workplaces and industries.[10] Consequently, Barcheisi notes, full-time jobs are 'likely to reflect the material conditions of a shrinking minority of workers' in South Africa.[11]

TEMPORARY EMPLOYMENT SERVICES AND THE EMERGENCE OF THE LABOUR BROKING SYSTEM

By driving recruitment into the labour market since independence in 1994, authorizing and encouraging contractors to replace employers with brokers, TES has had a significant influence on the South African political economy and working class. Accordingly, rather than generating social equity by

Table 5.1   Sectoral distribution of employment change in South Africa, 1995–2014

Sector	1995		2001		2014		Average annual growth 1995–2014		Change
	000s	%	000s	%	000s	%	000s	%	%
Primary	1696	7.9	1732	15.5	1135	7.5	−2.1	−561	−10.0
Agriculture	1247	13.2	1178	10.5	710	4.7	−2.9	−537	−9.5
Mining	449	4.8	554	5.0	424	2.8	−0.3	−25	−0.4
Secondary	1988	21.0	2348	21.0	3138	20.8	2.41	150	20.4
Manufacturing	1452	15.4	1620	14.5	1808	12.0	1.2	356	6.3
Utilities	860	9.0	940	8.0	1300	9.2	24.0	4	0.8
Construction	449	4.8	634	5.7	1200	8.0	5.3	751	13.4
Tertiary	5774	61.0	7058	63.1	10808	71.7	3.4	5034	89.5
Retail	1684	17.8	2454	22.0	3195	21.2	3.4	1511	26.9
Transport	483	5.1	546	4.9	897	5.9	3.3	414	7.4
Finance	592	6.3	1035	9.3	2050	13.6	6.8	1458	25.9
Community, social, and personal services	2205	23.3	1989	17.8	3433	22.8	2.4	1228	21.8
Household	809	8.6	1034	9.2	1234	8.2	2.2	425	7.6
Totals	9458	100.0	11179	100.0	15081	100.0	2.5	5623	100.0
TES	199	2.1	398	2.6	970	6.4	8.7	771	13.7

Source: Derived from data from Statistics South Africa, October Household Survey (1995), Labour Force Survey (September 2001), and Quarterly Labour Force Survey (Quarter 1, 2014).

socializing major industries, the South African economy decidedly turned towards neoliberal reform, specifically removing the established relationship of the worker to the firm, which formerly bestowed employer responsibility over wage scales, working conditions, and human resources.[12] In a range of industries, TES interposes a third party into the labour–management scheme, whereby the worker is no longer employed by the producer, but by a labour contractor. Labour brokering is a neoliberal scheme corresponding with structural reform under neoliberalism, and reduces the capacity of the worker to contest wages and conditions directly with the producer, thus losing a significant degree of power to contest wages and conditions through job actions and strikes. See Table 5.1 for the sectoral distribution of employment change in South African industries from 1995 to 2004 and for temporary services as a share of total employment. Figure 5.2 shows the expanding share of TES output across industries in the South African

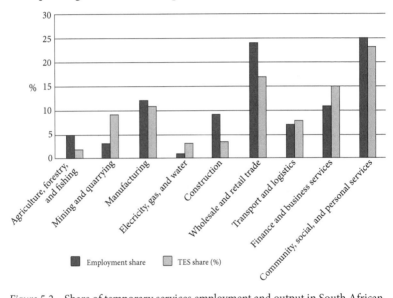

Figure 5.2　Share of temporary services employment and output in South African labour market, 2013

Note: The ratio is based on the share of formal, non-TES employment to TES employment reported by Statistics South Africa, Statistical Release P0211, *Quarterly Labour Force Survey*, Quarter 4, 2014, www.statssa.gov.za/publications/P0211/P02114thQuarter2014.pdf, accessed 11 May 2019.

Source: Calculated from Statistics South Africa, Quarterly Labour Force Survey, Quarter 1, 2014.

labour market, revealing that instability has been injected into community and social services, the wholesale and retail trade, manufacturing, construction, and transport and logistics.

As a result of the rise of the neoliberal policies of TES and labour broking, the post-apartheid labour market in South Africa has become increasingly inequitable, dashing the high hopes of closing the income and wealth gap and forging an inclusive and democratic society. Thus, the South African state has not only failed to nationalize major industries and provide essential services for the broad masses, as envisioned by the Freedom Charter, but has supported socially regressive programmes which have further imperilled the lives of the black South African majority.

RANK AND FILE MOBILIZATION AND ORGANIZATIONAL RESPONSES: NUMSA AND CWAO

By 2010, the erosion and breakdown of economic conditions did not go unnoticed by the majority of workers across the economy as rank and file dissent began to break out throughout the country where conditions had deteriorated markedly. The existing unions had largely neglected to respond to worker unrest, particularly in the mining and industrial sectors, where an autonomous labour movement had become more and more militant in confronting employers and unresponsive unions. Some labour scholars saw the unrest as a sign of a return of a rank and file leaderless workers' movement embedded in anarchist, syndicalist, and autonomist activism. As the organized trade unions and Left parties were betraying the interests of the workers or otherwise imploding all around the world, some could draw succour from identifying worker participation in anti-capitalist activism, conventionally signified as 'bottom-up change' in context (see Chapter 2) rather than in the development of strong and militant organization.[13] Autonomism had become the motive force behind a new kind of Left in South Africa which didn't require power, but was content with the expression of militancy based on contemporary evidence of renewed working-class dynamism. Above all, syndicalists and autonomists, considered the workers as operating independently of compromised bureaucratic labour leaders and capable of stimulating change on their own. If the benchmark is worker militancy, observers could then assert that evidence of a recent upsurge of unauthorized strikes, protests, and occupations revealed the extent of opposition to the state and capital. Perhaps workers could capture a modicum of bargaining power *vis-à-vis* employers, or strike to improve wages and conditions.

In the South African context, who would lead the struggle against temporary employment and labour broking, as well as the erosion of a principled labour leadership? In the 2010s, two major forms of resistance emerged:

- autonomous labour organizations and workers' assemblies in opposition to capital, the state, and corrupt union bureaucracies;
- detachment of the labour movement emerging to contest capital, the state, and existing unions which failed their members.

The decline and failure of existing trade unions to contest capital have brought a rise of rank and file labour militancy and the resurgence of a segment of the labour unions. This case study of South African labour broking examines the activities of both autonomous organizing and militant organizational forms.

The exemplar of rank and file organizing is the Casual Workers Advice Office (CWAO) of the industrial corridor on the East Rand. This rejects all South African trade unions as aligned with capital and the state, and serves as the autonomist organization for workers against existing unions.[14] CWAO serves as a mobilizing force behind workers who were not represented by trade unions and the National Union of Metalworkers of South Africa (NUMSA), a militant union which was expelled from the dominant COSATU federation following its decision to break with the ANC in 2014. In view of the dramatic growth of contract and outsourced labour from 1995 to the present and the rise of highly exploited workers in temporary employment services, rank and file activity is re-emerging in a growing range of economic sectors neglected or overlooked by unions. In this chapter, we will explore the competing positions of both CWAO and NUMSA, a union which maintains ties to unorganized workers, yet, after having been banished from the major union movement, has fewer resources to mobilize these militant workers into unions.

The next section of this chapter analyses the scant capacity of existing unions and the rise of rank and file militancy in South Africa before turning to the organizational responses of the CWAO and NUMSA.

TRADE UNIONS, AUTONOMOUS ORGANIZATION, WORKERS, AND POWER

Robust research on the South African political economy must include examination of the changes in material relations of the working class and how gains or losses bear on labour struggles. The neoliberal restructuring of labour–management relations through subcontracting and outsourcing has severely undercut wages throughout the global South and has had exceptionally pernicious consequences for the organization of South Africa's working class. Temporary workers tend to fill jobs in expanding sectors of the economy. Short-term TES contracts have reduced the capacity of trade unions to represent workers as they have done traditionally. In the absence of trade unions, autonomous organizations have filled a deep vacuum for a growing number of workers needing advice, advocacy, and assistance in pressing struggles against rapacious third-party managers who are not the direct employers. Autonomist representation tends to entail the most competent workers as activists in workplaces challenging third-party employers for improved wages, conditions, and direct employment. As such, existing trade unions are frequently viewed as an exogenous force that has failed to represent a growing number of workers. As unions are increasingly removed from temporary labourers, NUMSA is representing, advocating, and challenging the laws in the labour courts, and leading strikes for the right to represent workers. As such, NUMSA is an alternative to the fledgling autonomist organizations. This chapter will now compare the activities of both the CWAO and NUMSA in advancing the struggles of contingent workers in South Africa's current informal economy.

Autonomist Struggles against Labour Broking: The Casual Workers Advice Office

The CWAO was founded in 2011 as a non-profit independent organization, funded by foreign NGOs as an alternative to established unions which had not advanced the interests of contract workers employed by labour brokers. The CWAO provides advice and support for casual, contract, labour broker, and other precarious workers who mostly live in impoverished townships. The organization was formed by labour activists who recognized that the traditional labour movement was incapable of and unwilling to organize contingent workers who had largely replaced full-time manufacturing workers in the major industrial East Rand region and throughout South Africa. The withdrawal and lack of enforcement of labour protections had allowed new firms to emerge staffed by labour brokers who paid workers low wages and offered no benefits or job security. As neoliberal policies took hold, labour brokers proliferated throughout South Africa as a means to increase corporate profitability by supplying non-union labourers to major multinational and national employers. These neoliberal policies were promoted by the South African government as a means to increase competitiveness and support businesses seeking to seize on a lower-wage regime.

Decline of Existing Unions

Following the two decades from 1990 to 2010, COSATU – South Africa's primary union federation which had affiliated with the ANC and SACP, and emerged in the post-apartheid period as a major organizational force for South Africa's working class – had lost much of its lustre. It was viewed by both labour and management as a largely ineffective and depleted force, functioning as a political exponent of the government's neoliberal policies and being out of touch with most of the labour movement. As Devin Pillay notes:

> the federation has gradually moved from a more robust 'social movement unionism' towards a narrower form of party-led 'political unionism'. While retaining its independence and continuing to engage in policy contestation on issues inside and outside the workplace, COSATU has not dared to push the envelope too far, and forge links with social movements antagonistic toward the ANC. Nor has it had much success in shaping ANC policy. Rather than build an alternative counter-hegemonic Left project, COSATU has chosen to 'swell the ranks' of the ANC [...] COSATU has revived elements of its historical 'social movement unionism', but this co-exists schizophrenically with its narrower 'political unionism'.[15]

Only NUMSA, the largest union in COSATU before its expulsion in 2014, remained in resolute opposition to the erosion of wages and labour rights in South Africa. But NUMSA was the exception among COSATU unions, and by the 2010s it had actively opposed the implementation of neoliberal reform and was actively criticizing the ANC for serving the interests of MNCs and national capitalists.

This perception of COSATU and its constituent trade unions as a spent force in the South African government also informs the emphasis CWAO places on the necessity of precarious workers organizing outside the contours of a union. At its formation in 2011, the industrial model of organization through existing trade unions was viewed as in decline in North America and Western Europe, especially among contingent and part-time workers. As labour brokers increasingly entered the established unionized industrial sectors, existing trade unions appeared less suitable for traditional workers, as full-time employment cut into employer profitability. In the same way as new forms of worker organization formed in the West, CWAO constituted itself as a new representational form devoid of a stated plan to expand the power of a workers' organization. The CWAO staff offered legal and strategic advice, space for weekly meetings, and logistical support. Instead, contingent workers who joined the CWAO from the surrounding area of the East Rand would publicly hold meetings to independently determine actions and strategy outside of the traditional union model. In the ensuing years, CWAO activists founded the Simunye Workers' Forum (SWF) as the principal labour organization of most members, while relying on CWAO staff and legal support to conduct campaigns to improve the wages and rights of workers employed by the labour brokers, which had expanded dramatically throughout the region.[16] The key question is how the CWAO, as a labour consultant, could advance worker conditions through developing a community base by tapping into the spontaneous power of workers expressed every day without organizational subjectivity. Would an organization funded by foreign NGOs have the capacity to act independently without interference? Incontrovertibly, South Africa's working class, growing increasingly impoverished under apartheid, required a vision and organizational capacity to overcome the unchallenged power of state-supported corporations and MNCs exploiting workers in South Africa.

The defining moment in the struggle for labour rights was the platinum workers' struggle in the South African mining belt in Northwest and Limpopo Provinces, culminating in the Marikana Massacre by South African State Police.[17] In part, the worker insurgency which began in the same year as the formation of the CWAO in the mining belt to the north of the East Rand and Gauteng would transform the shape, structure, and

future of the South African labour movement and national politics. Pre-
sumably organized to contest the existing order in the manufacturing belt
surrounding Johannesburg, CWAO could not have anticipated the mineworker insurgency that broke out in 2011 and continues into the 2020s, a
development which would rend the power of COSATU and the National
Union of Mineworkers (NUM). In part, CWAO drew upon justifiable anger
and energy from Marikana, as many of the workers in temporary services
were directly recruited from rural areas by labour brokers. Nkosinathi
Godfrey Zuma observes that:

> brokers travelled to rural areas 'to reduce the cost of labour by reversing
> the established wage standards won by the organised labour'. [...] Rural
> recruitment should be distinguished from the migrant labour system as a
> form of labour recruitment in a sense that with the migrant labour system
> it includes the recruitment of labour across one country.[18]

The massacre of 34 striking platinum miners by the South African Police
Service on direct orders from state authorities on 16 August 2012 gave
substance and authenticity to the perception among black South Africans
that COSATU and the established trade unions had accommodated to the
logic of neoliberal capitalism, in which the interests of finance and capital
took precedence over the wages and conditions of labour. The Marikana
Moment led to a range of responses from labour and the left. One sector
of the Left, inspired by the global decline of unions and the rise of rank
and file labour organizing as a source of working-class power, generated
a movement for 'new forms of labour organising' outside existing unions
through workers' centres and autonomous unions.[19] To be sure, Marikana
was led by workers' assemblies that formed to challenge the NUM in the
platinum belt of the Northwest.[20] The force behind the workers' movement
was indeed the thousands of workers who organized independent formations outside the existing structures of South African trade unions. Thus,
not only did Marikana challenge the NUM, but all unions in the COSATU
federation of unions, which not only lost control of their own members,
but formed part of the Tripartite Alliance which had effectively ordered the
massacre against black South African workers.

The absence of an authentic South African trade union opposition to
COSATU led to the rise of worker centres as alternatives to established

unions. Both Leftist organizers and workers recognized the severe limitations of trade unions and a tainted relationship with the governing coalition. As a consequence, dispossessed workers would have to take matters into their own hands and form unions and organizations independent from the state or combat the state or form new forms of labour organization. The Association of Mineworkers and Construction Union (AMCU) formed to largely replace the NUM as representative of platinum miners. CWAO, an NGO founded just one year before Marikana, emerged as a major oppositional force to COSATU unions among unorganized workers in the urban areas, most prominently, the Johannesburg East Rand region. CWAO is not a formal registered union, but a community centre for organizing, and almost exclusively represents the interests of unorganized workers outside government-recognized unions who seek to improve wages, job security, and working conditions throughout a range of industries. Yet concomitantly, CWAO represented a direct challenge to the existing trade union establishment linked to the South African government.

Organizing Precarious TES and Contract Workers

As an independent labour organization in Germiston, on the East Rand, an old manufacturing centre in Gauteng Province undergoing industrial restructuring and the recomposition of its labour force from formal to informal sector workers, the CWAO attracted workers from the surrounding townships with grievances against employers. A decade earlier, large factories and mills employing hundreds of workers began to be replaced by smaller facilities that employed non-union and temporary workers. Still, the East Rand remains in the industrial core of South Africa and is a major community centre for labourers in the surrounding townships and settlements. Located in downtown Germiston, CWAO supports and advances the demands of the lowest-waged workers in the Gauteng region through legal and organizational campaigning.[21] The primary campaigns have focused on mobilizing the growing number of impoverished workers living in settlements seeking equity with full-time workers in major private businesses, including subsidiaries of major MNCs. In many instances, workers have migrated to the region in the post-apartheid era, lacking stable employment. As such, CWAO seeks to fill a major gap that established unions neglected in the period 1995–2010, especially the vastly increasing numbers of workers

157

employed by labour contractors, brokers, and in small and dispersed factories and retail outlets.

While COSATU had been critical of the rise of labour brokers from 2000 to 2010, following Marikana and the expulsion of NUMSA the federation's defence of non-union workers employed for labour brokers has largely vanished. The labour brokering practice is supported by leading South African business interests seeking to lower the cost of labour in manufacturing, services, and logistics. As a key member of the Tripartite Alliance, COSATU has not criticized the practice of labour brokering, as it is viewed by the state as a means to increase business competitiveness by lowering wages and increasing profitability. CWAO has filled the organizational gap and seized on the rise of labour brokers as a major threat to the black South African labour force at a time when trade unions have become more submissive and have largely neglected the burgeoning sector of workers employed by subcontractors.

CWAO provides support to workers living in informal settlements who are employed by labour brokers. Ighsaan Schroeder, CWAO's founder, argues that traditional unions have completely neglected the majority of workers who do not have regular employment, as a result of neoliberal industrial restructuring and the failure of trade unions to organize workers.

Schroeder joined the South African trade union movement in the 1980s, and stated that two decades ago, shop stewards were active and engaged. Now, Schroeder laments that many workers do not even know who their stewards are:

> Due to the massive industrial restructuring, the working class has been smashed at a social level. There is also a struggle that the movement faces of building a layer of militants, a strong social layer, and the accumulation of militancy is scattered. I am surprised daily by the material force of labour fragmentation. [...] We find people working at the same factory, working on their own legal case without considering those workers at their side who may be involved in the very same struggle. We have found maintaining a core of activists in the work areas very difficult. People just move on, even after winning major battles, to another job or back to their rural area. Another issue is that we are not really even close to linking permanent workers with labour broker workers, but instead we struggle to even link labour broker workers with each other.[22]

As a result of the fragmentation of labour and production, workers do not identify with unions of the 1980s–1990s which represented workers in large facilities with far better wages and conditions. Today, there are collapsed industries, and deindustrialization in auto, steel, and textiles. The decline in steel industries has had a disastrous effect on 'community organization'. Schroeder argues that even NUMSA and the newly formed South African Federation of Trade Unions have abandoned the interests of informal contract workers, despite the union having engaged in its own organizing and legal campaigns to end the practice of labour brokers. Schroeder asserts: 'All unions, from COSATU to NUMSA and the independent unions, have become small scale and regional and are incapable of representing the South African working class.'[23]

Simunye Workers' Forum

Workers attending weekly meetings have formed the Simunye Workers' Forum as the organizational agency attending weekly meetings to press worker demands and engage in mass labour actions. Every Saturday and Sunday morning, the SWF holds a general meeting of workers employed in the East Rand at CWAO's offices in Germiston, a space that holds up to 300–350 people. The number of workers attending each meeting depends on the status of specific worker disputes against management, and key labour law decisions affecting the legality of labour broker actions are decided by the Commission for Conciliation, Mediation and Arbitration (CCMA).[24]

Schroeder has little confidence in existing labour unions seeking to mobilize South African workers, and sees autonomous organizations like CWAO as the major force for labour mobilization in the future:

> The labour movement has failed to deliver or meet the needs of the majority of black South African workers. As the first labour centre in South Africa, CWAO has spurred the formation of other centres and informal labour organizations throughout the country.[25] And we view labour brokers as the dominant force in South Africa.[26]

CWAO represents workers in production, distribution and logistics, warehouses, and beyond to challenge the labour brokers who are contracted by those businesses Schroeder sees as the dominant force in South African labour today. Schroeder does not believe trade unions are equal to the task of challenging employers across the South African economy:

> For instance, among private security workers, trade unions and employers have established bargaining councils, and unions are actively working against the interests of workers, allowing the average work week to rise from 40 to 60 hours a week. They have effectively become yellow unions, and the labour movement actively works against the interests of workers.[27]

At a meeting on 9 July 2017, Schroeder informed the 300 workers assembled, who were employed by labour brokers, that they had very few rights when enterprises close:

> The company has the right to shut down the factory under the law. You comrades have an understanding that you must work Monday to Friday or Monday to Thursday. They can't just shut down the factory without giving workers notice. On a day-to-day basis, companies shut down. In contrast to permanent workers, you do not have a provident fund, equivalent wages, and other benefits and allowances. So you have to fight for equity with permanent workers.[28]

The CWAO meeting is chaired by worker organizers with the assistance of CWAO staff and volunteers. The meetings provide information to workers about their legal rights and the inadequacy of South African law in protecting their rights, and has mobilized labourers employed by leading brokers in manufacturers, retail outlets, logistics, and service firms throughout the East Rand. In addition, the CWAO helps lead work stoppages and strikes among many of the workers to protest against low wages, poor conditions, violation of labour laws, and other abuses by labour brokers.

In a very short period of time, CWAO has become a leader in organizing informal workers to legally challenge systemic violations in labour broking in South Africa, whereby labourers employed at an enterprise for more than three months are not conferred formal job status. In some cases, workers have been employed by labour brokers for more than ten years. CWAO mobilizes workers to attend hearings at the CCMA, and has legally advocated on behalf of their legal claims. On Saturday 15 July 2017, nearly 500 workers attended an informational and organizing meeting at the

CWAO hall in Germiston.[29] Workers were drawn to an open mass meeting by the CCMA judgment on 10 July stipulating that workers could not work longer than three months for labour brokers without being granted formal employment status. The ruling also specified that strikes among workers employed for more than three months are only directed against employers, not labour brokers and contractors.[30] The CCMA decision was appealed by labour brokers and ultimately decided in the workers' favour one year later, in July 2018.

A notable feature of the CWAO and SWF is that workers come to the CWAO meeting in Germiston from surrounding townships and settlements of the East Rand. Workers are employed by contractors spread throughout Gauteng. At the meetings, a high level of worker participation and enthusiasm are palpable. One leader of the SWF pleaded, 'Comrades – let us be disciplined,' and by pleading for restraint and order among the workers, revealed a strong interest in organization. Yet questions remain concerning how directives endorsed by workers can be enforced without organization, and whether the SWF, which unambiguously rejects the term 'union,' is in fact a proto-workers' organization which takes actions and has established nebulous relations with workers. The organizational question was also raised by Ighsaan Schroeder at the meeting:

> We have a need for organization if we are to have a chance for success. We need a workers' council and a workers' committee. The bosses will resist the demands [...]. It is much harder for bosses to do this if we mobilize. Otherwise, the bosses would not give us our rights.

He continued that without organization, workers would face victimization, dismissal, and retrenchment.[31]

In assessing the influence of CWAO and the SWF, we must also evaluate the activism by NUMSA, the nation's largest union, in opposing labour brokers and also mobilizing temporary service workers. Even with this favourable ruling that labour brokers cannot employ workers for more than three months, contractors retained the right to dismiss workers and then hire new workers to fill these jobs, rendering the job a permanent temporary position. Moreover, some brokers claimed they were labour contractors providing essential ancillary services to corporations.

CASE STUDY: CAMPAIGN TO REGULARIZE
SIMBA CHIPS WORKERS

Among the most significant campaigns waged by CWAO/SWF is the organization of workers employed at Simba Chips, a South African subsidiary of the international conglomerate PepsiCo. Simba workers are predominantly black South African women who are employed as contractors, receive no minimum wage, and do not earn enough for daily survival expenses.[32] Simba Chips employs 500–600 temporary employees on rotating shifts through NAMPAK, a labour broker. Founded in 1957, the Simba (Swahili for 'lion') company was purchased by PepsiCo Food Production. PepsiCo claims to adhere to a code of conduct, stating: 'Our Global Code of Conduct describes the "purpose" behind our performance and is designed to help us meet our obligations, show respect to one another in the workplace and act with integrity in the marketplace.'[33]

Yet, despite this ostensibly principled code of conduct, Simba Chips and PepsiCo secure labour brokers to seek out the lowest-wage workers by contracting all workers. Simba Chips sought to recruit women, and as reported in *The New Worker*, some workers believed they faced discrimination if the employer knew they had children:

> A lot of us women didn't say that we had kids, because we thought they would fire us. In time, we learned that having kids, being single mothers, was in some cases a guarantee that we would be even more exploited. They knew we needed the money.[34]

The breakdown of formal labour–management relations at Simba Chips has stimulated the temporary service employees there to directly mobilize with the sustained support of CWAO and SWF. By providing legal and organizational guidance to workers, a synergy developed between Simba Chips labourers and CWAO/SWF. Workers were energized by the support, and engaged in sustained actions to end the oppressive TES labour regime which consigned the workers to low wages, oppressive conditions, and lack of job stability.

The Simba Chips workers campaign was a long and drawn-out struggle of organizing for legal rights and recognition from PepsiCo. From 2016 through 2018 and beyond, Simba Chips workers engaged in spontaneous strikes to protest against low wages and their conditions of subordination. To demonstrate their frustration with the labour contracting system, over 300 Simba Chips workers left their jobs to attend a conciliation hearing at the CCMA in Benoni, South Africa, on 13 September 2017. The militant protesters, mostly comprising women, spontaneously stopped work at the Isando factory to attend the hearing. They demanded that the long and drawn-out process by the labour commissioners be resolved in favour of their equalization and regularization as employees. The crowd forced the commissioners from their rooms as nervous Simba lawyers requested a postponement of the hearing.[35]

According to CWAO newspaper *The New Worker*:

> On returning to the factory later in the day, the workers found their line managers packing chips in a desperate attempt to meet their production targets. This confirmed what worker leader Nandi Grobler said in a general meeting just days before the event: 'We are the most important people and management should bow before us when they walk past. They must lie down like the Venda people. Because we are important, we do the job for them. Say all of us don't go to Simba today, there will be no money for them!'[36]

In response to the workers who had attended the CCMA hearing, Simba Chips sent written warnings to the 170 activist workers for walking off the job.[37]

It is notable that the Food and Allied Workers Union (FAWU) was the delegated representative of workers at the Simba Chips factory, but through the labour broker system non-union workers were recruited to all the positions. As a consequence, the capacity of FAWU to represent the workers was severely compromised. FAWU had presided as the union of record during the transition to the labour broker system, and was unsuccessful in organizing the workers employed at the factory.[38] In sharp contrast to FAWU, CWAO/SWF, which had emerged as the major force in mobilizing Simba Chips workers, was instrumental in mobilizing the workers who were contracted through labour brokers. Ironically, FAWU is the second-largest affiliate of the South African Federation of Trade Unions (SAFTU), the breakaway federation from COSATU, which is pledged to worker empowerment, militancy, and redistributive policies.[39] FAWU had waged a long strike against Simba in the summer of 2002 demanding higher wages and improved working conditions.[40] Subsequently, Simba had contracted out most of its workers.

Women have played a central role in the struggle for temporary service employees, and the struggle for regularization at Simba Chips helped build strong leadership. On Saturday 10 March 2018, 446 workers attended a SWF/CWAO meeting to commemorate International Women's Day and to protest against the informal status and poor conditions at Simba Chips and PepsiCo, which also contracted labourers in Argentina, where workers waged a major struggle against the labour broker system.[41]

As a consequence of the very poor wages, lack of job security, and oppressive conditions at Simba, TES workers employed at the expansive Isando plant near OR Tambo Airport began organizing for a strike against the company for alleged attempts to contravene labour laws by arbitrarily contracting them from a third-party temporary employer. CWAO claimed that Simba and PepsiCo South Africa colluded with labour broking company Adcorp Blu to evade the requirements of section 198 of the Labour Relations Act. This legislation stipulates that after a three-month period, a labour broker-employed worker must become a direct employee of the company, in this case Simba. Adcorp Blu defines its mission to use contracting to reduce labour costs as follows:

> When your Outsourcing partner sees the future before you do, they can help you craft an idyllic future. And when they embody your business's own personality, it becomes ever easier to co-create solutions: to accelerate productivity, ensure business continuity, and reduce costs. That's us. That's Adcorp Outsourcing.[42]

CWAO organizer Ronald Wesso explained that the Simba Chips workers' campaign rallied worker support against the labour brokerage scheme, which denied fundamental protections under South African labour law, leading workers to recognize their exploitation and engage in spontaneous industrial unrest leading up to a call to strike in April 2018:

> the labour-brokered workers want to put an end to the neoliberal approach adopted by almost all big companies, in which labour broking is used to undermine temporary workers and to treat workers as temporary while

they are doing permanent work. As a consequence, workers are denied living wages, fair treatment and the right to collective bargaining.[43]

The notice of the strike was sent to the CCMA on Monday, and the strike would start on Thursday 19 April 2018, with up to 600 workers expected to participate. According to a statement from CWAO and SWF, in response to workers' demands that their conditions of employment be restored, including their transport allowances, salaries, and roles, Simba's strategy was to delay the legal process as much as possible, to intimidate and victimize the workers in order to demobilize them, and to change the way production was managed in order to undermine the legal claims of the workers. The CWAO/SWF statement said that the strike formed part of a longer struggle at Simba. In addition to the failure to directly employ the workers, CWAO/SWF charged that the conditions at the packing plant in Isando were rife with sexual discrimination and harassment. The Simba workers' complaint stated:

Women are forced to work in the cold storage areas when they are pregnant and they are put on night shift all the time, which puts their safety at risk in the plant and during their travels between work and home.[44]

On 19 April, the SWF/CWAO organizing campaign achieved its most important goal when Simba Chips met the workers' demands to change their casual jobs into permanent ones, ending a long, drawn-out conflict over employment status.[45] SWF/CWAO's successful organizing campaign is all the more remarkable because the workers achieved their goals three months before the South African Constitution Court ruling ordered an end to the abuse of the TES programmes, meaning that all workers hired by third-party contractors would be required to be made permanent after three months of work. But in the meantime, NUMSA was engaged in its own struggles against the TES industry, being the major plaintiff in a key case against a major labour broker contracting workers for the multinational steel corporation ArcelorMittal.

South African Constitutional Court Ruling

NUMSA was the plaintiff in the legal case against the labour broker system at the South African Constitutional Court on 26 July 2018 in a decision affirming the rights of labour broker workers against the TES industry.[46]

In the case, the Constitutional Court ruled in favour of NUMSA that workers earning R205,000 (approximately US$11,300) per year or less who are contracted through a labour broker to a client firm for more than three months become employees of the firm. The court ruled that they should be: 'employed on the same terms and conditions of similar employees, with the same employment benefits, the same prospect of internal growth and the same job security'.[47] After three months, the labour broker is no longer the employer of the worker.

In the court case between NUMSA and Assign Services (Pty) Limited, a labour broker, the court ruled that marginal workers are deemed to be employees of the temporary service employer only for three months, and that these same vulnerable workers must become employees of the broker's client after the completion of three months.

In South Africa, the Left looks to NUMSA as the union which will transform the turgid labour movement into a mobilizing force for change and militancy.[48] NUMSA has demonstrated its resolve by opposing the ANC and the Tripartite Alliance, leading to its expulsion from COSATU in 2014. NUMSA leaders recognize that it holds a crucial position in tangibly upholding the principles of the Freedom Charter by building a socialist, anti-imperialist bloc. The union's leadership understands that achieving a multiracial socialist South Africa requires strong bonds with community social movements and the establishment of a political party to challenge the dominant power. Upon NUMSA's expulsion, it called for the building of a United Front and a socialist political party to expropriate and nationalise national resources, redistribute land, and challenge the South African power structure controlled by the ANC. In this way, NUMSA would have to form a Tripartite Alliance of a party, social movement, and militant union that would contend for political power.

Thus, while NUMSA as a trade union emerged as the militant union force aligned with Left forces in opposition to the ANC, SACP, and COSATU, it also needed to build a unified national coalition to challenge neoliberal capitalism. The transformation could not emerge immediately in 2014, as the process of creating a union federation, social movement, and socialist party takes time and requires significant internal and external struggles. Consequently, NUMSA has fitfully built an opposition by immediately forming a coalition with the United Front (UF), a coalition of social movements throughout South Africa established by SAFTU in 2017 as a Left federation of unions, and the main force in building the Socialist Revolutionary Workers Party (SRWP) as an independent force in 2019. These efforts can easily be belittled and disparaged as too little too late, but NUMSA must be given credit for taking these initial steps. Establishing a viable socialist political party to challenge the ANC and other forces will take many years, and its viability must be assessed on a long-term basis, rather than on short-term electoral results.

To gain popular support as a reliable force for change, NUMSA has engaged in political struggles throughout the country, extending its organizing beyond its core manufacturing sector and devoting resources to building labour support within communities, waging legal campaigns, and supporting and leading worker mobilizations and strikes. Even though NUMSA has opponents on the Left, it has become the key social organizational force in defending the South African working class, including unorganized and non-union workers. Though CWAO/SWF contend that established unions have failed to mobilize informal workers, NUMSA has replaced COSATU as the main trade union force in opposition to the labour brokerage system.[49] NUMSA has successfully organized workers beyond the metals industry and manufacturing sector, extending its reach to other industries. While NUMSA, the United Front, SAFTU, and the SRWP advocate principles of socialism and anti-imperialism, they must secure the support of the broader black South African working class to coalesce as a major force to viably challenge the ANC and the current capitalist state.

Background: NUMSA, Left Union Challenge to Conformist Unions, 2013–present

By the early 2010s, most South African workers believed that COSATU was not advancing the needs and demands of labour in South Africa and that the Tripartite Alliance with the ANC and SACP was a failure. Most felt that COSATU, the major labour federation of South Africa, formed part of a capitalist state that did not espouse working-class rights, but rather advanced the South African capitalist status quo. The Tripartite Alliance, which led the government, did not keep promises to redistribute wealth from the minority white population to the black majority. The tripartite government leadership was permitted to administer government-owned enterprises, but left the white South African capitalist class, and whites in general, alone; meanwhile, its leaders were gaining access to economic resources in exchange for maintaining the inequitable system. The strategic mineral sector was dominated by a comprador bourgeoisie which profited from its exclusive connections to finance capital and the dominant global supply chains in the mineral industry. The South African state did not nationalize this crucial sector, preferring to retain the status quo, which primarily maintained wealth and profits in the hands of a white comprador class, multinational mining firms, and financiers. In the period since the end of apartheid, a thin layer of black South African elites gained leadership positions in government, was awarded lucrative contracts for government projects, and secured private control over state-owned enterprises. Government bureaucrats with networks in the interstices of the South African state personally benefited economically from securing government-controlled assets and enterprises. This practice became known as 'state capture', whereby even the public pretence of developing society for the benefit of the black South African majority had ceased to exist.[50]

COSATU and its affiliate unions generated massive wealth for trade union leaders in these key sectors, and lost the vibrant militancy it had earned in the apartheid era. Cyril Ramaphosa, president of South Africa, was formerly the general secretary of the National Union of Mineworkers. He left to become a member of the board of trustees of the foreign-dominated mining conglomerate Lonmin, and presided over the Marikana Massacre on 16 August 2012.[51] Thus, the stagnation of economic growth and the growing inequality and lack of opportunity created an image of a disengaged black South African leadership. Unlike ostensibly developing states, South Africa primarily transformed into an extractive society directed at profiting its dominant white capitalists and those blacks who were part of the governing leadership.

The black South African majority was excluded from this calculus, and was deeply conscious that economic apartheid had deepened inequality, poverty, and a common consensus. Unlike socialist projects in the twentieth century, South Africa lacked a moral pretext as a nation serving a common purpose. It was a charade that persisted as a consequence of its break with formal apartheid. The abject disregard for poverty and social dislocation has created a sense of frustration and cynicism among South Africa's population against the black elite.

The Marikana Massacre

Marikana represented the major break in the post-apartheid era.[52] Low wages and poor conditions in the platinum mining industry, which was the major source of foreign exchange earnings, had expanded in the 2000s and 2010s as unionized mineworker salaries had stagnated. Most workers in the mining sector did not consider the NUM an authentic representative of their interests. Collective bargaining did not produce wage growth, but stagnation and decline as mining conglomerate profits rose steeply thanks to the growth in the value of platinum. Workers in turn organized themselves in opposition to the union, demanding significant wage increases from approximately US\$500 to US\$900 a month. In the minefields of the Northwest and Limpopo, the Amalgamated Mining and Construction Union emerged as a counterforce against the NUM, led by its charismatic leader, Joseph Muthunjwa. Yet the mineworking movement had already become a social force with a rank and file leadership which sought both wage gains and transformation of South African society.[53] The discontent expanded, and wildcat strikes emerged on a regular basis in the mining fields, as well as competition for members between the NUM and AMCU from around 2010. This culminated on 16 August 2012 with the Marikana Massacre, when 34 workers congregating at two locations on a hillock (*koppie*) in Marikana were deliberately shot dead by South African Police on orders from the Tripartite ANC-SACP-COSATU government, working in consort with Lonmin, the mining conglomerate. Marikana became the largest massacre of protesting black South Africans since the gunning down of about 200 students protesting against inferior education policies in Soweto on 16 June 1976, a youth movement that spread throughout South Africa.[54]

NUMSA, whose presence was primarily in the urban region among manufacturing workers, viewed the massacre as a concrete example of the rapacious South African state. A member of the COSATU labour federation, NUMSA held a congress in December 2013 at which it broke with the ANC ruling government and called for the creation of a revolutionary party to unify South Africa's working class in challenging the capitalist state by remaining faithful to the demands of the anti-apartheid movement. NUMSA opposed cosmetic and unimplemented policies to ameliorate the black working class (e.g. GEAR), instead committing itself to social transformation, nationalization of the mining industry, redistribution and collectivization of lands, and opposition to the economic imperialism which pillaged Southern Africa's natural resources. Following its break with the ANC and the Tripartite Alliance, NUMSA was expelled from COSATU on 8 November 2014.[55]

NUMSA's expulsion followed its decision to oppose the ANC in the 2014 General Election.[56] COSATU General Secretary Zwelinzima Vavi called for a special national congress, but Irvin Jim, General Secretary of NUMSA, did not back down from the decision to end support for the ANC and Tripartite Alliance. HCOSATU president S'dumo Dlamini refused to call a special national congress. Jim told the meeting:

> NUMSA emerges as the militant union force aligned with left forces in opposition to Tripartite Alliance: ANC, SACP, and COSATU. The split reflects not only an ideological divergence but programmatic differences among SA trade unions. Key question: do unions mobilize SA's working class?[57]

Jim said that NUMSA would play a leading role in forming a 'revolutionary socialist organ of the working class'. Speaking at the December 2013 NUMSA General Congress, he continued:

> While knowledge and wealth are socially created by billions of human beings, ownership is private and individual, and concentrated in a tiny minority. [...] *We can end the exploitation of one by another. We can and must work towards a society in which there are no classes among us!*[58]

NUMSA AND THE FORMATION OF THE UNITED FRONT, SAFTU, AND SRWP, 2014–20

The split in the labour movement had clarified the necessity to establish an alternative union-movement-political formation to counter South Africa's neoliberal system that had failed to lift the black majority. Irvin Jim of NUMSA pondered the prospects for the creation of an alternative left front to the Tripartite Alliance:

> We at Numsa think all this is possible. Which is why we resolved to form a United Front last year in December, to begin the tough journey of uniting

all South Africans, of all races, male and female, from all walks of life but especially the working class and their communities, into a United Front to resist, to fight, and to defeat the plague of our system of private greed which imprisons us all.[59]

In addition, in 2014, NUMSA called for the formation of a new party to challenge the ANC in South African elections, a task which would take five years.[60] The union also committed itself to building ties to peasant workers in rural regions, and to supporting community unionism. According to Jim:

We of Numsa invite all of us to go out to all the corners of our country, to the remotest rural most dwellings, in our slums, in our townships, in our suburbs, to loudly proclaim and shout at the top of our voices that the time has come to reclaim our humanity, to restore dignity to all the oppressed, to give back their freedom to the exploited, to return the Earth to all its peoples, to rebuild our country into the paradise it can become![61]

In building a mass organization, the NUMSA leadership envisioned establishing strong social ties to existing community organizations throughout South Africa, which the union set in motion even before its expulsion in 1994. The United Front was founded in December 2014 following a summit of 350 delegates from trade unions, social movements, civics, women's organizations, student and youth associations, and other membership-based organizations of the mass popular anti-capitalist associations. It officially launched in April, 2015:[62]

We then resolved that NUMSA was going to lead the establishment of a *new United Front*, whose task would be to coordinate struggles in the workplace and in communities, in a way similar to the UDF [United Democratic Front] of the 1980s.

The task of this Front will be *to fight for the implementation of the Freedom Charter and to be an organisational weapon against neoliberal capitalist policies such as the NDP*.[63]

Jim emphasized that the United Front was not a political party, but a mass organization which would represent the aspirations of the broader working class of South Africa:

Clearly, the United Front is not a political party – it is simply an *orga-nizational weapon against neoliberal policies and for the demand for the radical implementation of the Freedom Charter.* The fundamental purpose of the United Front is to *coordinate struggles in the workplace and in com-munities.* [...] In our Resolutions, we clearly stated that the United Front will be an organization similar to the United Democratic Front (UDF) [...]. We repeat: *the United Front is not a political party! It is a democratic umbrella coordinating structure of the shopfloor and community struggles to resist neoliberalism and to fight for the radical implementation of the Freedom Charter.*[64]

Work and Campaigns of the United Front

As a broad democratic fund, the United Front organizers encouraged trade unions, community organizations, and social groups throughout South Africa to work together and join the coalition. As a democratic organiza-tion, the United Front has sought to build a broad organization to inject new ideas and amend the protocols established in December 2019. By doing so, Jim said, 'we all retain the right to contribute new ideas, to persuade one another to amend the protocols, and to advance the cause of creating a truly vibrant, united, democratic and effective United Front!'[65] The formation of the United Front has proven successful in mobilizing disparate work-ing-class organizations operating throughout South Africa to advance specific struggles for social rights, and to inspire a broader alliance on a nationwide, regional, and community level. The UF would fulfil the mission of the United Democratic Front, the social movement which disbanded after the end of apartheid. According to Zanoxolo Wayile, coordinator of the UF: 'we wanted to do the same as the UDF in the 1980s, through dealing with political and ideological discontent and building solidarity with broader worker and consumer struggles'. He continued that the UF would support jobs programmes for the youth, who were suffering from 70 per cent unem-ployment. The Left is fragmented in South Africa. People find themselves isolated and alone. They take destiny in their own hands. The United Front would serve as a civic movement unifying youth with struggles throughout South Africa.[66]

Formation of the South African Federation of Trade Unions

Plans to form SAFTU had been introduced in April 2016, and on 21 April 2017, precisely three years after the formation of the United Front, the Federation was formed by NUMSA and 20 union affiliates comprising 800,000–1 million members, led by NUMSA with 338,000 members and FAWU with 120,000 members. It was intended to represent trade unions and their members seeking a labour movement dedicated to the principles of socialism.[67] The creation of this major trade union federation in April 2017, led by the socialist Zwelinzima Vavi, former general secretary of COSATU, heightened the challenge to the established trade union movement and the Tripartite Alliance:[68]

> The Workers Summit and its call for concrete steps to be taken towards the launch of a new, militant, independent trade union federation, laid the basis for a massive growth in popularity of the moves towards workers' unity. 1500 trade union representatives, representing 52 unions attended the Summit. In addition 22 civil society organisations attended as observers. The Workers Summit agreed on the principles listed below.[69]

As we shall see, SAFTU joined NUMSA in a legal campaign to end the labour brokerage system, which has severely undermined the wages and job security of workers and the credibility of the South African trade union movement. SAFTU has supported NUMSA in its major organizing campaigns before and after the Constitutional Court ruling which banned labour broker control over informal contract workers after three months and clarified that low-wage temporary service workers must be regularized.

Constitutional Court Ruling against Labour Brokers

In July 2017, the CCMA had already ruled that labour brokers were operating illegally in South Africa and imposing severe economic strain on the poor. Despite the criticism of CWAO/SWF, NUMSA has been at the forefront of opposing the labour broker system in the courts and at workplaces. On 18 July, NUMSA General Secretary Irvin Jim asserted:

NUMSA is proud we took up this cause and we won. After three months, all workers will be supposed to be made permanent. We are going to mobilize our members, and all workers are going to be made permanent. We are going to organize non-union workers. All workers must be made permanent.[70]

On 26 July 2018, upon the historic judgment by the Constitutional Court banning the use of temporary service workers after three months, SAFTU spokesman Patrick Craven immediately issued a statement publicizing the significance of the ruling and warning of the importance that labour brokers and third-party employers comply and hire contract workers upon completion of a three-month period of employment.[71] However, the ruling would not prevent unscrupulous employers firing all temporary workers and replacing them with other temporary workers or hiring even more exploited trainee workers. Thus, enforcement was a crucial element of the struggle to rid South Africa of the entrenched labour broker system, as well as to prevent employers from violating the spirit of the new law. Patrick Craven of SAFTU hailed the ruling in no uncertain terms:

The Court has dealt a deadly blow against labour brokers and is the biggest victory for workers in recent times. The federation congratulates its affiliate NUMSA on the successful conclusion of its long court battle against labour brokers. [...] SAFTU has consistently held that employers have been using labour brokers to avoid having to comply with laws which safeguard workers' rights and minimum conditions of employment. It has led to a form of human trafficking under which labour brokers hire out workers to their client companies, with no job security, lower wages and worse conditions.[72]

SAFTU, in support of the decision supporting NUMSA, forewarned that labour brokers remained a threat to the South African working class as they would continue to operate as suppliers of low-wage labourers, noting the statement of an attorney for Assign Services that labour brokers:

would continue to perform other functions in terms of the contract of employment and income tax law, among other legislation. No matter what this court rules, the labour brokers are not falling out of the picture completely as the unions have said.[73]

As such, SAFTU stressed that trade unions had to remain attentive to efforts by labour brokers to evade the law by the 'back door', thereby unmistakeably revealing its steadfast support for NUMSA, FAWU, and all constituent unions in the federation.[74] Indeed, NUMSA was to face a major confrontation with labour brokers after the Constitutional Court ruling.

CASE STUDY: NUMSA CHALLENGES LABOUR BROKERS AT STEEL CONGLOMERATE ARCELORMITTAL

SAFTU certainly outflanked COSATU in the Constitutional Court ruling, as NUMSA secured a crucial victory. But the federation and union had to demonstrate a commitment to directly challenging employers who dodged the terms of the judgment and continued to employ labour brokers. Straight away, NUMSA would have to mobilize workers at the multinational steel conglomerate ArcelorMittal, where workers continued to be employed on a temporary basis.

NUMSA has a long-term commitment to mobilizing contract workers that goes back to 2006. On that occasion, it challenged labour brokers after about 1,700 Goodyear employees in Port Elizabeth waged a legal strike as the company refused to employ 300 temporary workers for a period of five years. According to NUMSA: 'These temporary workers have suffered repression from the labour broker – Kelly Temporary Staffing Agency – which allegedly denied them medical aid and provident fund benefits for five years.' NUMSA filed a notice to strike after Goodyear rejected the union's demand for the tyre maker to permanently employ the temporary workers.[75] At the same plant, NUMSA also charged Goodyear with misusing workers who were hired as interns at the plant for months without issuing employment contracts. According to a NUMSA spokesman:

These workers were sourced from unemployed people, but have not been granted work contracts since September 2005 [...]. NUMSA is also miffed at the treatment of these learners because they were forced to work normal shifts like full time employees and worked overtime during weekends for meagre wages of R2,000 a month.[76]

Thus, even though CWAO/SWF is correct to reproach most established unions for failing to enforce employment law, NUMSA has had an established record of opposing labour brokers and violations of employment through direct action and using the South African CCMA and Constitutional Courts.

NUMSA Mobilization at ArcelorMittal

Even before the Constitutional Court had decided that the indefinite labour contracting system had to end, NUMSA was engaged in mobilizing workers to challenge the multinational steel producer ArcelorMittal South Africa (AMSA) for abuse of the labour broker system, and to establish a higher wage scale that would compel the manufacturer to employ the workers on equal terms with all other workers.[77]

AMSA has a long and sustained record of contracting its services from labour brokers in South Africa. Following the decision by the Constitutional Court, NUMSA and workers escalated their effort to regularize all workers through mobilization and direct action in 2018 and 2019. Headquartered in Luxembourg, ArcelorMittal formed in 2006 through a merger of the French conglomerate Arcelor with Indian producer Mittal. In doing so, it became the world's largest steel producer, with operations in 20 countries, supplying the automotive, construction, household appliances, and packaging industries. Owned by Lakshmi Mittal of India, the multinational is controlled by a European and North American board of directors.[78]

In July 2018, NUMSA demanded that AMSA end the use of all labour brokers at its facilities in South Africa, while demanding an 11 per cent wage increase across the board, an increase in medical contributions, and a 1 per cent increase in provident fund contributions for all workers. The union called on AMSA to insource all workers employed via labour brokers: Excal, Scholts Transport, Workforce, and Real Tree Trading.[79]

In 2019, NUMSA charged AMSA with continuing to utilize a labour broker, Real Tree Trading, which contracted 1,000 NUMSA workers. According to AMSA, Real Tree was not a labour broker, but a 'service provider' offering ancillary staffing, and therefore not subject to the 2018 Constitutional Court ruling.[80] Service providers employed by Real Tree were paid half as much as AMSA workers.[81] NUMSA countered AMSA's position, asserting: 'Our members (employed by the contractors) work side by side with workers directly employed by ArcelorMittal who receive much higher pay and benefits. This kind of needless exploitation is unacceptable.'[82] NUMSA threatened a strike at AMSA's steel operations in Vanderbijlpark, an industrial centre approximately 70 kilometres (40 miles) southwest of Johannesburg, if the company did not comply with the ruling and regularize the workers. Mokete Makoko, NUMSA Regional Secretary for Sedibeng District in Gauteng, said:

> Our key demand is that ArcelorMittal must permanently employ all workers presently employed by the contractors who render their services to ArcelorMittal. The offer of employment must be on the same conditions of service and hold the same benefits as are applicable to employees of ArcelorMittal.[83]

AMSA countered NUMSA's demand for equal pay for all workers with an offer of 7.5 per cent for the lowest-paid workers, 6.5 per cent for the highest-paid workers, and a 6.5 per cent increase in the company's contribution to medical aid. NUMSA rejected AMSA's offer, saying that it would not 'make an impact on [workers'] lives', leaving the union with no choice but to embark on a strike. On 14 March, two days after the union called for the strike, *New Frame* reported that 'workers barricaded the east gate entrance to the company'.[84] The striking workers set up a picket, chanting '*Bophilo ba rona bo cheap*' ('Our lives are cheap').[85] The informal workers employed at the plant protested that AMSA and its labour brokers forced them to work under dangerous conditions, endangering their lives and causing some workers to be seriously injured. To counter the striking workers at Vanderbijlpark, AMSA called upon the South African Police Service (SAPS) to violently disperse protesting workers. One day later, SAPS arrested ten striking NUMSA workers, and the union charged SAPS with colluding with Real Tree and AMSA. In a statement the following day, NUMSA spokesperson Phakamile Hlubi-Majola announced:

> We condemn the South African Police Services and the management of ArcelorMittal for subverting workers' rights. On Friday the SAPS, acting on instructions from management at [AMSA], arrested ten of our members who were peacefully picketing near the offices of the company. They falsely claimed that they had violated the picketing rules. [...] We

view this as a gross abuse of power and harassment by the SAPS and the management of ArcelorMittal.[86]

In early April 2019, AMSA maintained its staunch position of refusing to insource all workers, but conceded to a programme to directly employ labour contractor workers viewed as having 'critical skills' over a period of three years.

Community Support for Striking AMSA Workers

In the following days and weeks, the striking workers were joined by community residents from Boipatong, a township nearby the Vanderbijlpark facility, in support of their strike against AMSA and Real Tree Trading. Community residents also faced harassment and violence from SAPS, which dispersed protesters with rubber bullets, leading to injuries and the hospitalization of a strike supporter.[87] In addition to supporting the striking workers, community residents protested against the three-week absence of electricity in the township. AMSA staunchly refused to relent to NUMSA and worker demands to insource all workers at the company, claiming that regularizing all workers would result in retrenchments and a reduction of the workforce. The union and strikers then turned to the Indian government to persuade ArcelorMittal to relent and comply with the law. On April 24, striking workers set up a picket in front of the Indian High Commission to protest against the sustained intransigence of the Indian-owned company.[88]

The strike continued into late May before some of the workers returned to work. But AMSA was on notice that it had to insource all workers at its four steel complexes, employing 8,379 labourers across the country. In addition, even after the Constitutional Court ruling, in 2019 the conglomerate stated that it employed '2,832 full-time equivalent jobs' through contractors.[89] Though the company was compelled to insource workers, it then followed through with its threat to retrench 1,000–2,000 workers in South Africa. In 2019, AMSA announced plans for a major retrenchment of workers.[90] But the company had already reduced the number of directly employed workers from 8,913 in 2017 to 8,379 in 2019.[91] In October 2019, AMSA announced a plan to retrench 1,000 workers throughout the country and begin closing the Saldanha Works in the Western Cape to reduce costs and increase profitability. The threat to close the Saldanha plant forced NUMSA into negotiations with AMSA and the government to improve the profit-ability of the multinational steel giant in order to preserve jobs in South Africa. NUMSA was called upon to work 'towards a viable solution', which would include more than US$10.5 million in productivity concessions from the union. The South African government would also guarantee an additional US$15 million in commitments to AMSA in return for suspending the retrenchment.[92]

The significance of the court ruling is reaffirmed by Ronald Wesso of the CWAO, who claims that, despite the growth in direct employment and permanent jobs, the conversion of temporary to permanent positions had been limited over the 15 months following the court order in July 2018.[93] Wesso estimates that:

> since this right came into effect, only about 12,000 workers got permanent jobs. But there are more than a million labour-brokered workers in the country. If you add in the fixed-term contract workers, we are talking about 40% of the workforce, five million workers who were supposed to get permanent jobs.[94]

As a result of South Africa's dependence on foreign MNCs, as we have seen in the case of Sumitomo in the Philippines in Chapter 4, multinationals like ArcelorMittal hold the power to discipline global South states, and their working classes who seek to improve the conditions of workers, by selling off stakes, retrenching, closing facilities, and withdrawing investments. To preserve strategic industries that are integrated into the global supply chain, the government and union had to concede to the demands of the MNC. In this way, the long struggle of workers and union to end labour broking in South Africa was successful in changing the neoliberal policies of the government, but multinational capital extracted gains by compelling states and workers to ensure the expansion of profits and capital accumulation.

Socialist Revolutionary Workers Party

The formation of a workers' party in South Africa by the breakaway movement led by NUMSA has been a major pillar of building a socialist opposition to the neoliberal Tripartite Alliance. A workers' party would be crucial in building a socialist and democratic opposition that would achieve the goals set forth by the Freedom Charter to nationalize industry and to oppose foreign imperialism. This sentiment is clearly stated by Irvin Jim, who views the past efforts as no more than rhetoric: 'Workers' party needed to advance the working class – we need the party to change the power relations in this country and ensure that the Freedom Charter is pursued.'[95] Though envisioned in 2014, the Socialist Revolutionary Workers Party was only officially formed in March 2019, just two months before the South African General Election on 8 May 2019. Building the SRWP is a long-term process, and its progress can only be assessed over a decade or more. In the May 2019, elections, the party garnered only a small fraction of the votes, yet it deepened its connection with the masses and the unions, participating in mass actions and mobilizing the working class in black South African settlements and townships. One can envisage that a highly committed and popular party linked to the union movement would have significant influence in helping to transform the country and implement multiracial democracy, nationalization of resources, and land redistribution.

CONCLUSION: WORKER SPONTANEITY, LABOUR
ORGANIZATION, AND REVOLUTIONARY SUBJECTIVITY

The expulsion from COSATU in 2014 allowed NUMSA to become the major advocate for eliminating the labour broker system. Though the union's own enforcement of the insourcing of all workers required greater monitoring, politically, the union was primarily responsible for challenging TES companies and established corporations. In doing so, it supported worker mobilizations and strikes for equal wages and permanent positions. Acknowledging the requirement for internal efforts at neutralizing labour brokers and major corporation efforts to circumvent the system among its own ranks, NUMSA was prepared to take on the system. Pushed by CWAO/ SWF as a critical autonomous opposition force, NUMSA made ending the labour broker system a priority. Expulsion from COSATU in 2014 was a clarion call for NUMSA to strictly enforce contracts for its members. Subsequently, the union has deepened its role as the major force for empowering the South African black working class. By way of response, managers are seeking to extend neoliberal policies, one of which entails NUMSA being forced into a defensive position to block the erosion of worker rights.

CWAO/SWF had become the most prominent exponent of ending the labour broker system. It prodded NUMSA and other unions to end the abusive practice and to enforce their own contracts. Some of the workers organizing with CWAO/SWF were members of trade unions which had not vigorously opposed the system and were therefore identified by a growing number of informal workers as part of the systemic problem. Still, the limitations of the CWAO/SWF model have been exposed by the inability of the autonomous labour organization to bargain and enforce agreements with employers. They could only encourage and support workers in strikes and job actions, wage legal actions, and publicize the abusive brokerage system which had been ignored by many trade unions which had not forcefully resisted the latter's emergence and growth. To date, CWAO/SWF has retained an inspection system through thousands of workers who depend on the organization as a watchdog of employer abuses. Clearly, the majority of workers in the informal sector want to join unions and are highly supportive of a stronger labour movement. The majority of workers in South Africa's settlements lack job security, and many are employed on a temporary basis and then dispensed with when employers identify cheaper labourers, whether migrant labourers willing to work for a fraction of South African labourers' wages or youth who are engaged as trainees at even lower wages.

In the meantime, from 2014 to the present, NUMSA has established the organizational infrastructure as a force in defending the South African working class, including unorganized and non-union workers, by taking a leading role in establishing the United Front, SAFTU, and the SRWP. It remains uncertain if this competing Tripartite Alliance can achieve major gains to challenge the entrenched neoliberal capitalist system which safeguards MNCs and the white labour aristocracy. SAFTU represents a national federation of sectoral unions, with NUMSA at the helm and expanding to organize beyond its core metals industry and manufacturing sectors, branching out to all other industrial sectors of the economy.

Even though the UF/SAFTU/SRWP alliance has grown slowly, and frequently lacks organizational cohesion, the front represents a crucial alternative to the ANC/SACP/COSATU Tripartite Alliance, which has proven over again that it is a spent force which is unwilling to challenge the neoliberal system. Not unlike analogous Left forces around the world, the Tripartite Alliance, while maintaining political power, has lost any patina of legitimacy as a socialist and transformative movement. Political rhetoric for redistribution is inchoate and lacks any concrete form, appearing as no more than a documentary list of all its failures.

Do the UF, SAFTU, SRWP, and NUMSA have the capacity to transform South Africa? To be sure, a strong organization is necessary if South Africa is to become an egalitarian society. The broader populist Left, including adherents of the Economic Freedom Fighters political party, will surely need to join forces to form part of a transformational movement towards socialism. Militant and radical politics have gained appeal for the broader working class throughout the South African economy. But if the new alliance fails, NUMSA does not have the capacity to transform the power structure alone, except as a social movement and political party. The NUMSA leadership has long understood the necessity for a social movement and political organization to transform the neoliberal state and end the dominance of MNCs and foreign economic imperialists, as shown in the case studies of PepsiCo and ArcelorMittal.

While the dominant order is discredited, the new socialist force has been deliberate in forming a counter-hegemonic bloc to challenge the ANC. The formation of the SRWP as a vanguard party has completed the development of a popular front capable of challenging capital in labour struggles, but does not have the power to counter the Tripartite Alliance. It is necessary for the fledgling new socialist force to stay committed to the practical application of a socialist system. If successful, the SRWP and its allied social and workers' movement will have a social base which mobilizes the broader working class outside established organizations. This was not evident in the 2019 elections, but building the party will require nurturing and time.

6
Conclusion: Labour Struggles and Political Organization

An assessment of the economic and political state of workers in the world political economy of the 2020s is far more dismal than it has been in over a century. The vast majority of the global working class, situated in the global South, are not permanent labourers, but remain tied to the rural and informal sectors of the economies. Labour conditions are marked by low wages, lack of job security, oppressive conditions, and hazardous and toxic workplaces. Though living standards of the working class in the global North have declined over the last 25 years, they are incomparably better off than those of far more workers in the global South, where income does not provide for the basic necessities. Over the same period, as Third World workers are increasingly drawn into the capitalist economy, workers have faced systemic oppression, poverty, and precarity.

As sociologist Jan Breman and historian Marcel van der Linden write:

The real norm or standard in global capitalism is insecurity, informality or precariousness, and the Standard Employment Relationship is an historical phenomenon which had a deep impact in a limited part of the world for a relatively short period of time. If, as we argue, the 'Rest' is not now becoming like the 'West', but the other way round, then the 'traditional' forms of collective action that have developed in the North Atlantic region during the last two centuries are gradually losing much of their impact. New forms of collective action are emerging, though these are often still at an embryonic stage. It is, therefore, high time to rethink the concept of the working class and the ways in which it can further its interests.[1]

In this volume's case studies of steelworkers producing kitchen and dining utensils in India, banana packing house workers in the Philippines, and

183

food service and steelworkers in South Africa, we have found the ubiquitous presence of labour conflict driven by workers' aspirations to improve wages and working conditions. Direct action by labour against capital has brought provisional, nebulous, and furtive gains which were inevitably withdrawn by employers in a range of industries. In each case, most workers understand that each hard-fought win will likely not be the last as employers in the steel, banana, and packaging industries of the Third World continuously seek to expand surplus labour by cutting labour costs and reducing job security. On an organizational level, this book has shown that workers are far more likely to act collectively with the support of a committed and militant labour union, backed by community social organizations and Left political forces. In response, workers are in a better position to improve and sustain their working and living conditions. In addition, the consolidation of labour union social power potentially sets the stage for the development of strong, transformative political movements wedded to establishing socialist states which are not dependent on the impulses of global capitalists in the First World.

Legal and organizational advances in wages, job security, and working conditions within the neoliberal global economy are typically only temporary as capital and multinational corporations can ineluctably extract surplus value by new means and forms. Thus, if workers succeed in organizing to increase wages and regularize informal workers, or changing the law, capital will demand concessions by threatening to retrench workers, close operations, or withdraw completely from investing. In this context, working-class organizations which are unmistakably committed to immediate and long-term revolutionary transformation are necessary in shifting the exploitative and repressive material subjectivity of workers. In each case, militant labour unions have emerged to advance the interests of oppressed informal and rural labourers so they will fight again to defend tenuous gains and build a stronger front for social transformation. Thus, in each instance, the workers' subjective conditions of weakness are converted into vigour.

On a systemic level, workers in the global South must defeat the neoliberal capitalist order to achieve a long-lasting victory over multinational capitalist firms that are dominated by global commodity supply networks benefiting people in the global North. Yet the implications of each of the three case studies is that it is far more likely that the working classes may achieve long-term gains through struggles in a single country rather than across states. Thus, the labour and working-class struggles in India, the Philippines, and South Africa are distinct and advance through the development of counter-hegemonic forces in each country. As such, while globalization has created growing integration of the world economy through the harmonization of oppressive conditions, capital takes advantage of the political, social, economic, and legal differences among a range of states as a means to extract greater profits. In the global South, conditions are far less standardized than in Western Europe and advanced economies of the global North. In this way, there is a propensity for states to compete among one another for foreign direct investment. Those states which offer products at the lowest possible cost will predictably gain greater foreign investments and market share for their goods and services.

RURAL AND INFORMAL SECTOR

A major contention of this book is that the rural and informal sector is the key driver of economies in most states of the global South, encompassing the vast majority of the world's population. The majority of global demographers and economists at the United Nations, the World Bank, and other multilateral economic organizations view the world as urbanizing, while neglecting the fact that the rural regions have also expanded dramatically over the last 50 years.[2] Moreover, urban areas are often rural zones that are engulfed by growing metropolitan areas, lacking basic services: running water, electricity, sanitation, and roads. Elsewhere in the global South, rural workers engage in circular migration to urban areas, returning home when their work is complete. As Breman shows, footloose labour is a predominant characteristic of workers in South Asia, where workers have no stable employment, but are employed in a range of occupations throughout the year. This form of precarious labour is unique to the global South.[3] Thus, the unstable nature of labour in the global South has implications for working-class organizing because workers are employed in a multiplicity of jobs and zones in the urban–rural frontier. As Karen Rignall and Mona Atia assert, capital mobility has blurred the boundaries between rural and urban zones:

How then do we grapple with these rapidly changing geographies of rural zones? Mobile, speculative capital has transformed rural spaces as sites for the creation of value by commodifying rural landscapes, restructuring economic and social life, and exacerbating long-standing inequalities. Poverty scholars can challenge the dominant discursive erasure of difference (especially between the urban and rural) endemic to poverty measurement by describing these processes in relational terms and attending to the lived realities of the poor. This entails viewing the people dispossessed by new regimes of accumulation as active agents embedded in inferior positions of power and particular historical conditions that limit their mobility while recognizing the globalized referents for these regimes of accumulation.[4]

Capitalist development in highly populated zones on the fringes of urban regions relies on a large rural proletariat which works in major industries of the economy. As the very nature of production in the informal and rural sectors of the economies of the global South is dominated by extraction, subjugation, and exploitation of labour, in the post-colonial era the imperialist domination has expanded even further. In effect, global capitalism has expanded the system of dependence on markets in the global North under highly unfavourable terms. Informal and rural labour in the South must conform to the principles of neoliberal capitalism, where the accumulation of profits is a prerequisite for investment in projects which exploit labour, despoil the environment, and transfer value from the global South to the global North.

Under these highly unfavourable conditions for the global South, it is necessary to build working-class organizations on a state and regional level that are capable of supporting labour campaigns to challenge capitalist oppression and educate and inculcate the working class for a socialist future. Thereby, workers can envision a new revolutionary subjectivity of a socialist society free of alienated labour. To varying degrees, the workers' movements in India, the Philippines, and South Africa have established the organizational basis to build a sustainable movement: labour organization, popular social fronts, and workers' parties, which are fundamental in challenging dominant capitalist norms and practices to concretely establish such a socialist future. Though each organizational force is in an incipient state of formation, we can see the basis of what a new movement must look like to wrest power from multinational corporations and local capitalists. Gramsci's refrain that 'The crisis consists precisely in the fact that the old is dying and the new cannot be born; in this interregnum a great variety of morbid symptoms appear'[5] can now be amended to include that we can in fact see early phases of the development of a new force for transformation. This analysis does not envision a global socialist transformation, but budding organizational forces in each state where labour, social organizations, and Left parties advance in small spurts and congeal and grow into popular movements and fronts.

GLOBAL ASSESSMENT AND PERSPECTIVE

The case studies in Part II of this book focusing on workers in key economic sectors in India, the Philippines, and South Africa demonstrate the dominant pattern in global commodity supply chains: the reliance on informal labour for businesses to retain profitability at every stage of production. Documentary ethnographic research demonstrates that informal relations of production are not exclusively practised by small, undercapitalized firms producing primary commodities in the agricultural or mining sectors, but are prevalent in steel and intermediate production processes for wholesale firms in India as well as the final-stage production of consumer goods in the food packaging industry for final consumption in South Africa. In the global South, capitalists prey on informal labour markets to ensure lower labour costs, creating a new labour regime of precarity that is quite different from the global North. In the case of South Africa, Ben Scully writes that the existence of precarious labour erodes the standards of workers in formal employment:

> In South Africa, the rise of precarity does not seem to have driven sections of the working class apart to the same degree. Instead, precarious workers and the unemployed live their social and economic lives alongside many of the remaining formally employed workers. Their interdependence signals a material link between precarious workers and formal wage work. At the same time, formal workers' ties to their precarious family members likely make their economic situations less stable and secure than they seem if we look only at the workplace.[6]

The dominant perspective in research on global commodity supply chains across countries and regions is that firms have the highest profits the closer they are to final production of goods for consumption. But the research on three supply chains shows that workers do not benefit from proximity to consumption in the global South. Rather, dominant multinational firms exercise extensive control over each stage of production across a range of industries. The three case studies of labour–management conflict reveal that wages and working conditions are not related to their situational location to multinational firms nor to the stage of production in the commodity chains. Thus, Indian steelworkers in Wazirpur are engaged in all stages of stainless steel utensil fabrication, yet their wages and conditions remain onerous, whether they are engaged in the purification of steel in the hot-rolling or cold-rolling mills, the fabrication of utensils in the moulding plants, or the transport of products between each of these facilities.

THE REQUIREMENT FOR ORGANIZATION

Leadership is crucial in advancing the struggle for the working class and the oppressed, yet it is often a difficult and complicated task to win the workers and masses over to joining a principled movement of the masses. This book has demonstrated that the working class must include informal and rural workers, who are so often neglected by most trade unions yet remain a powerful force for social transformation. This position is clearly asserted by Lenin, who stresses the significance of rural (informal) workers in the revolutionary transformation to socialism and anti-imperialism.

By necessity, leading from below requires a detachment of the working class to assume the responsibility of carrying out the demands of the masses of peasants by participating in trade unions. This detachment must be drawn from the working classes and understand and reflect the revolutionary subjectivity of oppressed workers. Revolutionary subjectivity is an educational process in which workers produce an understanding of their conditions of oppression and the requisite path to social emancipation from the capitalist system. In this process, the detachment recognizes the immediate and long-term interests of oppressed classes, and comprehends the probability of surmounting the urgent challenges, along with understanding the aspirations of a class as a whole for liberation from the oppression of capitalism. The three case studies of India, the Philippines, and South Africa survey how working-class detachments operate in the context of similar contestations to address the pressing needs of workers and hold longer-term strategies for

transformation. Though each case study analyses organizations with dispro-
portionate power, they all are committed to the common goal of the present
demands and future goals, which in unity reflect the revolutionary subjectivity of the workers.

Lenin remarked on spontaneity and leadership:

> The spontaneous upsurge of the masses in Russia proceeded (and
> continues) with such rapidity that the young Social Democrats proved
> unprepared to meet these gigantic tasks. This unpreparedness is our
> common misfortune, the misfortune of all Russian Social-Democrats.
> The upsurge of the masses proceeded and spread with uninterrupted con-
> tinuity; it not only continued in the places where it began, but spread to
> new localities and to new strata of the population (under the influence
> of the working class movement, there was a renewed ferment among the
> student youth, among the intellectuals generally, and even among the
> peasantry). Revolutionaries, however, lagged behind this upsurge, both
> in their 'theories' and in their activity; they failed to establish a constant
> and continuous organisation capable of leading the whole movement.[7]

Leftists have endlessly pointed to the present and coming workers'
movement, but in the modern stage of neoliberal capitalism, these protests
and rebellions are uninterrupted and reflect both immediate and long-term
dissent against a system that has abandoned the pretence of bourgeois
democracy. Thus, it is insufficient to report on major strikes and political
movements protesting against states at a time when the evidence shows
protest movements forming and gaining strength. Indeed, while it is crucial
to recognize changes in the rate or potency of protests, protests and social
activism cannot be applied as a measure of political transformation. The significance of protests can only be measured through the presence and strength
of social organization which directs and conducts the working-class forces.
Thus, the significance of protests can only be correlated to the organization.
In this way, we can clearly see that most protests today are mobilizations
against state and capitalist power, and do not determine, indicate, nor even
reflect, the potency of the movement.

In the last 30 years, as the power of trade unions has diminished
worldwide, scholars have taken succour in the autonomy of spontaneous
worker insurgencies and a diminished organizational presence in these

struggles. As a consequence of the proliferation of autonomous work-ing-class organizations, the literature has tended to praise and advocate ephemeral organizations as the new form of class struggle. By some means, these fleeting organizations will have the capacity to seriously challenge the dominance of neoliberal capitalism and multinational corporations.

Much of the literature contrasts these new unions as more democratic rank and file forms than the trade unions which rose to power in the Fordist era of mass production and, over many years, have become bureaucratic organizations. The notion that workers will resist oppression is not a new development among contemporary workers, but has persisted throughout history. This book contends that concentrating attention on weak organi-zational forms is essential to comprehend the unfolding of contemporary labour conflict in a time of highly compromised and weak trade unions. Yet mobilization is not sufficient. These new forms of autonomous movements may indeed improve worker conditions, as in the case of the Casual Workers Advice Office in South Africa, but they are insufficient in challenging employers and building social movements capable of challenging powerful capitalist firms, no less building revolutionary working-class movements capable of challenging state power. To achieve lasting power, organization and political parties are crucial in developing a political movement.

How can an effective workers' organization be created and sustained? It is crucial to understand how an organization develops from initial workers' struggles based on material need, and on a strong and successful organiza-tion which is committed to building power for the working class beyond immediate economic necessity. Why should workers support an organiza-tion which is not rooted in material need, but based on building power? How does the organization build trust among workers who are not nec-essarily interested in building an organization on the needs of the broader working class?

This book has attempted to demonstrate that workers are always engaged in political opposition in response to oppression. Autonomous unions and workers' assemblies spring up continuously under capitalism. It is palpably clear that the working classes and rural peasant labourers in the global South are in motion today as they face neoliberal globalism and capitalist supply chains. Mass movements of workers are expanding dramatically in the contemporary period of neoliberal capitalism. The evidence of this can be seen in the numerous social protests that occur in the Global South on an increasing basis.

Workers often rise up and mobilize to defend and improve their wages and working conditions, yet this book shows that successful transformation requires organizational and political sustenance to survive and grow beyond protests into powerful movements.

Notes

Introduction: Forging a New Global Workers' Movement

1. See Beverly Silver, *Forces of Labor: Workers' Movements and Globalization Since 1870* (New York: Cambridge University Press, 2003), and Ronaldo Munck, *Rethinking Global Labour after Neoliberalism* (Newcastle, UK: Agenda Publishing, 2018).

Chapter 1   The Labour Atlas: The Southern Working Class Holding Up the World

1. Jan Breman, *Footloose Labour: Working in India's Informal Economy* (Cambridge, UK: Cambridge University Press, 1996).
2. Mike Davis, *Planet of Slums* (London: Verso, 2004).
3. World Bank, *Systems of Cities: Harnessing Urbanization for Growth and Poverty Alleviation* (Washington, DC: World Bank, 2009), http://documents.worldbank. org/curated/en/877591468163481401/Systems-of-cities-harnessing-urbaniza-tion-for-growth-and-poverty-alleviation, accessed 28 December 2019; United Nations: Department of Economic and Social Affairs, *Population Dynamics*, https://population.un.org/wup/, accessed 28 December 2019; David E. Bloom and Tarun Khanna, 'The Urban Revolution', *Finance and Development*, vol. 44, no. 3 (2007), pp. 9–14, www.imf.org/external/pubs/ft/fandd/2007/09/bloom. htm, accessed 31 December 2019.
4. See United Nations, *World Urban Prospects: The 2018 Revision* (New York: United Nations, 2019).
5. Arne L. Kalleberg and Steven P. Vallas (eds), *Precarious Work, Research in the Sociology of Work*, vol. 31 (Bingley, UK: Emerald Publishing, 2018); Guy Standing, *The Precariat: The New Dangerous Class* (New York: Bloomsbury, 2016).
6. Kim Moody, *On New Terrain: How Capital Is Reshaping the Battleground of Class War* (Chicago, IL: Haymarket Books, 2017).
7. Jason Hickel, *The Divide: Global Inequality from Conquest to Free Markets* (New York: W.W. Norton, 2018).
8. Ronaldo Munck, 'Workers of the World Unite (at Last)', *Great Transition Initiative*, April 2019, www.greattransition.org/publication/workers-of-the-world-unite, accessed 19 April 2019.

9. Standing, *The Precariat*; Arne L. Kalleberg, *Precarious Lives and Well-being in Rich Democracies* (Oxford, UK: Polity Press, 2018).

10. Marissa Brookes, *The New Politics of Transnational Labor: Why Some Alliances Succeed* (Ithaca, NY: Cornell University Press, 2019).

11. Approaches to stem the decline of the working class have been directed to persuade capital and corporations to allow workers' representation and a modicum of wage concessions to create labour peace or prevent work stoppages. In most cases, labour unions have failed to win these campaigns, but the campaigns all exchanged restrictions on working-class militancy for higher wages or improved working conditions. Even then, unions had trouble enforcing these agreements. But the very process of organizing campaigns to moderate the exploitation of capital cedes overall power to capital and the state. Eventually, all these recognition and bargaining campaigns have been overturned by management actions to whittle away at the gains. Nonetheless, the prescriptions for a renewal of labour are continuously propagated, and do not really tell us anything new about worker mobilization and working-class representation, but just reiterate the same old arguments. In the USA, see, for instance, the work of Andrew Stern, Dan Clawson, Jane McAlevey, Joel Rogers, Stewart Acuff, and countless others. In reality, these measures tell us nothing new, and more often obscure the structural obstacles to establishing improved conditions for workers. All these formulas were motivated by increasing union density as the principal goal, rather than improving the lives of the working class. As long as the union succeeded in gaining recognition and a collective bargaining agreement that would help fund its leadership, organizing campaigns was considered a success. No attention was paid to the conditions that ensued. Andrew Stern, former president of the Service Employees International Union, has subsequently sat on corporate boards and gone on to a career in business.

12. Recognizing the 20 years of failure to transform the calculus heavily weighted against workers, in the 2010s, some scholars lowered expectations in documenting what they viewed as transnational campaigns at UNI Global Union and elsewhere to mobilize highly vulnerable low-wage workers as the optimal solution. The new objective continued to view trade union representation as the optimal objective. See: Brookes, *The New Politics of Transnational Labor*; Jamie McCallum, *Global Unions, Local Power: The New Spirit of Transnational Labor Organizing* (Ithaca, NY: Cornell University Press, 2013).

13. Torkil Lauesen, *The Global Perspective: Reflections on Imperialism and Resistance* (Montreal, Canada: Kersplebedeb, 2018).

14. Zak Cope. *The Wealth of (Some) Nations: Imperialism and the Mechanics of Value Transfer* (London: Pluto Press, 2019).

15. Karl Marx, *Capital*, vol. I, trans. Ben Fowkes (London: Penguin Classics, 1990), pp. 874–5.

16. See United Nations, Department of Economic and Social Affairs, *World Urbanization Prospects, 2018 Revision* (New York: United Nations, 2019), https://

population.un.org/wup/, accessed 20 February 2020. This focuses on demographic population growth of major urban regions (cities over 300,000), projecting that while rural populations have grown in every era, the absolute numbers will moderate and slightly decline to just over 3 billion by 2050.

17. Jeffrey M. Paige, *Agrarian Revolution* (New York: Free Press, 1978).
18. Ibid., pp. 10–11.
19. Ibid., p. 19.
20. Karl Polanyi, *The Great Transformation* (New York: Farrar & Rinehart, 1944).
21. See: Ha-Joon Chang. *The East Asian Development Experience: The Miracle, the Crisis and the Future.* (London: Zed Books, 2007); James Cypher, *The Process of Economic Development*, 4th edn (New York: Routledge, 2014); Mark Weisbrot, *Failed: What the 'Experts' Got Wrong about the Global Economy* (New York: Oxford University Press, 2015).
22. Paige, *Agrarian Revolution*, pp. 10–11.
23. Utsa Patnaik, 'The Unacceptably High Cost of Free Trade', in Utsa Patnaik and Sam Moyo, *The Agrarian Question in the Neoliberal Era: Primitive Accumulation and the Peasantry* (Dar es Salaam, Tanzania: Pambazuka Press, 2011), pp. 34–46, p. 34.
24. Utsa Patnaik, 'Advanced Country Living Standards and Developing Country Lands', in Patnaik and Moyo, *The Agrarian Question in the Neoliberal Era*, pp. 14–19, pp. 15–17.

Chapter 2   Workers' Movements in the South: Inequality, Poverty, and Enduring Relevance of Rural Proletariat and Informal Sector Workers

1. See: Samir Amin, *Unequal Development: An Essay on the Social Formations of Peripheral Capitalism*, trans. Brian Pierce (New York: Monthly Review Press, 1976); L.S. Stavrianos, *Global Rift: The Third World Comes of Age* (New York: William Morrow, 1981).
2. Michael Hardt and Antonio Negri, *Multitude: War and Democracy in the Age of Empire* (New York: Penguin, 2004); John Holloway, *Change the World Without Taking Power* (London: Pluto, 2002); Immanuel Ness, *New Forms of Worker Organization: The Syndicalist and Autonomist Restoration of Class-struggle Unionism* (Oakland, CA: PM Press, 2014); Staughton Lynd, *Solidarity Unionism: Rebuilding the Union from Below*, 2nd edn (Oakland, CA: PM Press, 2015).
3. Stanley Aronowitz, *The Death and Life of American Labor* (New York: Verso, 2014); Steve Early, *The Civil Wars in U.S. Labor: Birth of a New Workers' Movement or Death Throes of the Old?* (Chicago, IL: Haymarket Books, 2011); Kim Moody, *On New Terrain: How Capital Is Reshaping the Battleground of Class War* (Chicago, IL: Haymarket Books, 2017).
4. Steven Greenhouse, *Beaten Down, Worked Up: The Past, Present, and Future of American Labor* (New York: Knopf, 2019); Jane McAlevey, *A Collective Bargain:*

Unions, Organizing, and the Fight for Democracy (New York: Ecco Press/ HarperCollins, 2020).

5. For empirical research and analyses on the rise of informal sector workers and collective mobilization, see: Rina Agarwala, *Informal Labor, Formal Politics, and Dignified Discontent in India* (Cambridge, UK: Cambridge University Press, 2013); Jan Breman, *On Pauperism in Past and Present* (New Delhi, India: Oxford University Press, 2016); Adrienne E. Eaton, Susan J. Schurman, and Martha A. Chen, *Informal Workers and Collective Action: A Global Perspective* (Ithaca, NY: Cornell University Press, 2017); Timothy Kerswell and Surendra Pratap, *Worker Cooperatives in India* (Singapore: Palgrave Macmillan, 2019).

6. Beverly J. Silver, *Forces of Labor: Workers' Movements and Globalization Since 1870* (New York: Cambridge University Press, 2003), p. 75.

7. Joshua Clover, *Riot. Strike Riot: The New Era of Uprisings* (London: Verso, 2016).

8. Rosa Luxemburg, *The Mass Strike, the Political Party and the Trade Unions* (Detroit, MI: Marxist Educational Society of Detroit, [1906] 1925), trans. Patrick Lavin, www.marxists.org/archive/luxemburg/1906/mass-strike/index. htm, accessed 20 June 2019.

9. V.I. Lenin, 'Better Fewer but Better', in *Lenin Collected Works*, 2nd English edn (Moscow, Russia: Progress Publishers, 1965), vol. 33, pp. 487–502, www. marxists.org/archive/lenin/works/1923/mar/02.htm, accessed 3 March 2020.

10. Janice Fine, *Worker Centers: Organizing Communities at the Edge of the Dream* (Ithaca, NY: Cornell University Press, 2006); Courtney Frantz and Sujatha Fernandes, 'Whose Movement Is It? Strategic Philanthropy and Worker Centers', *Critical Sociology*, vol. 44, nos 4–5 (2018), pp. 645–60; Immanuel Ness, *Immigrants, Unions and the New US Labor Market* (Philadelphia, PA: Temple University Press, 2005).

11. Callum Cant, *Riding for Deliveroo: Resistance in the New Economy* (Cambridge, UK: Polity Press, 2019); Sarah Kessler, *Giggled: The End of the Job and the Future of Work* (New York: St. Martin's Press, 2018); Jamie Woodcock and Mark Graham, *The Gig Economy: A Critical Introduction* (Cambridge, UK: Polity Press, 2020).

12. Susan L. Marquis, *I Am Not a Tractor! How Florida Farmworkers Took on the Fast Food Giants and Won* (Ithaca, NY: Cornell/ILR Press, 2017). For a critique of CIW and corporate-funded NGOs which claim to support workers' rights, see Feyzi Ismail and Sangeeta Kamat, 'NGOs, Social Movements and the Neo-liberal State: Incorporation, Reinvention, Critique', *Critical Sociology*, vol. 44, nos 4–5 (2018), pp. 569–77.

13. Peter Cole, *Wobblies on the Waterfront: International Unionism in Progressive-era Philadelphia* (Chicago, IL: University of Illinois Press, 2007); Melvyn Dubofsky, *We Shall Be All: A History of the Industrial Workers of the World* (Chicago, IL: Quadrangle Books, 1969); Joyce Kornbluh, *Rebel Voices: An I.W.W. Anthology* (Ann Arbor, MI: University of Michigan Press, 1968); Lynd, *Solidarity Unionism*.

14. Ralf Hoffrogge, *Working-class Politics in the German Revolution: Richard Müller, the Revolutionary Shop Stewards and the Origins of the Council Movement* (Leiden, the Netherlands: Brill, 2014); Peter J. Rachleff, *Marxism and Council Communism: The Foundation for Revolutionary Theory for Modern Society* (New York: Revisionist Press, 1976).

15. Dario N. Azzellini and Michael Kraft, *The Class Strikes Back: Self-organised Workers' Struggles in the Twenty-first Century* (Leiden, the Netherlands: Brill, 2018); Ness, *New Forms of Worker Organization*, pp. 6–8.

16. Don Kalb, 'Trotsky over Mauss: Anthropological Theory and the October 1917 Commemoration', *Dialectical Anthropology*, vol. 42 (2018), p. 37. Following the defeat of Trotsky's 1921 proposal for the militarization of labour, working-class enthusiasm and recruitment into the Communist Party and the Soviet Union expanded dramatically.

17. V.I. Lenin, 'Role and Functions of the Trade Unions', in *Lenin Collected Works*, vol. 33, 2nd English edn (Moscow, Russia: Progress Publishers, 1965), pp. 188–96. This text reveals that Lenin considered trade unions to be the quintessence of class power, as expressed through the socialist state: 'The main thing that socialists fail to understand and that constitutes their short-sightedness in matters of theory, their subservience to bourgeois prejudices and their political betrayal of the proletariat is that in capitalist society, whenever there is any serious aggravation of the class struggle intrinsic to that society, there can be no alternative but the dictatorship of the bourgeoisie or the dictatorship of the proletariat. Dreams of some third way are reactionary, petty-bourgeois lamentations.'

18. See Sidney Fine, *Sit-down: The General Motors Strike of 1936–1937* (Ann Arbor, MI: University of Michigan Press, 1969); Erik Loomis, *A History of America in Ten Strikes* (New York: The New Press, 2018).

19. Harry Braverman, *Labor and Monopoly Capitalism* (New York: Monthly Review, 1998); Michael Burawoy, *Manufacturing Consent: Changes in the Labor Process under Monopoly Capitalism* (Chicago, IL: University of Chicago Press, 1982).

20. Noam Scheiber, 'Volkswagen Factory Workers in Tennessee Reject Union', *New York Times*, 14 June 2019, www.nytimes.com/2019/06/14/business/economy/volkswagen-chattanooga-uaw-union.html, accessed 16 April 2020.

21. Eric Blanc, *Red State Revolt: The Teachers' Strike Wave and Working-class Politics* (New York: Verso, 2019).

22. See Anita Hammer and Adam Fishwick (eds), *The Political Economy of Work in the Global South: Reflections on Labour Process Theory* (London: Red Globe Press, 2020); Immanuel Ness, *Southern Insurgency: The Coming of the Global Working Class* (London: Pluto Press, 2015). Note that special economic zones (SEZs) and EPZs are synonymous, as they both represent state-supported infrastructural development and tax-free zones which attract foreign capital for the manufacturing of exported industrial products to foreign countries in the global North.

23. Zones are counted on the basis of their establishment by law. They exclude 8,368 zones (free points) found in 18 economies. SEZs in other developed economies (Australia, Israel, Japan, and New Zealand) and in Oceania were counted toward the respective economic group's aggregate and the global total.

24. Stanley Aronowitz, *The Death and Life of American Labor: Toward a New Workers' Movement* (London: Verso, 2014); Mike Davis, *Prisoners of the American Dream: Politics and Economy in the History of the Working Class* (London: Verso, 1986); Steve Early, *Save Our Unions: Dispatches from a Movement in Distress* (New York: Monthly Review, 2013); Bill Fletcher, Jr. and Fernando Gapasin, *Solidarity Divided: The Crisis in Organized Labor and a New Path Toward Social Justice* (Berkeley, CA: University of California Press, 2008); Ruth Milkman and Kim Voss, *Rebuilding Labor: Organizing and Organizers in the New Union Movement* (Ithaca, NY: Cornell University Press 2004); Kim Moody, *An Injury to All: The Decline of American Unionism* (New York: Verso, 1988); Ronaldo Munck, *Rethinking Global Labour after Neoliberalism* (Newcastle, UK: Agenda Publishing, 2018).

25. Mario Tronti, *Workers and Capital* (London: Verso, 2019). In Italy, the main expression of autonomism comprised Cobas (Committees of the Base): militant organizations representing the working class which emerged in tertiary sectors of the economy overlooked by larger unions. Among the most impoverished and disenfranchised Italian workers, Cobas have gained an independent voice and political force as opponents of the capitalist state and global capitalism. Rooted in a politics of refusal of the establishment, autonomist unions organized both labour strikes in workplaces and collective opposition to paying rent, electricity, taxes, and other expenditures. See Steve Wright, *Storming Heaven: Class Composition and Struggle in Italian Autonomist Marxism* (London: Pluto Press, 2014).

26. See Ana Cecilia Dinerstein, Alfonso García Vela, Edith Gonzalez, and John Holloway (eds), *Open Marxism 4: Against a Closing World* (London: Pluto Press, 2019); Steven Hirsch and Lucien van der Walt (eds), *Anarchism and Syndicalism in the Colonial and Postcolonial World, 1870–1940* (Leiden, the Netherlands: Brill, 2010); George Katsiaficas, *Asia's Unknown Uprisings: South Korean Social Movements in the 20th Century* (Oakland, CA: PM Press, 2012); George Katsiaficas, *Asia's Unknown Uprisings, Volume 2: People Power in the Philippines, Burma, Tibet, China, Taiwan, Bangladesh, Nepal, Thailand, and Indonesia, 1947–2009* (Oakland, CA: PM Press, 2013); James C. Scott, *The Art of Not Being Governed: An Anarchist History of Upland Southeast Asia* (New Haven, CT: Yale University Press, 2009).

27. V.I. Lenin, *What Is to Be Done?* (1902), Marxists Internet Archive, p. 23, www.marxists.org/archive/lenin/works/download/what-itd.pdf, accessed 9 April 2020.

28. Silver, *Forces of Labor*, pp. 1–40.

29. International Labour Organization, *World Economic Social Outlook, Trends 2019* (Geneva, Switzerland: International Labour Office, 2019).

30. John Holloway, *Change the World Without Taking Power: The Meaning of Revolution Today* (London: Pluto Press, 2019).

31. Under contemporary capitalism, the erosion of existing unions has given rise to new labour formations which challenge ineffective and corrupt traditional unions in India, Mexico, South Africa, and beyond. In their place, governments prefer subordinate unions and new party-controlled organizations which will permit corporate abuse of workers – known as 'paper unions'. As openings emerge, new workers' formations have taken shape in each of these countries, for example the New Trade Union Initiative in India, Frente Autentico del Trabajo in Mexico, and Casual Workers Advice Office in South Africa. But in the final analysis, these organizations do not have the capacity to mount a serious challenge against capital and the state. For an analysis of the deterioration of Mexican trade unions and current labour struggles, see Paolo Marinaro, '"We Fight against the Union!" An Ethnography of Labor Relations in the Automotive Industry in Mexico', in Maurizio Atzeni and Immanuel Ness (eds), *Global Perspectives on Workers' and Labour Organizations* (London: Springer, 2019), pp. 127–40.

32. Asia Monitor Resource Centre, *Resistance on the Continent of Labour: Strategies and Initiatives of Labour Organizing in Asia* (Hong Kong, China: AMRC, 2017), https://amrc.org.hk/sites/default/files/Resistance%20on%20the%20 Continent%20of%20Labour_AMRC%202017.pdf, accessed 10 April 2018; Gale Raj-Reichert, 'Global Value Chains, Contract Manufacturers, and the Middle-income Trap: The Electronics Industry in Malaysia', *Journal of Development Studies*, vol. 56, no. 4 (2020), pp. 698–716.

33. Abhinav Sinha, 'Problems of Indian Revolution: Prospects and Challenges', *Red Polemique*, 26 December 2014, https://redpolemique.wordpress.com/2014/12/26/problems-of-indian-revolution-prospects-and-challenges/, accessed 14 December 2020.

34. Ibid.

35. V.I. Lenin, 'Imperialism and the Split in Socialism', *Sbornik Sotsial-Demokrata*, no. 2 (December 1916), www.marxists.org/archive/lenin/works/1916/oct/x01.htm, accessed 21 March 2018.

36. V.I. Lenin, 'The International Socialist Congress in Stuttgart', *Proletary* (August/September 2007), in *Lenin Collected Works* (Moscow, Russia: Progress Publishers, 1972), pp. 75–81, www.marxists.org/archive/lenin/works/1907/oct/20.htm, accessed 10 April 2018.

37. Eric Hobsbawm, 'Lenin and the Aristocracy', *Monthly Review*, vol. 64, no. 7 (2012), https://monthlyreview.org/2012/12/01/lenin-and-the-aristocracy-of-labor/?v=38dd815e66db, accessed 20 May 2018.

38. Ibid. Hobsbawm notes: '[T]he more general argument about the dangers of "spontaneity" and "selfish" economism in the trade-union movement, though

illustrated by the historic example of the late nineteenth-century British labor aristocracy, retains all its force. It is indeed one of the most fundamental and permanently illuminating contributions of Lenin to Marxism.'

39. See Samir Amin, 'The Sovereign Popular Project: The Alternative to Liberal Globalization', *Journal of Labor and Society*, vol. 20, no. 1 (2017), pp. 7–22.

40. Pierre Bourdieu, 'Structures, Habitus, Practices', in *The Logic of Practice* (Stanford CA: Stanford California Press, 1990), pp. 52–65.

Chapter 3   Primitive Steel Manufacturing for the Global Consumer Market: Capital, Super-Exploitation, and Surplus Value in Wazirpur, India

1. This chapter was made possible thanks to 38 interviews of workers and organizers, political activists, observers, and employers in Wazirpur and Rohini districts of Delhi in July/August 2016 and January 2017.

2. Abhinav Sinha, 'New Forms and Strategies of the Working Class Movement and Resistance in the Era of Globalization', *Working Class Movement in India in the Twenty-first Century* (Lucknow, India: Arvind Memorial Trust, 2013), p. 50.

3. Ibid., p. 51.

4. Research for this chapter was conducted through interviews during 2016–17 with workers, organizers, and labour representatives of key strikes which shut down the local steel utensil industry (across hundreds of individual producers and employers).

5. Sumangala Damodaran, 'The Shape/ing of Industrial Landscapes: Life, Work and Occupations in and around Industrial Areas in Delhi', in Surajit Chakravarty and Rohit Negi (eds), *Space, Planning and Everyday Contestations in Delhi* (New Delhi, India: Springer, 2016), pp. 163–80.

6. Delhi Development Authority, 'Master Plans', https://dda.org.in/planning/mpd-2001.htm, accessed 3 August 2019. A new 'Master Plan' for Delhi is in the process of development in 2021 to replace Delhi's 'Master Plan 2001'.

7. S.C. Gupta and S.P. Bansal, 'Master Plan for Delhi vis-a-vis Industries, in Saigal, Omesh, Prakash Kumar', in R.K. Gupta and R. Mudgal (eds), *Problems and Prospects of Industrial Development in a Metropolitan City (a Case of Delhi)* (New Delhi, India: Mittal Publications, 1994), p. 34.

8. Mouleshri Vyas, *Public Arguments – 4: 'Dilli Door Hai' Migrant Labour in Manufacturing in the Megacity*, (Patna, India: Tata Institute of Social Sciences, August 2017), p. 4.

9. INR is the International Organization for Standardization code for the Indian rupee, also abbreviated as Rs. The US dollar equivalent of Rs 1,500–2,000 was US$20–30 per month in 2019 currency, in many cases for shared residences and facilities.

10. Vyas, *Public Arguments – 4*.

11. Bharat Dogra, 'Laws Ignored', *Economic and Political Weekly*, 12 August 1989, pp. 1,801–2, www.jstor.org/stable/4395189?read-now=1&seq=1#page_scan_

tab_contents, accessed 30 June 2019; People's Union for Democratic Rights (PUDR), 'Delhi: PUDR Report on Ongoing Wazirpur Struggle: Wazirpur Struggle Continues, as Factory Owners Refuse to Honour Written Agreement', 17 July 2014 (Delhi, India: PUDR, 2014), http://sanhati.com/articles/10470/, accessed 1 July 2019; Vyas, *Public Arguments – 4*.

12. Dogra, 'Laws Ignored'. For a recent account of dangerous working conditions in Wazirpur's steel industry, see Somya Lakhani, 'Workplace Injuries: Rage against the Machine', *Indian Express*, 20 August 2018, https://indianexpress.com/ article/cities/delhi/hardlook-delhi-aarah-machine-chowk-wazirpur-5314739/, accessed 11 July 2019.

13. Karl Marx, 'The General Law of Capitalist Accumulation', in *Capital*, vol. I, trans. Ben Fowkes (London: Pelican Classics, 1990), pp. 762–870.

14. Lakhani, 'Workplace Injuries'. In August 2018, the exchange rate of the Indian rupee to the US dollar was 68.3. Working a 12-hour shift in the Wazirpur machine shop would have netted a machinist approximately US$5.85 per day, as opposed to US$2.93 for other daily jobs in ample supply.

15. The rate of pay for a steelworker in Wazirpur is calculated as US$7.50 a day, or US$188 a month. In the industries with low rates of capital investment, average wages are about one third of those where industry-wide investments are higher, such as in electronics and auto production, where wages can rise to US$500 a month for full-time workers directly hired by major multinational employers. Note that the vast majority of workers employed in larger enterprises, such as auto, are not employed directly by MNCs and receive a fraction of the pay for permanent workers. Pay scales for workers outside manufacturing are typically half those of workers in the service sector.

16. Dogra, 'Laws Ignored'.

17. Friedrich Engels, *The Condition of the Working Class in England* (London: Penguin Classics, 2009). In 1838, Charles Dickens refers to owners' disdain for young migrant workers in the *Adventures of Oliver Twist*: 'What have paupers to do with soul or spirit? It's quite enough that we let 'em have live bodies. If you had kept the boy on gruel, ma'am, this would never have happened.'

18. Marx, *Capital*, vol. I, pp. 462–4.

19. Timothy Kerswell and Surendra Pratap, *Worker Cooperatives in India* (Singapore: Palgrave-Macmillan, 2019); Timothy Kerswell and Surendra Pratap, 'India's "Informal Sector": Demystifying a Problematic Concept', *Journal of Labor and Society*, vol. 19 (2016), pp. 229–50.

20. Vivek Chibber, *Locked in Place: State-building and Late Industrialization in India* (Princeton, NJ: Princeton University Press, 2003), pp. 110–45.

21. Alakh N. Sharma, 'Flexibility, Employment and Labour Market Reforms in India', *Economic and Political Weekly*, 27 May 2006, www.epw.in/journal/2006/21/ review-labour-review-issues-specials/flexibility-employment-and-labour-market, accessed 30 June 2020.

22. Indrani Mazumdar, *Unorganised Workers of Delhi and the Seven Day Strike of 1988* (Noida, India: V.V. Giri National Labour Institute, 2002).
23. Ibid., p. 3.
24. Ibid., pp. 75–82.
25. CITU, 'Delhi Workers Go on General Strike', *People's Democracy*, vol. 27, no. 13 (2003), https://archives.peoplesdemocracy.in/2003/0330/03302003_citu_strike.htm, accessed 3 May 2019.
26. Paranjoy Guha Thakurta, 'Workers' Rally in Delhi', *India Today*, 31 December 1988, www.indiatoday.in/magazine/economy/story/19881231-labour-militancy-arrives-in-industrial-belts-near-delhi-798101-1988-12-31, accessed 28 April 2019.
27. A *lathi* charge is the mobilization of police with batons to block and disperse workers and protesters by hitting them, often causing severe injury.
28. Arjun Ghosh, *A History of the Jana Natya Manch: Plays for the People* (New Delhi, India: SAGE Publications India, 2012), pp. 86–7.
29. Muzamdar, *Unorganised Workers of Delhi and the Seven Day Strike of 1988*, pp. 90–131.
30. See 'Wazirpur Hot-rolling Steel Plant Workers Call off Strike', *The Hindu*, 18 April 2013, www.thehindu.com/todays-paper/tp-national/tp-newdelhi/wazirpur-hotrolling-steel-plant-workers-call-off-strike/article4628854.ece, accessed 16 April 2020.
31. PUDR, 'Delhi: PUDR Report on Ongoing Wazirpur Struggle'.
32. 'Garam Rolla Mazdoor Ekta Samiti: All', *Newsclick*, www.newsclick.in/articles/Garam%20rolla%20mazdoor%20ekta%20samiti, accessed 1 July 2020. See also: 'Brilliant Victory of the Hot-rolling Steel Workers on the Third Day of Their Hunger Strike', *Garamrolla*, 8 July 2014, http://garamrolla.blogspot.com/2014/07/brilliant-victory-of-hot-rolling-steel.html, accessed 10 July 2019; Sarah Hafeez, 'Wazirpur Steel Factory Workers Call Off Strike', *Hindu Business Line*, 28 June 2014, www.thehindubusinessline.com/profile/author/Our-Bureau/, accessed 29 June 2019; Sarah Hafeez, 'Wazirpur Steel Factory Workers Continue Strike, Demand Rise in Wages. The Factories, Which Have Hardly Seen Manufacturing Utensils Since June, Have Been Running Losses of Up to Rs One Crore a Day', *The Indian Express*, 27 June 2014, https://indianexpress.com/article/cities/delhi/wazirpur-steel-factory-workers-continue-strike-demand-rise-in-wages/, accessed 1 July 2019.
33. PUDR, 'Delhi: PUDR Report on Ongoing Wazirpur Struggle'. See also Mithilesh Kumar and Ranabir Samaddar, 'Workers' Struggles and Autonomy: Strategic and Tactical Considerations', in Dario N. Azzellini and Michael Kraft (eds), *The Class Strikes Back: Self-organised Workers' Struggles in the Twenty-first Century* (Leiden, the Netherlands: Brill 2018), pp. 19–36.
34. For an examination of the unfolding labour actions in Wazirpur during 2014, see PUDR, 'Delhi: PUDR Report on Ongoing Wazirpur Struggle'.

35. Kim Moody, *On New Terrain: How Capital is Reshaping the Battleground of Class War* (Chicago, IL: Haymarket 2017).
36. For a discussion and critique of SEWA, which has gained international attention as empowering women in the garment sector and beyond to build labour cooperatives, see Kerswell and Pratep, *Worker Cooperatives in India*, p. 3: 'workers are politically demobilized and depoliticized with the support and encouragement of foreign NGOs, which serve as 'imperialist funding agencies'. The authors contend that 'Far from significantly improving the wages and working conditions of women workers, the cooperative appears to leverage the social prestige of the SEWA organisation, including amongst its members, to deliver pay and conditions which are weak even by capitalistic labour market standards. [...] SEWA as an organisation is a product of hegemonic forms of imperialism, both in the trade union imperialism [...] as well as hegemonic imperialism from the US government itself. We see SEWA's rise to significance in the spread of SEWA to various parts of India, but also importantly, to different countries in the global South.'
37. See Shankar Ramaswami, 'Forces of Truth: A Struggle of Migrant Workers in Delhi', *Ethnography*, vol. 13, no. 1 (2012), pp. 57–70.
38. Mithilesh Kumar and Ranabir Samaddar, 'Autonomy in India: Tactical and Strategic Considerations on the New Wave of Workers' Struggles', 19 February 2017, https://libcom.org/library/autonomy-india-tactical-strategic-considerations-new-wave-workers%E2%80%99-struggles, accessed 10 July 2019. See also *Faridabad Majdoor Samachar Faridabad Workers Newspaper*, http://faridabadmajdoorsamachar.blogspot.com/p/about-fms.html, accessed 30 July 2018.

Chapter 4   The Enduring System of Global Agricultural Commodity Production and First World Commodity Extraction: The Case of Mindanao, the Philippines

1. See Marion Werner and Jennifer Bair, 'Global Value Chains and Uneven Development: A Disarticulations Perspective', in Stefano Ponte, Gary Gereffi, and Gale Raj-Reichert (eds), *Handbook on Global Value Chains* (Cheltenham, UK: Edward Elgar, 2019), pp. 183–98; Edo Andriesse, 'Primary Sector Value Chains, Poverty Reduction, and Rural Development Challenges in the Philippines', *Geographical Review*, vol. 108, no. 3 (2018), pp. 345–66.
2. Kim Scipes, 'Another Type of Trade Unionism Is Possible: The KMU Labor Center of the Philippines and Social Movement Unionism', *Journal of Labor and Society*, vol. 21, no. 3 (2018), pp. 349–67.
3. Unyon ng mga Manggagawa sa Agrikultura (UMA), *Imperialist Plunder of Philippine Agriculture: A Research on the Expansion of Plantations through Agribusiness. Venture Arrangements in Mindanao* (Manila, the Philippines: UMA, 2019).

4. TheWorldBank,'RuralPopulation(%ofTotalPopulation)',https://data.worldbank. org/indicator/SP.RUR.TOTL.ZS?contextual=default&locations=PH,accessed17 April 2020.

5. For additional population estimates, rising to 110,000,000, see Philippine Statistics Authority, *Highlights of the Philippine Population 2015 Census of Population*, www.psa.gov.ph/content/highlights-philippine-population-2015-census-population, accessed 24 August 2019; World Population Review, 'Philippines Population 2020 Live', *United Nations Population 2020*, http://worldpopulationreview.com/countries/philippines-population/, accessed 4 May 2020.

6. For a history of US imperialism and manifold forms of resistance against colonization in the Philippines, see E. San Juan, Jr., *U.S. Imperialism and Revolution in the Philippines* (New York: Palgrave Macmillan, 2007).

7. David G. Timberman, *A Changeless Land: Continuity and Change in Philippine Politics* (Singapore: Institute of Southeast Asian Studies, 1991), pp. 182–4.

8. S.M. Borras, and J.C. Franco, 'Struggles for Land and Livelihood: Redistributive Reform in Agri-business Plantations in the Philippines', *Critical Asian Studies*, vol. 37, no. 3 (2005), pp. 331–61.

9. Elmer Bong Labog, 'KMU Slams Death Threat vs. Mindanao Labor Leader', 30 January 2014, https://laborrights.org/blog/201401/kmu-slams-death-threat-vs-mindanao-labor-leader, accessed 5 March 2019.

10. *By The President, Proclamation No. 216 Declaring a State of Martial Law and Suspending the Privilege of the Writ of Habeas Corpus in the Whole of Mindanao*, 23 May 2017, www.officialgazette.gov.ph/downloads/2017/05may/20170523-PROC-216-RRD.pdf, accessed 5 July 2019.

11. International Trade Union Confederation, *Workers' Rights Caught in the Crossfire in Mindanao, Philippines*, 14 December 2018, www.ituc-csi.org/Mindanao-Martial-Law-3rd-Extension, accessed 5 July 2019.

12. Arnold P. Alamon, *Wars of Extinction: Discrimination and the Lumad Struggle in Mindanao* (Iligan City, the Philippines: RMP-NMR, 2017), pp. 23–4.

13. Ibid., p. 46.

14. Daniel Workman, 'Bananas Exports by Country', *World's Top Exports*, 25 March 2020, www.worldstopexports.com/bananas-exports-country/, accessed 17 April 2020.

15. In March 2014, Chiquita merged with the Irish multinational Fyffes to become the largest banana producer in the world, consolidating the industry into major global corporate oligarchies. The Chiquita–Fyffes merger would further reduce competition and control over working conditions in plantations, packing houses, and logistics. See Dennis Klink, 'Compliance Opportunities and the Effectiveness of Private Voluntary Standard Setting – Lessons from the Global Banana Industry', in Axel Marx, Jan Wouters, Glenn Rayp, and Laura Beke (eds), *Global Governance of Labour Rights: Assessing the Effectiveness of Transnational Public and Private Policy Initiatives* (Cheltenham, UK: Edward Elgar, 2015) , pp. 230–56; Vanessa Wong, 'With Chiquita–Fyffes Merger, Dole

Will No Longer Be Top Banana', 10 March 2014, www.bloomberg.com/news/articles/2014-03-10/with-chiquita-fyffes-merger-dole-will-no-longer-be-top-banana, accessed 17 August 2019; Workman, 'Bananas Exports by Country'.

16. 'Mindanao Population', *Population.City*, http://population.city/philippines/adm/mindanao/, accessed 11 August 2019; Philippine Statistics Authority, *Highlights of the Philippine Population 2015 Census of Population*; 'Philippines Population 2019 (Live)', *World Population Review*, http://worldpopulationreview.com/countries/philippines-population/, accessed 11 August 2019.

17. For a population breakdown of Mindanao, see Eduardo Climaco Tadem, 'Development and Distress in Mindanao: A Political Economy Overview', *The Forum*, vol. 11, no. 3 (2010), pp. 1–2.

18. Ibid.

19. Eduardo Climaco Tadem, 'Development and Distress in Mindanao: A Political Economy Overview', *Asian Studies Journal*, vol. 48, nos 1–2 (2012), pp. 19–34, p. 31.

20. Ibid., p. 19.

21. Ibid., p. 33.

22. Ibid., pp. 21–4.

23. Onofre D. Corpuz, *An Economic History of the Philippines* (Quezon City, the Philippines: University of the Philippines Press, 1997), p. 143.

24. Alamon, *Wars of Extinction*, p. 42.

25. Republic of the Philippines, 'The Philippine Government Promotes the Rational Exploration, Development, Utilization and Conservation of Mineral Resources Guided by Its Commitment to Responsible Minerals Development' (Manila, the Philippines: Department of Environment and Natural Resources Mines and Geosciences Bureau, 2019), http://mgb.gov.ph/attachments/article/162/mining%20facts%20and%20figures%20updated%20March%202019.pdf, accessed 15 November 2019.

26. Joy Hasmin de los Reyes and Wim Pelupessy, *Agrarian Reform in the Philippine Banana Chain* (Antwerp, Belgium: Institute of Development Policy and Management, 2009), p. 8.

27. Katsumi Nozawa, *Banana Production and Co-operatives in the Philippines*, UPSE Discussion Paper, no. 2012-07 (Diliman, the Philippines: University of the Philippines, School of Economics, 2012), p. 42.

28. For a discussion of the global banana food chain, see Food and Agriculture Organization (FAO) of the United Nations, 'Banana Market Review: Preliminary Results for 2018' (Rome, Italy: FAO, 2018), www.fao.org/economic/est/est-commodities/bananas/en/, accessed 18 July 2020.

29. Jennifer Bair, *Frontiers of Commodity Chain Research* (Stanford, CA: Stanford University Press, 2008), p. 24.

30. Teresita O. De Leon and Gema Maria O. Escobido, *The Banana Export Industry and Agrarian Reform* (Davao City, the Philippines: Alternate Forum for Research in Mindanao, 2004).

31. Sonny Africa, 'Philippine NGOs: Defusing Dissent, Spurring Change', in Aziz Choudry and Dip Kapoor (eds), *NGOization: Complicity, Contradictions and Prospects* (London: Zed Books, 2013), pp. 118–43.

32. Prabhat Patnaik, 'Imperialism and the Agrarian Question', *Agrarian South: Journal of Political Economy*, vol. 3, no. 1 (2014), pp. 1–15.

33. Patnaik, 'Imperialism and the Agrarian Question', p. 14.

34. Ibid., pp. 1–15.

35. Zea Io Ming C. Capistrano, 'Japanese Banana Firm Concedes to Workers, Revokes Piece-rate Scheme', *Bulatlat*, 24 April 2015, www.bulatlat.com/ 2015/04/24/japanese-banana-company-concedes-to-workers-revokes-piece-rate-scheme/, accessed 19 October 2019. See also: Marya Salamat, 'Sumifru Banana Workers Regain Jobs after 9-day Strike', *Bulatlat*, 19 June 2015, www. bulatlat.com/2015/06/19/sumifru-banana-workers-regain-jobs-after-9-day-strike/, accessed 3 July 2019; 'Sumitomo under Fire over Labor Dispute and Rights Abuses at Philippines Banana Plantation Kyodo', *Japan Times*, 19 June 2019, www.japantimes.co.jp/news/2019/06/19/national/japans-sumitomo-fire-labor-dispute-philippines/, accessed 4 July 2019.

36. For an analysis of the inequities in trade between Japanese MNCs and the Philippines under neoliberalism in the banana industry, see Kae Sekine, *Resistance to and in the Neoliberal Agri-food Regime: A Case Study of Natural Bananas Trade between the Philippines and Japan*, http://kiyou.lib.aichi-gakuin.ac.jp/pdf/ kiyou_07F/07_55_3F/07_55_3_15.pdf, accessed 18 April 2020.

37. See 'An Inconvenient Truth about the Cavendish Industry in Asia and the Philippines', *Bapnet*, 10 February 2014, http://banana-networks.org/ Bapnet/2014/02/10/inconvenient-truth-cavendish-industry-asia-philippines/, accessed 17 August 2019.

38. For a comprehensive treatment of the exploitative conditions faced by rural workers in Mindanao, see Mahesti Hasanah, 'Between the Domination of Transnational Companies and its Discourse of Business and Human Rights: Contract Farming and Banana Small Farmers in the Davao Region (the Philippines)', PhD dissertation, Mahidol University, Thailand (2019), https:// apma-humanrights.org/wp-content/uploads/2019/11/mahesti-hasanah-cohort-2018.pdf, accessed 18 April 2020.

39. Ibid.

40. For analysis and critique of agrarian reform in the Philippines, see Andriesse, 'Primary Sector Value Chains, Poverty Reduction, and Rural Development Challenges in the Philippines'.

41. De los Reyes and Pelupessy, *Agrarian Reform in the Philippine Banana Chain*, p. 18.

42. Andriesse, 'Primary Sector Value Chains, Poverty Reduction, and Rural Development Challenges in the Philippines'.

43. Regletto Aldrich Imbong, 'Forging a Just and Lasting Peace in the Philippines', *Peace Review: A Journal of Social Justice*, vol. 31, issue 1 (2019), pp. 66–73; Gregg

R. Jones, *Red Revolution: Inside the Philippine Guerrilla Movement* (New York: Taylor & Francis, 1989).

44. UMA, *Imperialist Plunder of Philippine Agriculture*, p. 15.

45. Sarah Raymundo, 'Right on Time', *Bulatlat*, 28 September 2019, www.bulatlat.com/2019/09/28/right-on-time/, accessed 2 September 2019.

46. For an examination and critique of consumer market dependence on Filipino bananas, see Center for Trade Union and Human Rights, *The Labour and Environmental Situation in Philippine Banana Plantations Exporting to New Zealand* (Auckland, New Zealand: Oxfam New Zealand, 2013), www.oxfam.org.nz/sites/default/files/reports/Conditions%20in%20Philippine%20Banana%20Plantations%20Exporting%20to%20New%20Zealand%20(2).pdf, accessed 2 August 2019.

47. On the variation of the banana crops between high-quality Cavendish and lower-quality Lakatan bananas used for the domestic market in the Philippines, see R.V. Valmayor, R.R.C. Espino, and O.C. Pascua, *The Wild and Cultivated Bananas of the Philippines* (Los Banos, Laguna, the Philippines: PARRFI, 2002).

48. Kath M. Cortez, 'No Signs of Softening as Sumifru Workers Vow to Carry on the Fight for Rights', *Davao Today*, 14 April 2019, http://davaotoday.com/main/politics/no-signs-of-softening-as-sumifru-workers-vow-to-carry-on-the-fight-for-rights/, accessed 4 July 2019.

49. The Philippine government's anti-KMU initiatives included publicizing the formation of inauthentic unions. See, for example, Che Palicte, 'Labor Union Splits with KMU, Forms New Group', *Philippine News Agency*, 23 August 2019, www.pna.gov.ph/articles/1078556, accessed 14 April 2020.

50. Allan Nawal, 'AFP Sends Soldiers to "Prevent Chaos" at Japanese-owned Banana Plantation', *The Rappler*, 20 October 2013, www.rappler.com/nation/214206-soldiers-deployed-sumifru-banana-plantation-compostela-valley, accessed 3 July 2019.

51. Cortez, 'No Signs of Softening as Sumifru Workers Vow to Carry on the Fight for Rights'.

52. The NAMASUFA banana packaging union is an affiliate of the KMU. NAMASUFA-NAFLU-KMU is a legally registered local union in Mindanao and is the exclusive bargaining representative of all Sumifru workers in Compostela Region.

53. Daniel Blackburn, Director, International Centre for Trade Union Rights, 'Letter to Rodrigo Roa Duterte, President of the Republic of the Philippines', 18 November 2018, www.ictur.org/pdf/ICTUR_Philippines_NOV18.pdf, accessed 19 April 2020.

54. Interview with Paul John Dizon, 29 July 2019.

55. Ibid.

56. Ibid.

57. Interview with Ebenezer Chibo Tan, 29 July 2019.

58. See Chris Fabian, 'Tension Averted at SUMIFRU Farm', *Mindanao Times*, 9 August 2019, https://mindanaotimes.com.ph/2019/08/09/tension-averted-at-sumifru-farm/, accessed 22 October 2019.

59. Interview with Ebenezer Chibo Tan, 29 July 2019.

60. Ibid.

61. 'Sumitomo under Fire over Labor Dispute and Rights Abuses at Philippines Banana Plantation', *Japan Times*, 19 June 2019, www.japantimes.co.jp/news/2019/06/19/national/japans-sumitomo-fire-labor-dispute-philippines/, accessed 19 April 2020.

62. Interview with Paul John Dizon, 29 July 2019.

63. 'Sumitomo to Acquire Major Global Fruit Purveyor', *Nikkei Asian Review*, 10 December 2016, https://asia.nikkei.com/Business/Sumitomo-to-acquire-major-global-fruit-purveyor, accessed 19 October 2016.

64. See: Sumitomo Corporation, 'Announcement of Sale of Equity Stake in Sumifru Singapore Pte. Ltd', www.sumitomocorp.com/en/jp/news/release/2019/group/12020, accessed 19 October 2019; 'Sumitomo Sells Its Stake in Sumifru Philippines amid Allegations of Labour Rights Abuses', *BananaLink*, 8 July 2019, www.bananalink.org.uk/news/sumitomo-sells-its-stake-in-sumifru-philippines-amid-allegations-of-labour-rights-abuses/, accessed 18 September 2019.

65. See Robin Thiers, 'Flying Bananas: Small Producer Tactics and the (Un)making of Philippine Banana Export Chains', *Journal of Peasant Studies*, vol. 46, no. 2 (2019), pp. 337–57.

66. The KMU's website has been appropriated by a private company, and information on the union is derived from interviews with leading officials and from international labour websites, for example the International Trade Union Confederation and allied federations and associations. See especially 'Philippines: Action of Kilusang Mayo Uno (KMU)', 18 February 2015, www.ituc-csi.org/philippines-kmu, accessed 5 December 2020, and Maragtas S.V. Amante, 'Philippines Unionism – Worker Voice, Representation and Pluralism in Industrial Relations', in Hitoshi Ota (ed.), *New Labor Movement in Emerging Countries* (Tokyo, Japan: Institute of Developing Economies, 2019), pp. 63–103, www.ide.go.jp/library/Japanese/Publish/Download/Report/2018/pdf/2018_2_40_009_ch04.pdf, accessed 6 December 2020. The KMU is a member of regional and international networks and organizations such as the International Trade Union Confederation, International League of Peoples' Struggle, Workers International Struggle Initiatives, Southern Initiative on Globalization and Trade Union Rights, International Union League for Brand Responsibility, and the Asian Transnational Corporations Monitoring Project. The KMU is also an associate member of the International Migrants Alliance.

67. Interview with Sarah Raymundo, 18 August 2019.

68. Interview with Elmer Labog, 16 February 2019.

69. Ibid.

70. Ibid.

71. Elmer Labog, 'KMU Press Release', 24 November 2019; see also Mark Joy and
    G. Basallajes, 'Contractualization, Lack of Industries Are Causes of Job Losses
    in PH-KMU', *Davao Today*, 26 November 2019, http://davaotoday.com/main/
    politics/contractualization-lack-of-industries-are-causes-of-job-losses-in-ph-
    kmu/, accessed 19 April 2020.

*Chapter 5   Global Capitalism: Corporate Restructuring, Labour
Brokering, and Working-Class Mobilization in South Africa*

1. Rahul Anand, Siddharth Kothari, and Naresh Kumar, *South Africa: Labor
    Market Dynamics and Inequality*, IMF Working Paper 16/137 (Washington,
    DC: International Monetary Fund, 2016). For analysis dating back to the late
    1990s, see Servaas van der Berg and Haroon Bhorat, *The Present as Legacy of the
    Past: The Labour Market, Inequality, and Poverty in South Africa* (Cape Town,
    South Africa: Development Policy Research Unit, University of Cape Town,
    August 1999).
2. See: Patrick Bond, *Elite Transition: From Apartheid to Neoliberalism in South
    Africa* (London: Pluto Press, 2014); Hein Marais, *South Africa Pushed to the
    Limit: The Political Economy of Change* (London: Zed Books, 2011); John S.
    Saul, *A Flawed Freedom: Rethinking Southern African Liberation* (London: Pluto
    Press, 2014).
3. Peter Alexander, 'Rebellion of the Poor: South Africa's Service Delivery Protests
    – a Preliminary Analysis', *Review of African Political Economy*, vol. 37, no. 123
    (2010), pp. 25–40. For an update, see Carin Runciman, 'South Africa's Rebellion
    of the Poor, Conference Report', *Review of African Political Economy*, 14 July
    2016, https://roape.net/2016/07/14/south-africas-rebellion-poor/, accessed 23
    August 2020.
4. David Dickinson, 'Contracting out of the Constitution: Labour Brokers, Post
    Office Casual Workers and the Failure of South Africa's Industrial Relations
    Framework', *Journal of Southern African Studies*, vol. 43, no. 4 (2017),
    pp. 789–803, www.tandfonline.com/doi/abs/10.1080/03057070.2017.1316543,
    accessed 23 April 2020. For a study on labour broking in India, see Alessan-
    dra Mezzadri, 'The Informalization and Interlocking in Labour Contracting
    Networks', *Progress in Development Studies*, vol. 16, no. 2 (2016), pp. 124–39,
    https://journals.sagepub.com/doi/abs/10.1177/1464993415623120, accessed 23
    April 2020.
5. *Office of the President, No. 66 of 1995: Labour Relations Act*, no. 1877, 13
    December 1995, www.gov.za/sites/default/files/gcis_document/201409/
    act66-1995labourrelations.pdf, accessed 23 April 2020. The Labour Relations
    Act extended freedom of association, collective bargaining in all sectors of the
    economy to all workers, permitted strikes and lock-outs, trade union registra-
    tion and employer's organizations, and developed a cumbersome and
    time-consuming dispute resolution system through labour courts, which

favoured management around labour conflicts, including unfair dismissal for union activity.

6. *The Freedom Charter, Adopted at the Congress of the People at Kliptown, Johannesburg, on June 25 and 26, 1955* (Johannesburg, South Africa: Historical Papers Research Archive, 2013), www.historicalpapers.wits.ac.za/inventories/inv_pdfo/AD1137/AD1137-Ea6-1-001-jpeg.pdf, accessed 21 April 2020; Robert H. Davies and Dan O'Meara, *The Struggle for South Africa: A Reference Guide to Movements, Organisations and Institutions, Revised and Updated New Edition* (London: Zed Books, 1988).

7. See M. Mamobolo and T. Moyo, 'The National Development Plan (NDP): A Comparative Analysis with the Reconstruction and Development Programme (RDP), the Growth Employment and Redistribution Programme and the Accelerated and Shared Growth Initiative (ASGISA)', *Journal of Public Administration*, vol. 49, no. 3 (2014), pp. 946–59.

8. H. Bhorat, A. Cassim, and D. Yu, 'Temporary Employment Services in South Africa: Assessing the Industry's Economic Contribution' (Pretoria, South Africa: Labour Market Intelligence Partnership, 2016), www.lmip.org.za/document/temporary-employment-services-south-africa-assessing-industry%E2%80%99s-economic-contribution, accessed 12 April 2019. The research on TES shows that they have increased dramatically from 0.2 million in 1995 to 0.97 million in 2014, accounting for 6.4 per cent of total employment in South Africa, with more than 70 per cent of TES workers working in the tertiary sector, dominated by unskilled occupations. The TES industry contributed to an approximate 0.02 per cent reduction in the poverty headcount ratio in 2012 and 7.6 per cent of the country's Gross Domestic Product in 2014.

9. Franco Barcheisi, 'Informality and Casualization as Challenges to South Africa's Industrial Unionism: Manufacturing Workers in the East Rand/Ekurhuleni Region in the 1990s', *African Studies Quarterly*, vol. 11, nos 2–3 (2010), pp. 67–85, pp. 71–2, https://sites.clas.ufl.edu/africanquarterly/files/Barchiesi-Vol11Is2-3.pdf, accessed 9 April 2020.

10. Ibid., pp. 73–4.

11. Ibid., p. 79.

12. Bhorat, Cassim, and Yu, 'Temporary Employment Services in South Africa', p. 18.

13. See: Shawn Hattingh, 'Mineworkers' Direct Action: Occupations and Sit-ins in South Africa', *WorkingUSA: The Journal of Labour and Society*, vol. 13, no. 3 (2010), pp. 343–50, https://onlinelibrary.wiley.com/doi/abs/10.1111/j.1743-4580.2010.00294.x, accessed 24 April 2020; Kirk Helliker and Lucien van der Walt, 'Politics at a Distance from the State: Radical, South African and Zimbabwean Praxis Today', *Journal of Contemporary African Studies*, vol. 34, no. 3 (2016), pp. 312–31. For an exploration of informal workers' mobilization to improve conditions outside trade unions, see Omar Manky, 'Resource Mobilisation and Precarious Workers' Organisations: An Analysis of the

Chilean Subcontracted Mineworkers' Unions', *Work, Employment and Society*, vol. 32, no. 3 (2018), pp. 581–98.

14. For an examination of the history of the CWAO and the organization of temporary service employers in the East Rand, see Nkosinathi Godfrey Zuma, 'Contingent Organisation on the East Rand: New Labour Formations Organising Outside of Trade Unions, CWAO and the Workers' Solidarity Committee', Master's thesis, University of Witwatersrand, Johannesburg, 2015.

15. Devin Pillay, 'The Enduring Embrace: COSATU and the Tripartite Alliance during the Zuma Era', *Labour, Capital and Society/Travail, capital et société*, vol. 44, no. 2 (2011), p. 56, www.jstor.org/stable/43158405?seq=1, accessed 3 May 2020.

16. Data on CWAO derived from participant observation and interviews of its officials and workers. See also Zuma, 'Contingent Organisation on the East Rand'.

17. Peter Alexander, Thapelo Lekgowa, Botsang Mmope, Luke Sinwell, and Bongani Xezwi, *Marikana: A View from the Mountain and a Case to Answer* (Auckland Park, South Africa: Jacana Media, 2012).

18. Zuma, 'Contingent Organisation on the East Rand', pp. 79–80.

19. On the Marikana Moment, see Michael Neocosmos, 'Editorial Introduction: The Marikana Moment, Worker Political Subjectivity and State Violence in Post-apartheid South Africa', *Journal of Asian and African Studies*, vol. 51, no. 2 (2016), pp. 135–42, https://journals.sagepub.com/doi/abs/10.1177/0021909615605531, accessed 27 April 2020.

20. Luke Sinwell and Siphiwe Mbatha, *The Spirit of Marikana: The Rise of Insurgent Trade Unionism in South Africa* (London: Pluto Press, 2016).

21. Ironically in early September 2019 the CWAO office in Germiston was set on fire and looted during protests against immigrant-owned shops during a wave of xenophobic violence in South Africa. The damage to the office was repaired, and the CWAO remains in Germiston. See Zoë Postman, 'Worker Advice Office a Casualty of Joburg Looting: Casual Workers Advice Office Vows to Continue its Work, *New Frame*, 4 September 2019, www.newframe.com/worker-advice-office-a-casualty-of-joburg-looting/, accessed 3 May 2020.

22. Interview with Ighsaan Schroeder, 7 June 2017.

23. Interview with Ighsaan Schroeder, 9 July 2017.

24. Casual Workers Advice Office, 'Non-unionised Workers and Advice Offices Win Representation at the CCMA', press release, 20 September 2016.

25. Other advice offices include the Association for Community Advice Offices of South Africa and National Alliance for the Development of Community Advice Offices Advice Office. It is noteworthy that the advice offices are supported by NGOs, including the Mott Foundation and the Industrial Aid Society.

26. Interview with Ighsaan Schroeder, 10 July 2017.

27. Ibid.

28. CWAO General Meeting, observation of comments of speaker, 9 July 2017.

29. General Membership Meeting of Simunye Workers' Forum, CWAO, Germiston, South Africa, 15 July 2017.

30. Observation of CWAO and SWF meeting, 15 July 2017.

31. Ighsaan Schroeder, CWAO/SWF General Meeting, 10 July 2017.

32. Ighsaan Schroeder, 9 July 2017, CWAO, Germiston, South Africa.

33. 'Simba Code of Conduct', www.simba.co.za/our-company/code-of-conduct, accessed 14 July 2017.

34. Editorial, *The New Worker*, March–April 2018, p. 2. In the sprawling Simba Chips factory in Isando, workers earned the equivalent of US$1 hour (R18) for 12-hour shifts, seven days per week.

35. '300 Simba Workers Capture CCMA', *The New Worker*, no. 3, October 2017, p. 4.

36. Ibid.

37. Ibid. Nandi, the leader of the workers, remained defiant in the face of management's threats: According to *The New Worker*, Nandi's words indicate that the workers are confident in their collective power under the leadership of a stronghold of women comrades: 'If the Titanic is sinking, we are sinking together. Unfortunately it is not going to sink, we are going forward. Because the one thing I like about my company: the women are powerful!'

38. International Union of Food, Agricultural, Hotel, Restaurant, Catering, Tobacco and Allied Workers' Associations (IUF), 'Pepsi Simba Shop Stewards in South Africa Discuss National Recognition, Casualization', 30 March 2010, www.iuf.org/w/?q=node/301, accessed 28 April 2020.

39. SAFTU, 'Affiliates', http://saftu.org.za/affiliates/, accessed 2 May 2020.

40. 'Chips Down as Simba Strike Drags On', *Independent Online*, 9 July 2002, www.iol.co.za/news/south-africa/chips-down-as-simba-strike-drags-on-89415, accessed 29 April 2020.

41. Lynford Dor and Jacob Potlaki, 'Workers on Strike at Simba Chips', *The New Worker*, March–April 2018, p. 8.

42. Adcorp, 'Clients', www.adcorpgroup.com/clients/, accessed 2 May 2020.

43. Ronald Wesso, 'SA's Labour-broker System Does Not Favour Unemployed Youth', *Huffpost*, 1 February 2018, www.huffingtonpost.co.uk/ronald-wesso/sas-labour-broker-system-does-not-favour-unemployed-youth_a_23348800, accessed 20 April 2020.

44. Sarah Smit, 'Chips Are Down at Simba as Workers Prepare to Strike', *Mail & Guardian*, 17 April 2018, https://mg.co.za/article/2018-04-17-chips-are-down-at-simba-as-workers-prepare-to-strike, accessed 20 January 2019.

45. 'Simba Chips Workers Have Decided to Suspend Strike Action', *Political Analysis South Africa*, 20 April 2018, www.politicalanalysis.co.za/simba-chips-workers-have-decided-to-suspend-strike-action/, accessed 6 May 2020.

46. Constitutional Court of South Africa; Case CCT 194/17, Constitutional Court Judgment Dlodlo AJ (Majority), heard 22 February 2018, decided 26 July 2018, *Assign Services (Pty) Limited* v. *National Union of Metalworkers of South Africa*

and Others [2018] ZACC 22, www.saflii.org/za/cases/ZACC/2018/22.pdf, accessed 29 April 2020.

47. New Frame, 'Constitutional Court Ruling on Labour Brokers a Victory for the Working Poor,' *Daily Maverick*, www.dailymaverick.co.za/ article/2018-07-27-constitutional-court-ruling-on-labour-brokers-a-victory-for-the-working-poor/, accessed 10 April 2019.

48. Kally Forrest, *Metal That Will Not Bend: The National Union of Metalworkers of South Africa, 1980–1995* (Johannesburg, South Africa: Wits University Press, 2011).

49. Since 2010, COSATU's opposition to labour brokering focused on advocacy rather than direct organizing of workers. At COSATU's national congress in December 2015, the union endorsed a ban on brokers. See Bheki Ntshalintshali, 'Cosatu Demands Ban on Labour Brokers', *Independent Online*, 18 December 2015, www.iol.co.za/business-report/opinion/cosatu-demands-ban-on-labour-brokers-1961638, accessed 30 April 2020.

50. Sarah Bracking, 'Corruption and State Capture: What Can Citizens Do?', *Daedalus*, vol. 147, no. 3 (2018), pp. 169–83, www.mitpressjournals.org/doi/ abs/10.1162/daed_a_00509, accessed 29 April 2020; Trevor Ngwane, 'South Africa's Shrinking Sovereignty: Economic Crisis, Ecological Damage, Sub-imperialism and Social Resistances', *Vestnik Rudn, International Relations*, vol. 20, no. 1 (2020), special issue *Decolonization, Neocolonialism and Recolonization: 60th Anniversary of the Year of Africa*, pp. 6–88, http://journals.rudn.ru/international-relations/article/view/23323, accessed 29 April 2020.

51. See *Miners Shot Down*, documentary film, 2014, www.minersshotdown.co.za/, accessed 30 April 2020.

52. Alexander, Lekgowa, Mmope, Sinwell, and Xezwi, *Marikana*; Sinwell and Mbatha, *The Spirit of Marikana*.

53. Ibid.

54. For a detailed historical account of the unfolding Soweto uprising against the imposition of Afrikaans language on black South Africans, see 'The June 16 Soweto Youth Uprising', *South African History Online*, www.sahistory.org.za/ article/june-16-soweto-youth-uprising, accessed 21 April 2020.

55. 'NUMSA Expelled from COSATU', *Mail & Guardian*, 8 November 2014, https://mg.co.za/article/2014-11-08-numsa-expelled-from-cosatu, accessed 8 November 2019.

56. The secret ballot COSATU vote was 33 votes in favour of expelling NUMSA and 24 votes against. See Alan Cowell, 'South African Union Breaks from A.N.C. as Alliance Frays Further', *New York Times*, 27 October 2014, www.nytimes. com/2014/10/28/world/africa/union-breaks-from-anc-as-south-africa-alliance-frays-further.html, accessed 9 April 2019).

57. Qaanitah Hunter, 'Numsa Expelled from Cosatu', *Mail & Guardian*, 8 November 2014, https://mg.co.za/article/2014-11-08-numsa-expelled-from-cosatu/, accessed 8 November 2020.

58. Irvin Jim, 'What Is the United Front, and Why Is It Needed?', *Politics Web*, 13 December 2014, www.politicsweb.co.za/party/what-is-the-united-front-and-why-is-it-needed--irv, accessed 7 December 2020.
59. Ibid.
60. Penelope Mashego and Olebogeng Molatlhwa, 'Numsa to Oppose the ANC with New Party', *Sunday Times*, 16 May 2014, www.timeslive.co.za/news/south-africa/2014-05-16-numsa-to-oppose-the-anc-with-new-party/, accessed 3 April 2019.
61. Jim, 'What Is the United Front, and Why Is It Needed?'.
62. 'South Africa: Radical NUMSA-backed United Front declares "Enough is Enough!"', *Links: International Journal of Socialist Renewal*, 14 December 2014, http://links.org.au/node/4199, accessed 1 May 2020.
63. The NDP is the National Development Plan to eliminate poverty and reduce inequality in South Africa by 2020. See Jim, 'What Is the United Front, and Why Is It Needed?'.
64. Ibid.
65. Irvin Jim continued his address to state that key campaign areas include the following: (1) mass poverty, (2) extreme inequalities, (3) nationwide unemployment, (4) inferior and low-quality jobs, (5) the apartheid wage gap, (6) minimum wage, (6) labour brokers, (7) crime, especially its violent forms, (8) gender discrimination, (9) cultural poverty and exclusion, (10) inferior education, health, sanitation, and other social services for the working class, (11) environmental destruction and global warming, (12) sex discrimination, (13) the NDP, (14) e-tolls, (15) the abominable youth wage subsidy, which the bosses and the ANC want to use to divide and weaken the working class while giving free money to the bosses, (16) the South African colonial wage structure and lack of workplace transformation, (17) the apartheid geography of human settlement and economy, (18) poor service delivery or non-delivery, and lack of access to basic goods and services in adequate quality and quantity to working-class communities by the state (housing, public transport, electricity, water, education, healthcare), (19) the violation of the rights of children, women, the lesbian, gay, and transgender community, the aged, and people with disabilities, including general criminality and moral decay, and (20) formation of SAFTU. See: SAFTU, '2016 Workers Summit', http://saftu.org.za/the-federation/, accessed 9 November 2019; 'SAFTU – This Is What We Stand For: Declaration of the Launching Congress of the South African Federation of Trade Unions', *SP The Bullet*, 25 April 2017, https://socialistproject.ca/2017/04/b1401/, accessed 9 November 2019.
66. Interview with Zanoxolo Wayile, 18 July 2017, Newtown, Johannesburg.
67. For an assessment of SAFTU and the South African labour movement, see: Trevor Ngwane, 'South Africa: Transforming Crisis into Uprising', *Green Left Weekly*, no. 1231 (2019), p. 13, https://search.informit.com.au/document Summary;dn=558025928057160;res=IELHSS, accessed 21 August 2020; Bridget

Kenny, 'The South African Labour Movement: A Fragmented and Shifting Terrain', *Tempo Social, Revista de Sociologia da USP*, vol. 32, no. 1 (2020), pp. 119–36, https://orcid.org/0000-0001-6255-4971, accessed 1 May 2020; Alternative Information Development Centre, 'South African Federation of Trade Unions [SAFTU] Launch', 21 April 2017, https://aidc.org.za/south-african-federation-trade-unions-saftu-launch/, accessed 18 December 2020.

68. Kally Forrest, 'New South African Federation Prioritises Marginalised', *International Union Rights*, vol. 24, no. 2 (2017), pp. 22–3, www.ictur.org/pdf/IUR_FORREST_SAFTU.pdf, accessed 1 May 2020.

69. SAFTU, '2016 Workers Summit'.

70. Interview with Irvin Jim, General Secretary of NUMSA, 18 July 2017, Newtown, Johannesburg.

71. Patrick Craven, 'Historic Court Victory against Labour Brokers Celebrated – SAFTU', *PoliticsWeb*, 26 July 2018, www.politicsweb.co.za/politics/historic-court-victory-against-labour-brokers-cele, accessed November 8, 2019.

72. Ibid.

73. SAFTU, 'SAFTU Hails Historic Court Victory against Labour Brokers', https://saftu.org.za/saftu-hails-historic-court-victory-against-labour-brokers/, accessed 1 July 2020.

74. Craven, Historic Court Victory against Labour Brokers Celebrated – SAFTU'.

75. NUMSA, '1,700 NUMSA to Go on Strike over Exploitation of Temporary Workers by Labour Brokers', press release, 26 March 2006, www.numsa.org.za/article/1-700-numsa-to-go-on-strike-over-exploitation-of-temporary-workers-by-labour-brokers/, accessed 7 November 2019.

76. Ibid.

77. NUMSA, 'NUMSA Embarks on Strike at ArcelorMittal over Labour Brokers!', press release, 12 March 2019, www.numsa.org.za/article/numsa-embarks-on-strike-at-arcelor-mittal-over-labour-brokers/, accessed 7 November 2019.

78. ArcelorMittal, *ArcelorMittal Annual Corporate Report 2019*, www.arcelormittalsa.com/Portals/0/ArcelorMittal%20AR_2019_Lores.pdf, accessed 3 May 2020.

79. NUMSA, 'NUMSA Lodges a Dispute against ArcelorMittal', press release, 17 July 2018, www.numsa.org.za/article/numsa-lodges-a-dispute-against-arcelor-mittal/, accessed 5 May 2020.

80. Dineo Faku, 'So. Africa: Union Threatens to Shut Down Operations at ArcelorMittal Mine Due to Alleged Poor Working Conditions; Company Comments', *Business and Human Rights Resource Centre*, 17 March 2019, www.business-humanrights.org/en/so-africa-union-threatens-to-shut-down-operations-at-arcelormittal-mine-due-to-alleged-poor-working-conditions-company-comments, accessed 22 April 2019; Real Tree Trading 1 (PTY) Ltd, 'Services', https://realtree.vesco.co.za/services.html, accessed 2 May 2020.

81. 'Union Condemns Plans to Retrench 2,000 Workers at ArcelorMittal South Africa', *IndustriALL Global Union*, 18 July 2019, www.industriall-union.org/

union-protests-plans-to-retrench-2000-workers-at-arcelormittal-south-africa, accessed 3 May 2020.

82. NUMSA, 'NUMSA Embarks on Strike at ArcelorMittal over Labour Brokers!'.

83. Ibid.

84. Musawenkosi Cabe, 'Labour Brokers Are Sidestepping the Law, Says NUMSA', *New Frame*, 20 April 2019, www.newframe.com/labour-brokers-are-sidestepping-law-says-numsa/, accessed 10 November 2020. The report quoted NUMSA shop steward for permanent workers Motlasti Potsane: 'We are here today because our management is exploiting our fellow [workers who are on contract]. We are here as leadership and workers to support that [contract workers] should be signed permanently as well and should enjoy the benefits that the permanent employees are enjoying, so that they can have the same treatment as permanent people.'

85. Ibid.

86. 'ArcelorMittal South Africa strike Will Continue, Says NUMSA', *The Citizen*, 19 March 2019, https://citizen.co.za/news/south-africa/protests/2103974/arcelormittal-south-africa-strike-will-continue-says-numsa/, accessed 30 April 2019.

87. 'NUMSA to Open a Case of Police Brutality against SAPS in Sedibeng', *Polity*, 30 March 2019, https://www.polity.org.za/article/numsa-numsa-to-open-a-case-of-police-brutality-against-saps-in-sedibeng-2019-03-30, accessed 3 May 2020.

88. Pavan Kulkarni, 'Workers of ArcelorMittal South Africa Demonstrate before the Indian High Commission', *Peoples Dispatch*, 27 April 2019, https://peoplesdispatch.org/2019/04/27/workers-of-arcelormittal-south-africa-demonstrate-before-the-indian-high-commission/, accessed 30 April 2019.

89. ArcelorMittal, *ArcelorMittal Annual Corporate Report 2019*.

90. Theto Mahlakoana, 'NUMSA Slams ArcelorMittal for Not Consulting Workers about Retrenchments', *EWN*, 13 July 2019, https://ewn.co.za/2019/07/13/numsa-slams-arcelormittal-for-not-consulting-workers-about-retrenchments, accessed 8 November 2019.

91. ArcelorMittal, *ArcelorMittal Annual Corporate Report 2019*.

92. 'Statement on ArcelorMittal South Africa', *Brand South Africa*, 13 November 2019, www.brandsouthafrica.com/investments-immigration/statement-on-arcelormittal-south-africa, accessed 3 May 2020.

93. Interview with Ronald Wesso, 22 September 2019.

94. Ibid.

95. Interview with Irvin Jim, General Secretary of NUMSA, 18 July 2017.

Chapter 6   Conclusion: Labour Struggles and Political Organization

1. Jan Breman and Marcel van der Linden, 'Informalizing the Economy: The Return of the Social Question at a Global Level', *Development and Change*, vol. 45, no. 5 (2014), p. 920.

2. See, e.g., United Nations Department of Economic and Social Affairs, *World Urbanization Prospects: The 2018 Revision* (New York: UN, 2019); World Bank, *Urban Development*, www.worldbank.org/en/topic/urbandevelopment/overview, accessed 23 May 2020.

3. Jan Breman, *Footloose Labour: Working in India's Informal Economy* (Cambridge, UK: Cambridge University Press, 1997).

4. Karen Rignall and Mona Atia, 'The Global Rural: Relational Geographies of Poverty and Uneven Development', *Geography Compass*, vol. 11, no. 7 (2017), p. 5.

5. See Antonio Gramsci, 'Past and Present', in *Prison Notebooks Volume II*, Notebook 3, 1930 (New York: Columbia University Press, 2011), pp. 32–3.

6. Ben Scully, 'Precarity North and South: A Southern Critique of Guy Standing', *Global Labour Journal*, vol. 7, no. 2 (2016), p. 167.

7. V.I. Lenin, *What Is to Be Done? Burning Questions of Our Movement*, www.marxists.org/archive/lenin/works/1901/witbd/ii.htm, accessed 27 May 2020.

Index

Thanks to our Patreon Subscribers:

Abdul Alkalimat
Andrew Perry

Who have shown their generosity and comradeship in difficult times.